City of Dispossessions

POLITICS AND CULTURE IN MODERN AMERICA

Series Editors: Keisha N. Blain, Margot Canaday, Matthew Lassiter, Stephen Pitti, Thomas J. Sugrue

Volumes in the series narrate and analyze political and social change in the broadest dimensions from 1865 to the present, including ideas about the ways people have sought and wielded power in the public sphere and the language and institutions of politics at all levels—local, national, and transnational. The series is motivated by a desire to reverse the fragmentation of modern U.S. history and to encourage synthetic perspectives on social movements and the state, on gender, race, and labor, and on intellectual history and popular culture.

CITY OF DISPOSSESSIONS

Indigenous Peoples, African Americans, and the Creation of Modern Detroit

Kyle T. Mays

PENN

UNIVERSITY OF PENNSYLVANIA PRESS

PHILADELPHIA

Published by
University of Pennsylvania Press
Philadelphia, Pennsylvania 19104-4112
www.upenn.edu/pennpress

Printed in the United States of America on acid-free paper
10 9 8 7 6 5 4 3 2 1

Library of Congress Cataloging-in-Publication Data
Names: Mays, Kyle, author.
Title: City of dispossessions : indigenous peoples, African Americans, and the creation of modern Detroit / Kyle T. Mays.
Other titles: Politics and culture in modern America.
Description: Philadelphia : University of Pennsylvania Press, [2022] | Series: Politics and culture in modern America | Includes bibliographical references and index.
Identifiers: LCCN 2021039333 | ISBN 9780812253931 (hardcover) | ISBN 9780812298543 (eBook)
Subjects: LCSH: Indians of North America—Michigan—Detroit—History. | African Americans—Michigan—Detroit—History. | Indians of North America—Michigan—Detroit—Social conditions. | African Americans—Michigan—Detroit—Social conditions. | Detroit (Mich.)—History. | Detroit (Mich.)—Race relations—History.
Classification: LCC F574.D457 M36 2022 | DDC 305.8009774/34—dc23
LC record available at https://lccn.loc.gov/2021039333

CONTENTS

Preface vii

Introduction. Dispossession, Detroit! 1

1. The Roots of Dispossession: From Waawayeyaattanong to Detroit 11

2. Performing Dispossession: Detroit's 1901 Bicentenary 46

3. Reclaiming Detroit: Blackness and Indigeneity During the Age of Fordism 64

4. Citizenship and Sovereignty: Black Nationalism and Indigenous Self-Determination 94

5. Black Indigeneity and Urban Indigenous Feminism in Postwar Detroit 114

6. Dispossession and the Roots of Culturally Relevant Education 135

Conclusion. "Where Have All the Indians Gone?": The Afterlife of Dispossession, Detroit 165

Notes 179

Index 209

Acknowledgments 219

PREFACE

Over the years, I have given dozens of talks on my research for this book. The audiences and venues have varied from academic conferences to bars to my auntie in her living room. When speaking to academic audiences, I begin by acknowledging my great-grandmother, Esther Mays, and my aunt Judy Mays, and their roles in shaping cultural and educational history in postwar Detroit. Then I ask the audience, "What do you know about Detroit?" I implore them to yell things out at me; predictable answers emerge. Someone will shout out "Motown!"; another will say "the Bankruptcy"; a person hip to Detroit's radical Black history will proclaim "the Rebellion!" Then someone will shout, "Factories! Cars!" I usually have to follow up, reminding them of Detroit's great sports history, making sure that they acknowledge the Detroit Pistons, the team, led by Isiah "Zeke" Thomas, that went 3–1 against Michael Jordan's Chicago Bulls. The audience will usually laugh, perhaps reminiscing about those 1980s Bad Boys, including Dennis Rodman, John Salley, Bill Laimbeer, Rick Mahorn, Vinnie "the Microwave" Johnson, Mark Aguirre, and Joe Dumars beating Jordan's Bulls, and knocking him to the ground. Similar to the erasure of the Pistons as one of the great basketball teams in NBA history, what audiences also don't mention is the Indigenous people who also made the city. Detroit has a long Indigenous history and a continuing Indigenous presence, with representations everywhere in the city. The Pontiac brand, for example, is named after the Odawa chief, Pontiac. Although there are numerous other examples at the Detroit Historical Museum and at the Detroit Public Library, this history has been neglected.

The Indigenous histories of modern Detroit remain invisible for a host of cultural and political reasons. My aim in this book is to unpack why this happened and to reconstruct this history, offering examples of Indigenous history and Black history and their presence in Detroit from the late nineteenth century to the present. My aim is not to write a long, boring history book. This book is not a tribal history; I am not interested in proving how many Indigenous people live in Detroit and how they're going to decolonize everything today. My aim is to encourage the reader to think long and hard about their local place, especially urban spaces, and how the Indigenous people in that area are recognized or not recognized—or, worse, erased.

I first decided to write about Detroit's Indigenous history as an undergraduate at James Madison College, which was not necessarily a haven for first-year students, especially students of color, on the campus of Michigan State University. While I gained a great deal of knowledge there, the experience was still challenging because several Black students and I believed the campus was hostile to Black people, and we protested. I learned from my experience to delve deeply into something and always figure out how to reconstruct history from below.

Though my family, Saginaw Chippewa, came to Detroit in 1940, writing about them was not on my intellectual radar. But Gitchi-Manidoo (the Great Spirit) works in mysterious ways. On a cold, January day in 2006—and I mean Michigan cold—I attended my first day of class in Native American history, taught by Anishinaabe professor George Cornell. He had a reputation on campus as a tough grader, one who would never bend for students. As a cocky nineteen-year-old, I was determined not to be intimidated. I went to class, sat down in the front with a hoodie on, and cocked my head back, ready for the intellectual battle. He went over the syllabus and basically told us that we would have to unlearn U.S. history. Twenty minutes later, he dismissed the class. A line of students quickly formed in front of Dr. Cornell so that students could discuss matters related to the class, while I tried to sneak out the back door.

As I was leaving, Dr. Cornell stopped me and said, "Mays!" Damn, I thought, what does he want? I went up to him, with the annoyed look of a sophomore undergraduate student, repelled at unwarranted conversation with a professor. He shook my hand, the way a tall, dignified Indigenous uncle would, and said, in a deep voice, "I know your whole family! I used to work with your grandmother on Indian policies and activism back in the day!"

"Oh, that's cool," I replied, feigning interest.

"She was great. She didn't take shit from nobody," he stated glowingly.

I left that day with deep respect for Dr. Cornell. After all, most of the Indigenous men I knew or heard about from back in the day took all of the credit, ignoring the contributions of Indigenous women. I walked back into that cold, grey Michigan winter day, full of intellectual vigor. In retrospect, my intellectual destiny—to honor my family, to honor my great-grandmother, and to honor Detroit's Indigenous community—was forever set.

After finishing my undergraduate degree, I began to pursue a doctorate in the African American and African Studies Program at Michigan State. I had plans to write a dissertation on the relationship between Black and Indigenous activists in the Red and Black Power Movements. After a year, I became disillusioned with my ability to do the comparison well. I wanted and needed to learn more about Black and Indigenous relations, and I wasn't necessarily able to do that there. I found another intellectual path, however, in the form of a book I discovered online about Detroit's Native American History: Emund Danziger's *Survival and Regeneration: Detroit's American Indian Community* (1991).

I flipped the book open to the middle. On that page was a black-and-white photo of my aunt Judy Mays. I was stunned. She never told me about this. I devoured the book—underlining every word, reading every footnote, determined to retrace the historical research of the author, and trying to figure out why my auntie was in there. From that moment, I knew I wanted to write on Native Americans in the Motor City. I also wanted to place at the center the histories of Afro-Indigenous people, like me and the members of my family, who were often erased from mainstream narratives. What follows is the culmination of my efforts—to understand how Indigenous people became invisible in cities and to tell the stories of the Indigenous men and women who have lived and continue to live in Detroit.

City of Dispossessions

INTRODUCTION

Dispossession, Detroit!

In the public imagination, Native people were removed from Detroit a long time ago. Europeans moved in, then Black people moved in and later "destroyed" the city. White people moved out but returned with the goal of reclaiming and revitalizing the city. They wanted to make the city great again—to restore it to its former glory. So the story goes. Yet this narrative, upheld by the media and still embraced by many Americans, overlooks the central role Black and Indigenous people have played in making Detroit a great city—despite its many economic challenges. The exclusion of these groups in mainstream narratives captures the theme and main argument of this book: Dispossession—in the form of narratives and stories, displacement and removals, and memorializations and performances—is a central mechanism that has defined the Black and Indigenous experience in Detroit from the late nineteenth century to the present.

This book grapples with two main questions. First, how does a history of Black and Indigenous dispossession help us understand the current state of Detroit? Second, and more broadly, how has dispossession impacted the development of modern U.S. cities? In July 2013, the city of Detroit declared bankruptcy following years of financial mismanagement by the city's capitalist elite. It was the largest municipality in U.S. history to declare bankruptcy. In order to understand Michigan's 2013 emergency takeover of Detroit, and the city's bankruptcy just four months later, we must examine the longer histories of Black and Indigenous dispossessions in this place. At its most basic, dispossession is a process of settler capitalists taking land, removing people, developing that land, and creating and reproducing narratives and symbols that serve to explain why certain populations deserve to be removed, who can belong to the metropolis, and who profits off that land.[1] In this way, dispossession helps us to understand the construction of cities, to see social relations in urban environments, and to connect the original dispossession of Native people with contemporary forms of dispossession affecting both Indigenous and Black urban residents.[2] *City of Dispossessions* is a cultural, intellectual, and social history situated at the nexus of urban history, urban studies, and critical ethnic studies. It argues that the physical, discursive, and political forms of dispossession have been central to Detroit's modern development. In turn, dispossession has shaped the larger idea of the Motor City's political and cultural imagination in the United States. More broadly, it reveals that modern U.S. cities have developed in conjunction with the presence of Indigenous people—in both a real and an imagined sense. Dispossession is a process that has undergirded the development of urban America, and it is a process that continues to permeate cities well into the present.[3]

Understanding the meaning and legacy of dispossession in Detroit offers a window into the ongoing structures of racial capitalism and settler colonialism and demonstrates how these structures shape the development of modern U.S. cities, especially with regard to the fundamental question of who belongs and who does not.[4] Moreover, looking at the meaning and legacy of dispossession in Detroit illustrates how certain histories and peoples are portrayed in cultural realms in order to further the process of dispossession. Finally, understanding the history of dispossession will help us appreciate and recover the erased history and presence of Indigenous peoples, who were central to the original takeover of Detroit. I describe these different processes as "sites of dispossession."

We can think of a site in both material and ideological terms. A site can be a place, a process, an outcome, a situation. Black and Indigenous peoples in Detroit have experienced dispossession in particular places and at different moments. At times, their experiences overlap; at other times, they don't. The sites of dispossession include, but are not limited to the following: displacement, removal, and disappearance from land; discourses, narratives, and memorializations; economic exploitation; pageantry and performance; and second-class citizenship. While I won't cover every facet of these in detail, all are sites of dispossession.

Scholars of settler colonial studies continue to use the late anthropologist Patrick Wolfe's formulation that settler colonialism "is a structure not an event," one designed to eliminate the Indigenous population.[5] This formulation of settler colonialism is not capacious enough to capture the development of modern cities like Detroit. Though we might call Detroit a settler colonial space at its founding in 1701, as settler populations moved in and changed the land, Black and Indigenous peoples experienced a multitude of dispossessions from the late nineteenth century to the present. These sites of dispossession have persisted after the settler colonial process, and this book reveals how.

The field of urban Indigenous studies has not adequately confronted the issue of race, especially blackness and Black people, and their interaction with Indigenous people. Moreover, Afro-Indigenous studies continue to focus on the important topics of African enslavement and Indigenous dispossession in the nineteenth century and, in particular, how these processes played out among the Five Tribes.[6] Perhaps no one sums up the differences between Black and Indigenous peoples better than Wolfe himself. Wolfe argues that the key differences between how people of African descent and Native people are treated are rooted in the idea of removal from land and labor. Colonialism seeks Indigenous disappearance and the exploitation of African labor.[7] However compelling this explanation may be, it ignores some crucial histories and forces us to ask challenging questions about when and where Black Americans, the descendants of Indigenous Africans, lose their indigeneity. As historian Robin D. G. Kelley has argued, Wolfe's argument erases African indigeneity.[8]

Some scholars who broach the topic of Black and Indigenous relationships in Detroit have argued that Black people have used the language of white settlers to argue for their own belonging or as part of a larger pattern of historical resentment against Native people.[9] Other scholars have tended to focus on these relationships at the level of theory.[10] Tiffany Lethabo King's excellent work offers a method for thinking about Black and Indigenous encounters using what she describes as the "shoals." The "shoals," she argues, reveal "the ways that some aspects of Black and Indigenous life have always already been a site of co-constitution."[11] King's book has offered us a way forward in thinking about these histories and intellectual connections offshore. I want to momentarily bring Black and Indigenous studies back to land and examine these histories in the metropolis. By exploring Black and Indigenous urban histories together, we can better understand that dispossession as an analytic can explain the connections between racial capitalism and settler colonialism, as well as indigeneity and racialization in urban spaces.[12]

With a few exceptions, urban studies scholars and geographers continue to neglect the process of dispossession of Indigenous and Black peoples as a part of modern metropolitan development, instead leaning on discussions of neoliberalism.[13] They might demonstrate that Indigenous dispossession was the original one, and then move along to their analysis, ignoring it as an ongoing process that exists beyond the nineteenth century. This approach naturalizes

Indigenous dispossession and erases the process from the present.[14] Indeed, it is not enough to simply begin with the dispossession of Indigenous peoples and then leave them behind; we must continue to write of Indigenous people in the present, otherwise we risk perpetuating the major goal of settler colonization: the removal of Native people from the present, allowing them to remain stuck in the past. Dispossession did not happen to Indigenous people alone, once upon a time; rather, it has been an ongoing process in which property, citizenship, and narratives are taken while someone else comes into possession of them.[15] Dispossession is not just the removal of Indigenous people and the taking of their land, nor is it simply the slum clearance and segregation of Black Americans. Dispossession as an ongoing process in the making of urban America has many tentacles, and Detroit is a place rooted in multiple sites of dispossession.[16]

Although dispossession might seem like a totalizing force, Black and Indigenous peoples have produced sites of resistance. They resist displacement and removal by reclaiming land and creating sites of fugitivity. They resist discourses of their erasure by producing counter narratives that assert their presence and produce their own versions of history through education. In order to challenge the pageants and memorializations of dispossession, they produce expressive culture, including protest art, performance, and music. In this book, I chronicle not only the variety of Black and Indigenous sites of dispossession but also the way they resist. Indigenous peoples and African Americans have long experienced and resisted dispossession in urban America.

The African American experience in Detroit remains a pendulum of resisting dispossession and an attempt to create belonging. Rooted in Black Nationalist and class-based activism since at least the early part of the twentieth century, African Americans' attempt at resisting exploitation, segregation, and second-class citizenship was framed as a struggle for freedom. They struggled for self-determination in both personal and political terms. They sought to create pockets of belonging in a city where they experienced economic, political, and social exclusion.

Indigenous people in Detroit have experienced colonization and dispossession, and they continue to do so. White settlers removed them through treaties, while, in the contemporary era, settler capitalists continue creating dispossession narratives and celebrating Indigenous peoples of the past, relegating them to archives and museums. Indigenous people have resisted and continue to resist these sites of dispossession in the beast of the colonial belly. They have used public education, organizational work, and cross-racial alliances to better their condition. Indigenous people are asserting that they will continue to exist in the aftermath of the original dispossession.

Understanding Detroit, Then and Now

A common phrase used by pundits and others in the mid-twentieth century to describe Detroit went something like this: "If Detroit sneezes, the American economy catches a cold." The origin of the phrase is unknown, but it aptly describes the importance of Detroit to the U.S. economy at the time. Now, it could be said that when the United States catches a cold, Detroit gets pneumonia. Detroit might no longer have the same importance to America's economy, but its past glory still holds sway over the public imagination. It remains a special place—an iconic part of America's past.

Detroit, Michigan, has many histories. In the preface to *Landmarks of Wayne County and Detroit*, written in 1884, nineteenth-century Detroit historian Silas Farmer noted that at least three nation-states claimed Detroit as their own.[17] The city was also an important part of the region's history, serving as a meeting point between Indigenous nations and European settlers, and it was the gateway to the west. Detroit remains important to the popular imagination as a symbol to the rest of the United States and the world.[18]

What makes Detroit unique from other cities? That question is borne of the continuum of history and contemporary reality. From 1901 until the postwar era, with the factories of Chrysler, Ford, and General Motors (GM), Detroit was a manufacturing boomtown. The factories, which were central to the U.S. economy, rapidly changed America. Henry Ford's assembly line and his policy of paying his workers $5 a day changed labor in the United States forever. Along with Ford, GM, which created the Pontiac brand, became two of the largest companies in the United States. In this way, Detroit's automobile companies served as a central force in the creation of U.S. identity and modernity. They helped create the national landscape of highways, motels, and even fast-food restaurants.

During World War II, President Franklin Delano Roosevelt declared Detroit the "arsenal of democracy." The Chrysler, Ford, and GM factories shifted their focus to producing for the war effort. The need for labor increased, and African Americans migrated again from the South as they had done during World War I. By 1950, Detroit was home to nearly two million people, and it was majority white. While Detroit of the 1940s experienced a boom, the economy began to change. The city lost more than 134,000 jobs; unemployment was rampant. Four recessions impacted the city.[19] Detroit lost its workforce, and manufacturers closed plants and relocated to other parts of the United States.[20] The McCarthy era also impacted Black protest. In the 1940s, Black organizations had been able to actively protest. By the 1950s, some groups began to seek gradual change so that they would not be accused of being communist.[21] The 1950s also saw the rise of conservatism in Detroit. Any call for racial progress coincided with conservative accusations equating such calls with communism or socialism.[22]

During the Black Power era, culminating with the Detroit Rebellion of 1967, the city began to change yet again. Whites had been moving out of the city since at least World War II when affirmative action was white, when the suburbs were aided by government subsidies and created the wealth disparities that exist between African Americans and white Americans today. With the conservative backlash, the law-and-order rhetoric of the 1970s, and Detroit's transformation into a majority-Black city, signified by the election of Mayor Coleman A. Young, the city would forever be different, embroiled in a matrix of deindustrialization, disinvestment, poverty, and racism.[23] Today, Detroit remains the largest majority-African American city in the United States.

This is the narrative of Detroit's twentieth-century history, dominated as it is by discussions of unions, class, and Black-white racial conflict.[24] In this tale, Detroit represents the American dream and nightmare personified. After the 1967 Rebellion, after the factories left, after white people took their capital with them, the city suffered rampant poverty and unemployment, culminating in bankruptcy.

By contrast, accounts of Detroit today depict it as a place of endless possibility—led by Dan Gilbert, the billionaire owner of the Cleveland Cavaliers and Quicken Loans. A 2013 article in the *New York Times* captures this well. Titled "An Anatomy of Detroit's Decline," the article rehearsed the familiar story of twentieth-century Detroit before pivoting to observe that white people are moving back into the city and resettling it. Backed by Gilbert and the rhetoric of Detroit 2.0, which suggests that they are "saving" the city and developing it, returning it to its past glory. This discourse is reminiscent of nineteenth-century pioneer logic, where whites would go west and encroach on Indigenous lands, looking for a better life.[25] This frontier imagery is also an organizing discourse, which demonstrates that the dispossession of Native land in the eighteenth and nineteenth centuries is not much different from what is happening today.[26] Elites use frontier discourse to frame urban spaces like Detroit as places of

Table 1. Detroit's Population, 1880–2010.

Year	*Detroit (total)*	*Native*	*Black*	*White*
1870	79,577	4	2,235	77,338
1880	116,340	34	2,821	113,475
1890	205,876	11	3,431	202,422
1900	285,704	16	4,111	281,575
1910	465,766	41	5,741	459,926
1920	993,678	155	40,838	952,065
1930	1,568,662	350	120,066	1,446,656
1940	1,623,452	434	149,119	1,472,662
1950	1,849,568	730	300,506	1,545,847
1960	1,670,144	1,426	482,229	1,182,970
1970	1,511,482	2,914	660,428	838,877
1980	1,203,339	3,420	758,939	413,730
1990	1,027,974	3,655	777,916	222,316
2000	951,270	3,319	775,729	116,672
2010	713,777	2,636	590,226	75,758
2020	639,111	2,556	500,424	93,949

Source: Bureau of U.S. Census, United States Census of Population, 1870–2010 (Washington D.C., U.S. Government Printing Office, various years).

opportunity, ripe for settlement. The local population no longer matters and is quickly removed. This process is, again, dispossession, in twenty-first-century form. Even considering the populations of Indigenous peoples can be an issue. For instance, how do we know that there were only four Native people in Detroit in the 1870s? While the census record might reveal the number of people in a given place, for Native people those numbers were largely unreliable because the general American population believed that Native people were "vanishing." The census, as a narrative of dispossession, was used to imply that a city like Detroit was a white-settler city, which hardly had room for Native people.

Urban history and theory have yet to reveal how Indigenous peoples and histories shape these narratives. Earlier studies focused on cultural assimilation versus cultural maintenance, modernity versus tradition, and Indigenous-white relations.[27] There was also an assumption that when Indigenous people moved to cities, they lost their traditions. Recent scholarship has shifted for the better. These studies have found more creative ways to tell the story of urban Indigenous communities.[28] *City of Dispossessions* builds on this scholarship but moves in a different direction by using dispossession as a theoretical tool in order to demonstrate how, throughout Detroit's history,

Black and Indigenous peoples have experienced forms of dispossession and, although tense, have attempted to create belonging in the city.[29]

Black and Indigenous people experience dispossession in the realm of cultural and historical memory. As decolonial theorist Frantz Fanon writes, "Culture under colonial domination is a culture under interrogation whose destruction is sought systematically."[30] In attempting to further dispossess people, the city elite and new population create icons for consumption; for example, in this case, Black and Indigenous historical figures, as in the case of Pontiac.[31] Dispossession narratives like Pontiac's remain an iconic part of Detroit's past and, ironically, now no longer a part of the city's future. How Black and Indigenous people are represented or not represented within these symbols and meanings impact how they are treated. Popular representations are important.[32]

Dispossession forces Black and Indigenous peoples to engage in radical resurgent freedom dreams.[33] They protest. They resist. They create new educational spaces—and they seek to improve the ones that already exist. They try to challenge racial capitalism at the point of production. They attempt to not only better their everyday lives but also act in order to challenge the foundational processes of dispossession. Above all, they hope—imagining and putting into practice alternative institutions, and always resisting by any means necessary.

My Point of View

City of Dispossessions is not a strict chronological history of Detroit. Rather, each chapter grapples with a specific form of dispossession. This organizational strategy allows me to focus on key moments of dispossession. Time periods might overlap from chapter to chapter in order to demonstrate the ongoing nature of dispossession and how the dispossession of Black and Indigenous peoples, as well as their resistance to it, can be disorienting and disruptive and can change depending on time, circumstance, and place.[34] It analyzes how elites assert narratives of dispossession and how they impact Black and Indigenous peoples. It also demonstrates how Black and Indigenous peoples resist dispossession through political activism and expressive culture.

The first chapter, "The Roots of Dispossession: From Waawayeyaattanong to Detroit," offers a brief history of Detroit's development as a French colony, founded in 1701. It reminds readers that the first modern takeover of

Detroit is rooted much earlier than the twentieth century and that Indigenous peoples were the first to be dispossessed. It also illustrates the processes of dispossession, especially how, as the city developed, white settlers used narratives of dispossession in order to construct Detroit as a modern place, through the memorializations of Indigenous peoples. Because the archives are scarce regarding Indigenous people who lived in Detroit, this chapter also includes the movements of Walpole Island First Nations who traveled back and forth to Detroit, including those who attempted to reclaim Belle Isle.

While Chapter 1 covers more than two centuries of the city's history, Chapter 2, "Performing Dispossession: Detroit's 1901 Bicentenary" dives deep to analyze the three-day, two-hundred-year celebration of Detroit's history. I argue that, through this celebration, elite white men attempted to create a cultural idea of Detroit as a white man's space. It allowed for them to further solidify white men as the "indigenous" people of Detroit. However, Black and Indigenous peoples challenged this notion by trying to assert their belonging in how Detroit's history would be remembered.

Chapter 3, "Reclaiming Detroit: Blackness and Indigeneity During the Age of Fordism," explores the history of Black and Indigenous protest and organizations during the interwar years. It explains the history of the Society of American Indians and it chronicles Dakota writer Charles Eastman's time in Detroit. It also explores the history of Black and Indigenous organizations and their attempt to create relevance in the key sites of their dispossession during the time: racial subjugation and invisibility.

Chapter 4, "Citizenship and Sovereignty: Black Nationalism and Indigenous Self-Determination," explores the processes of Black removal from certain parts of the city with the introduction of the federal Housing Act of 1949 and its impact on further constraining Black peoples' lives. It also demonstrates the political activities of Indigenous peoples from the 1940s through the 1960s.

Chapter 5, "Black Indigeneity and Urban Indigenous Feminism in Postwar Detroit," investigates Black and Indigenous radicalism in Detroit during the post-1967 Rebellion. In the contested terrain of peoples' right to the city, it argues that Black radicals constructed a sense of belonging through their labor that was at odds with Native peoples' ideas of land. It also analyzes how Indigenous women asserted their idea of feminism within the urban context.

Chapter 6, "Dispossession and the Roots of Culturally Relevant Education," considers the development of culturally relevant education in Detroit. Beginning with the Afrocentric educational movement in Detroit, Indigenous activists took up this mantle and helped establish the third public school in U.S. history with an Indigenous curriculum. Responding to rampant crime and poverty, educators believed that culturally relevant education would sustain the culture and lives of youth in Detroit.

I conclude the book by looking at how discourses of erasure continue to exist in the city. I make recommendations about the ways Detroit might engage with its Black and Indigenous populations, with the hope of undoing the longer history of dispossession in Detroit by honoring its Indigenous and Black inhabitants and by returning the land.

Together, the six chapters of this book capture the parallel urban experiences of Black and Indigenous people in Detroit—placing these two histories in conversation that is often disconnected. In doing so, I hope to capture the long history of dispossession and how it has shaped both Black and Indigenous struggles for liberation.

CHAPTER 1

The Roots of Dispossession: From Waawayeyaattanong to Detroit

A history of dispossession in Detroit must begin with European settlers' occupation and forced removal of Native people in the eighteenth century. This is the original dispossession—the most familiar one—but not the only one. Even before this moment of encounter, we must account for the people who were already in the Great Lakes area. According to Anishinaabeg oral histories, the Anishinaabe migrated from the eastern part of the United States. Gitchi-Manidoo (the Great Spirit) prophesied that they would make seven sacred stops, and they would find food growing on water (which is manoomin, or wild rice).

Moving along the St. Lawrence River, they stopped at present-day sites of Montreal; Niagara Falls; Manitoulin Island; Sault Ste. Marie; Duluth, Minnesota; and Madeline Island. The third sacred stop is present-day Detroit, which also includes the many islands in the Detroit River. Detroit was one of a few central meeting places for Indigenous people to negotiate and settle disputes.

Detroit is a French word that translates to "the straits." Anishinaabeg had their own name for the space: "wawaiiatan," which translates to "round" or "circular."[1] Other Indigenous names referenced the geographic nature of the space.[2] Beginning with the Frenchman Antoine de la Mothe Cadillac's landing in July 1701, wawaiiatanong would change from an Anishinaabe space, including its name, to an occupied, European space. The French occupation changed the area from a meeting place to a site of dispossession. The Anishinaabeg attempted to maintain their way of life and find ways to deal peacefully with the French and British and the competition for land, furs, and supremacy.

Even before the French arrived, they were entering an already fragmented Indigenous world. Disease had killed thousands of Indigenous people.

Multiple Indigenous nations were embroiled in warfare. The Haudenosaunee had attacked many Algonquian-speaking peoples throughout the Great Lakes region. The Haudenosaunee wanted beaver and replacements for their people lost to battle. Disease and conflicts created refugees throughout the Great Lakes area. Historian Helen Hornbeck Tanner notes that, prior to Fort Detroit's founding, "no tribal group was settled in the region south of Detroit on the western and southern shores of Lake Erie." Detroit was on the "fringe of an apparently vacant area."[3] The French, wanting in on the fur trade, were able to walk into Detroit and occupy the land.[4]

Cadillac, along with dozens of men, came to Detroit in July 1701. They chose that location because of its close proximity to the Detroit River. As a political choice, the French also chose it to ward off advancing Haudenosaunee and British aggression during the fur trade; in addition, it served as a site of negotiation and peace, as well as a fur-trading post. However, Cadillac quickly realized that he needed Indigenous allies in order to thrive.

Between 1701 and 1703, Cadillac beckoned different Indigenous bands, including Wyandot and Michilimackinac, who would join the already present Tionontati, a tribal group that spoke Huron, to come live near the fort. A few years later, other Indigenous bands would join, including the Odawa from Mackinac and two Anishinaabe bands, the Saulteur and the Mississaugi. Finally, a group of Potawatomi and Miami came from the southeastern shore of Lake Michigan. This collection of Indigenous groups would then provide protection from hostile Haudenosaunee and British, food for military personnel, and furs for traders. By 1705, there were about 2,000 Indigenous people living in the area, including 400 warriors. By 1712, only four tribal communities remained in the area: the Anishinaabe, the Odawa, the Potawatomi, and the Huron. The Mississaugi moved to the Thames River in Canada; other Anishinaabe moved to Lake St. Clair and would eventually become known as the "Chippewa of Saginaw Bay."[5]

Detroit continued as a place of cultural exchange and violence throughout the eighteenth century. It was a part of what historian Richard White called "the *pays d'en haut.*" Although scholars have challenged, developed, and deemed White's definition of the "middle ground" incomplete, it is still useful.[6] It was a space in which "the older worlds of the Algonquians and various Europeans overlapped, and their mixture created new systems of meaning and exchange."[7] These encounters and relationships were filled with fear, cultural and political misunderstandings, miscommunications, and violence. In this middle ground occurred "the breakdown of accommodation and common meanings and the re-creation of the Indians as alien, as exotic, as other."[8]

Detroit and violent conflict were synonymous for almost two centuries. It is perhaps known best for Pontiac's so-called conspiracy. In the spring of 1763, led by the Odawa war chief Pontiac, hundreds of warriors attempted to retake British forts throughout the Great Lakes region, including Detroit. Pontiac and Indigenous people were able to retake some forts, but at Detroit the conflict ended in a stalemate. Pontiac then left the area and moved to present-day Illinois, where he was eventually murdered. Detroit continued to be a place of importance well into the nineteenth century. Pontiac's rebellion occurred there, as did the War of 1812. Indigenous people were more than a sideshow to those important histories of U.S. expansion and Indigenous dispossession.

As the United States expanded following the Revolutionary War, it sought more land. Thomas Jefferson, author of the Declaration of Independence and the third president of the United States, oversaw large portions of U.S. land expropriation. Following the Louisiana Purchase, which Jefferson acquired for the United States from the French in 1803, Jefferson also desired control over more land, including Detroit. Detroit was important because of its close proximity to the British occupation of what is now Canada.

In the context of Detroit, one of the first treaties signed was the Treaty of Detroit in 1807.[9] On November 17, 1807, William Hull, who was appointed by Jefferson to be the governor of Michigan territory, negotiated the treaty between the Ojibwe, Odawa, Potawatomi, and Wyandot tribal nations and the United States, which ceded lands in present-day southeast Michigan and Northwest Ohio to the United States. This treaty would later cause problems with Shawnees and Tecumseh, who waged an epic struggle to form an Indigenous state in Ohio, and it contributed to the War of 1812.[10] Article 2 of the treaty states that the United States, with the consent of the Senate, would pay $3,333.33 and four mills to the Odawa and Ojibwe nations and $1,666.06 and six mills to the Wyandot and Potawatomi nations. This treaty and others, in addition to African enslavement, were early examples of racial capitalism in the United States.[11] Just as African enslavement was essential to the development of the U.S. political economy, so too were treaties with Indigenous nations. The U.S. government was able to not only acquire land but also engage in land speculation for the purpose of profit. This profit in turn helped fund the U.S. government.[12] For the United States, negotiating the dispossession of Indigenous land and using Detroit as the meeting place for this exchange largely benefited the white settler capitalists. Of course, treaties do not fully negate

Indigenous agency and the attempts by Indigenous people to negotiate a livelihood as best they can; however, the history of the United States is rooted also in land dispossession. Other treaties included an 1855 agreement between Anishinaabeg and Odawa bands and the United States, which led to further dispossession, and the modern reservations that now exist in Michigan.

Detroit was also a place rooted in both enslavement and dispossession. It was a borderland bound between the reality of slavery and the possibilities of freedom. Slavery was a common feature in early Detroit, and the majority of the enslaved were Indigenous. Historian Tiya Miles's *The Dawn of Detroit: A Chronicle of Slavery and Freedom in the City of the Straits* captures the complexity of the city in the eighteenth and nineteenth centuries. Miles notes, "In the mercantile settlement that would eventually become an American urban behemoth, hundreds of people," including Blacks and Indigenous people, were "kept captive, stripped of autonomy, and forced to labor for others."[13] Indigenous removal and African enslavement built Detroit.[14] In 1750, 25 percent of French families enslaved Indigenous people, and that enslaved group made up 7 percent of the population.[15] The enslavement of Indigenous peoples was not the same as some might imagine about southern slavery. Many enslaved Indigenous people worked in the fur trade and as domestics.

One of the most important parts of legislation connected to the history of Michigan, dispossession, and enslavement was the Northwest Ordinance of 1787. After the British had surrendered the Ohio Country following the Revolutionary War, it remained a place in limbo. U.S. settlers began to move into the Ohio Country, causing rifts with Indigenous peoples. At the legislative level, it set the stage for U.S. expansion, statehood, and the meanings of citizenship. One could only become a citizen after living there for three years and holding 200 acres of land. Although the Northwest Ordinance maintained that Native "lands and property shall never be taken from them without their consent" and that "there shall be neither slavery or involuntary servitude in said territory," it did not halt Indigenous dispossession, nor did it include people of African descent as citizens. The ordinance effectively determined that citizens would be property-owning white settler men; it solidified who could be a citizen and who could not.

This set the stage for further forms of Black and Indigenous dispossession in Michigan throughout the nineteenth century. For example, one of the Michigan Territory laws enacted in 1827 was designed to halt Black settlement in the territory; it required Black migrants to show valid papers demonstrating their freedom or proof of birth before the state would allow them to settle in Michigan.[16] Michigan Territory created dispossession laws before Black migrants could even settle.

Black people, although dispossessed, also found ways to resist. For example, there was the case of Thornton and Ruth Blackburn. In July 1831, the Blackburns escaped from Louisville, Kentucky. They arrived in Detroit shortly after and made it their home. Two years later, their enslavers discovered that they were in Detroit. In June 1833, they were apprehended under slave codes that would require fugitives to be returned to their enslavers. On June 15, the court found them guilty, placed them in jail, and planned to ship them back to Louisville. Mrs. Tabitha Lightfoot, the wife of Madison Lightfoot, who co-founded the Detroit Anti-Slavery Society, and Mrs. Caroline French, two prominent members of Detroit's Black community, visited Mrs. Blackburn in jail. During the visit, Mrs. French switched clothing with Mrs. Blackburn. Disguised as Mrs. French, Blackburn walked out of the jail with Mrs. Lightfoot. They immediately helped get her over to Canada. Mr. Blackburn was still imprisoned, but a group of Black men ripped him away from his captors and immediately sent him across the Detroit River to be with his wife. This was a triumphant, albeit short-lived, victory with devastating consequences. A combination of citizens, police, and the military patrolled the streets with guns, knives, and swords, jailing any Black person they saw and attacking and terrorizing them. Whites violently attacked and burned Black businesses, forcing prominent Black families to flee their properties or sell them, many going across the Detroit River into Ontario, Canada.[17] After the riot, whites treated Blacks worse than before. They would not employ them. Black people had to post a $500 bond in order to show that they would obey the law; if they could not pay, they would be forced to leave.[18]

Dispossession in the form of second-class citizenship was a fundamental part of the Black experience after the so-called Blackburn riots. The 1835 Michigan Constitution stated that voters would include "every white male citizen above the age of twenty-one years" who had "lived in the state for six months before an election."[19] Being a voter was a fundamental basis of U.S. citizenship. The African American population would not increase again until after statehood.

Detroit was the capitol of Michigan from 1807 through 1847, during which time major changes swept over the Midwest.[20] Perhaps the most significant event that changed the landscape of cities like Detroit was the opening of the Erie Canal in 1825, which facilitated an increase in the number of white settlers because they now had an easy way to access Michigan Territory.

In addition to waterways being opened and transformed, so too was the land. Roads were improved, all of which made transportation of goods, people, and resources from the east much easier. Detroit's population grew from 2,222 in 1830 to 9,102 by 1840.

In the 1850s, Detroit was caught between the dispossession of Indigenous peoples, a place of enslavement for Black and Indigenous people, and a locus of freedom through the Underground Railroad. For example, before infamous white radical abolitionist John Brown and a dozen or so formerly enslaved Africans unsuccessfully tried to take over Harpers Ferry in October 1859, he made two stops in Detroit. The first was in 1858, when he met with members of the Colored Vigilant Committee, which consisted of notable members of the Black elite, such as William Lambert, William Monroe, and George DeBaptiste. A year later, he would return and try to convince these folks to help raid Harpers Ferry.[21] Although DeBaptiste objected to Brown's plan, he offered a more radical idea of using gunpowder to blow up fifteen of the largest churches in the South.[22]

At the same time, on the eve of a civil war, in the fight to end African enslavement, Indigenous people were thought to be disappearing, including from Detroit. On April 29, 1853, the *Detroit Daily Free Press* published an article that mentioned the quickly vanishing Detroit Indigenous community. "We noticed four aborigines yesterday, on seeing whom we could not but reflect on the great changes that have taken place in our city in fifteen years." Reflecting on the situation only fifteen years previously, the article remarked, "In 1838, a person by merely glancing through almost any street, could see parties of these children of the forest scattered throughout its entire length." Detroit's citizens could hear Indigenous people right across the way in the nearby forests, apparently keeping up those who stayed at a local hotel: "Horrible were the grimaces, and discordant yells, of the dusky-featured performers, as they hopped and writhed with the utmost agility, destitute, as they were of nearly every article of clothing. Now, it is comparatively rarely that one of them is to be seen. They are almost gone, and in a short time, their former existence among us will be known only through the medium of tradition. Farewell, 'Injuns,' 'Niitchees,' a long farewell!"[23] This long farewell was more than just hyperbole; it was an attempt to erase Indigenous people from the public imagination.

From newspapers to books such as James Fenimore Cooper's *The Last of the Mohicans* (1826), whites throughout the United States believed that Native people were going to disappear. These narratives not only continued the long-held idea of Indigenous savagery and disappearance from the land but also cemented the vanishing Indian trope. Settlers spread these stories, as White Earth Anishinaabe historian Jean O'Brien observes, throughout the country as a "generalized trope and disseminated not just in the form of the written word but also in a rich ceremonial cycle of pageants, commemorations, monument building, and lecture hall performance."[24] With the assumption that Native people were disappearing, elite white men in Detroit began to memorialize their Native historical figures. And yet, at the same time as they sought to memorialize the Native past, they continued to experience the visits and migrations of Native peoples in the present. But that did not stop white settlers from creating further narratives of dispossession to remake Detroit as a white space.

Storying Dispossession

Settler narratives, or dispossession narratives, serve as a key site of dispossession. They are discourses, histories, speech acts, and other stories that white settlers use to construct their own sense of belonging. Importantly, they explain *how* and *why* a particular geographical space became theirs. In this process, they often ignore or make invisible the accompanying colonial violence that was fundamental to their conquest of land and containment of Indigenous peoples and the enslavement of Black peoples. In addition to removing Indigenous peoples, settlers use stories of the past to construct a future for white citizens while simultaneously erasing an Indigenous presence and, just as important, an Indigenous future.

One of the most influential settler narrators of early Detroit was Friend Palmer. Palmer was the cousin of Senator Thomas W. Palmer, a notable character in Detroit who served as president of the 1893 Columbian Exposition in Chicago, Illinois. Friend Palmer was born in Canandaigua, New York, on May 7, 1820, to Friend Palmer and Thankful Palmer, and came to Detroit at the age of seven. He would later marry Miss Harriett C. Witherell, of Detroit, with whom he had two children. She was the daughter of Judge Benjamin F. H. Witherell, who was territorial judge of Michigan. Friend Palmer served for several years as quartermaster in the army during the Mexican-American War, after which he returned to Detroit. He also served in the Civil War as assistant quartermaster general of the state of Michigan, and, later, as quartermaster general. He was also an active Republican and was engaged in the book trade for a number of years.

In his old age, Palmer dedicated himself to sharing with the (white) citizenry what he believed to be the true history of Detroit. In his view, citizens should know how the city developed in order to know where they could take it in the future. Palmer recounted to a reporter his memories of Detroit, from a small town to a booming city. In his book titled *Early Days in Detroit*, Palmer details a variety of stories about Detroit's past. He believed that central to a city's development, as well as the education of its citizens, was historical memory. Interestingly, Palmer included several anecdotes about Indigenous histories of Detroit.

Native people were central to Palmer's retelling of Detroit's past. He discussed a story about a lion's head knocker that was fixed on the door of General Lewis Cass's home. Cass was the longtime governor of the Michigan Territory (1813–31) and served as secretary of war under the notorious killer of Indigenous people, President Andrew Jackson. There was a deep mark on the lion's face. A rumor circulated that the lion's head was made by the Odawa chief Pontiac. Apparently, he drew his tomahawk in a rage and hit the bronze lion head.[25] Palmer also reported that Native people were present in Detroit throughout the early and mid-part of the nineteenth century. In 1807, Palmer suggested that "Indians of the surrounding wilderness were even then seriously threatening."[26] He also points out that men such as Pontiac, Tecumseh, and others, "from time to time were held by dwellers of the town in the direst dread, and were familiar figures on the streets of both the old and new town and the country here after my advent."[27] Native people, suggests Palmer, were common figures in Detroit, walking the streets, visiting with whites. The important question here is why would Palmer feel the need to mention these Indigenous folks, given that they walked the paths and trails of Detroit long ago? What function did it serve for Palmer and, more importantly, for the audiences he was hoping to reach with his recollections? For Palmer, recollections about Indigenous peoples were akin to ghosts. As anthropologist Colleen Boyd and historian Coll Thrush argue, Indigenous ghosts "express the moral anxieties and uncertainties provoked by the dispossession of a place's Indigenous inhabitants." Indigenous recollections for Palmer also demonstrate the "remarkably complex facets of the experience of colonialism and highlight the ways in which knowledge of place and past are constructed, produced, revealed, and contested."[28] Highlighting particular Indigenous people unique to American and Detroit history further connects settlers to the land and, in some way, asserts their claim to constructing histories of place, moving from savagery to civilization. It solidifies dispossession in the realm of popular discourse, creating a past and future in which Indigenous dispossession then becomes inevitable, or a matter of fact, instead of a process that settlers produced, furthering the Indigenous disappearance narrative.

Still, Palmer stated, "streets thronged with them during spring, summer and autumn, but they were always most peaceable and friendly."[29] Palmer, like many whites during his time, believed that Native people were disappearing, and he therefore deemed it important to make sure Detroit citizens knew about their Indigenous past. Palmer continued, even mentioning some discovered Indigenous bodies during an excavation: "I presume there is hardly a rod square of ground underlying the city from Beaubien Street to First, and from the river back to Fort Street and in the immediate vicinity of the latter, that does not contain the remains of a human being. When the Cass farm front was excavated into the river over a hundred dead bodies of Indian warriors were exhumed. Their bones went into the dirt carts, the implements of war and the chase, as also the various ornaments buried with them becoming the spoil of the lucky finder." The fact that there was an excavation is not necessarily important; however, for Palmer, the story illustrates how white men in the early twentieth century believed they could control Indigenous bodies, could narrate their histories, and could do with those narratives as they pleased. The bones, histories, and artifacts of these Indigenous people have become a part of the lost history of Detroit—a thing locked deep in the crevices of history but still remaining—like an omnipotent present that remains unclaimed and unverified.

In addition to telling other stories about Detroit's past, Palmer also recalled a history of the Sauk Warrior Black Hawk. Black Hawk remains a prominent symbol of resistance for Indigenous communities. He led a revolt against U.S. encroachment on Sauk and Fox lands in present-day Illinois. Black Hawk, throughout his life, disputed the Treaty of St. Louis (1804) between the Sauk and Fox Nations and Governor William Henry Harrison of Indiana Territory.[30] In June 1831, he and his warriors lost a battle with the Illinois Militia and were forced to sign a treaty that moved them west of the Mississippi. In April 1832, he returned, which led to the Black Hawk war. Black Hawk and the Sauk and Fox warriors lost and the Federal government incarcerated them and took much of their remaining land.[31] In April 1833, they were sent east, and their first stop was Washington D.C., where they met with President Andrew Jackson and Secretary of War Lewis Cass.

Friend Palmer recounted Black Hawk's visit to Detroit. In the summer of 1833, Black Hawk and his delegation were traveling home from Washington,

D.C.[32] He was imprisoned for a time at Fort Monroe in Hampton, Virginia. After his release from prison, U.S. officials took Black Hawk on a tour of eastern U.S. cities so that he could see the power of the United States. On his way home, he stopped at Albany, Buffalo, and then Detroit. Black Hawk, in his autobiography, stated that, upon their arrival in Detroit, "I had spent many pleasant days, and anticipated, on my arrival, to meet many of my old friends, but in this I was disappointed."[33] Traveling with his son, Whirling Thunder, and others, Black Hawk came during the Fourth of July and stayed at the Mansion House. Augustus Woodward, the Chief Justice of the Michigan Territory, owned the Mansion House, which he had built in 1824. It was three or four stories tall and had a huge open porch in the front. The Mansion was destroyed in 1834 to make room for riverfront development. This this was one of two hotels in Detroit at the time; mostly people of notoriety stayed there.

Palmer recalled that he saw "the Indian warrior and chief, the celebrated Black Hawk, and party" at the Mansion House. Perhaps in order to authenticate the fact that he actually saw Black Hawk, he quoted an Englishman who described Black Hawk as a "slight-made man, about 50–55 years old, and stands five feet five or six inches tall." His son was apparently a "fine looking young man, with what might be called an open countenance" and he "carries his head high and looks about him." Palmer wrote, "I have seen many good specimens of the Indian brave, but I think this son of Black Hawk excelled them all, a noble specimen of physical beauty, a model for those who would embody the idea of strength."

It is ironic, however, that Palmer had such fond memories of Black Hawk's visit. According to historian Kerry Trask, Detroiters were not thrilled. While Black Hawk and his entourage experienced a great reception in the eastern cities of Buffalo and Philadelphia, Detroit was not kind to Black Hawk. Trask notes, "Effigies of Black Hawk and other members of his party were burned in a hostile display of collective hatred."[34] The difference in reception, according to Trask, is likely because of the close proximity white Detroiters had to Native people: "The malice in the voices clearly indicated that the myth of the 'noble savage' flourished only in the part of the nation where real Indians had ceased to exist."[35] Trask is perhaps correct, illustrating the huge difference between how European Americans, within the context of settler colonialism, understand Indigenous people. They can remember Indigenous people fondly if—and only if—those Indigenous people have been conquered and white society has been enacted. If Detroiters like Palmer had fond memories of the city's past, they were even more ecstatic to meet real-life Indigenous people, who they assumed were fading away.

Sitting Bull, Buffalo Bill's Wild West, and Detroit

Like Black Hawk, Sitting Bull, perhaps one of the most recognizable names in U.S. history, also passed through to Detroit and stayed only briefly. He came to the city as a part of Buffalo Bill's Wild West show.[36] The show traveled to Detroit for a two-day performance held on September 4 and 5, 1885. The female shooter Annie Oakley came, the Cowboy Kid, and Indigenous performers were all part of the show. One of those performers was Hunkpapa Lakota Medicine Man, Sitting Bull. Though the local newspapers advertised the event, the actual performance was not well documented. However, a meeting held between Sitting Bull and elite Detroit politicians at Recreation Park was. Although Sitting Bull's stay was brief, the encounter between Sitting Bull and these elites, as well as their discursive representation of him, reveal the larger attitudes that white settlers of Detroit had about Indigenous peoples upon encountering them. They viewed Sitting Bull through the lens of their own settler masculinity.

"Settler masculinity" is the way settler populations, especially men, create an ideological condition whereby the epitome of manhood is rooted in modernity. That is, those who are "men" are "civilized," white, and urban, and they perform a certain type of work. This is in contrast to the "Natives," who are "uncivilized," not white, not urban, and not modern, and they are disappearing. White men believed that a major reason Indigenous people could not be modern is because, in the process of dispossession, white men placed Indigenous men in a particular time and space, affixing them in a particular ideological matrix from which they could never escape.[37]

It is not surprising that Sitting Bull came to Detroit. Historian Robert Utley explains that during the last six years of Sitting Bull's life, he traveled extensively.[38] Sitting Bull only participated in one season of Buffalo Bill's show. His travels, though, expanded Sitting Bull's view of the world, and, while he marveled at aspects of modernity, he found it difficult to shake settler imaginings of him. Sitting Bull came during the end of the so-called Indian wars on the plains, and five years before the Wounded Knee Massacre and his own death. It was during a time when whites for the most part no longer feared armed Indigenous resistance. Simultaneously, settlers began memorializing Indigenous peoples of the past.[39] Yet, Sitting Bull was one of the few Indigenous people lauded by settlers before he died. He was praised—in an ironic and twisted way—for his resistance to U.S. aggression and expansion. As a result, his coming to Detroit, and the magnificent way in which he was received, was not surprising.

On September 4, at 1:00 PM, a train left the Russell House to head to Recreation Park to meet the infamous "chief" Sitting Bull. Recreation Park was a baseball field, home to the Detroit Wolverines who played in the National League from 1881 through 1888. Those who came to meet Sitting Bull at the tent erected for him were government officials and businessmen of Detroit; they included Mayor Stephen Benedict Grummond (1884–85), President Augustus Kaiser of the Lower House, Senator Thomas W. Palmer (a descendant of early pioneer Detroit families), Michigan's secretary of state Harry Conant (1883–87), and Councilmen H. E. Champion and Theodore Rentz.

The public meeting between Sitting Bull and elite white men of the city was a public performance of dispossession. The tone of the meeting centered on the aftermath of dispossession and what the United States could do for the Native people. The encounter began with an afternoon lunch, which included beer, lemonade, and a rib roast. After the meal, introductions were made. Sitting Bull was accompanied by Crow Eagle, who stood to his left, and the interpreter Bill Halsey, who stood to his right, as well as Lakota. While smoking his cigar and looking around, Sitting Bull greeted each man with the masculine Lakota greeting, "hau." The visitors were eager to speak with the Lakota medicine man.

Sitting Bull was greatly admired and well respected by his visitors. "Tell Bull that he is one of our law-makers," said Senator Palmer. "We hope soon to place the entire Indian question in the hands of the War department, and . . . when we do the Indians will be honestly and liberally dealt with." The white men even seemed to seek Sitting Bull's approval. Councilman Rentz added, "The good time coming for the Indians, as predicted by our Mayor will be due to the honest and fairness of a good democratic institution." Pleased to hear such assurances, Sitting Bull responded, through Halsey: "The Bull says that he believes he is going to do the fair thing by the Indians." Halsey added, "He says that President Grover Cleveland sent Sheridan out to see the Cheyennes, and that action shows that the Democratic administration are bound to see fair play for the Indians." After making this brief dialogue, Secretary of State Conant was introduced to Sitting Bull and he said, "Hau! Big brave! Big, good brave!" Apparently, Sitting Bull's approval made Conant the most talked about person at the reception, besides Sitting Bull.[40]

Sitting Bull was not a passive object. Although he spoke through an interpreter, he was able to subtly critique Detroit and the society he saw growing around him. However, because Sitting Bull spoke through an interpreter, we should be careful about how his words were expressed. The historical record illustrates, though, that Indigenous people brokered as much leverage as they could for the future of their people. Like other performers in Wild West shows, Sitting Bull's encounter was a "contact zone" between Indigenous culture and performance and the settler cultural gaze and expectations.[41]

A young boy asked Sitting Bull if he was at Custer's last stand at the Battle of Little Big Horn. Sitting Bull replied, "Yes, I was near there, but not in the fight." Dissatisfied with the response—illustrating that settler imaginations reached even boyhood—the boy asked, "Did you kill Custer?" Sitting Bull replied, "I did not. I do not know who killed Custer." A reporter for the *Detroit Free Press* followed with an entirely different question. "What shall you say to your people when you go back to them, about white people?" This was a curious question, and Sitting Bull looked puzzled. But then his eyes opened wide, he changed his posture, and although his Lakota was unintelligible to everyone in his tent except for Crow Eagle and the interpreter, he said: "I have seen the white people and their great chief. I have seen how they live and my eyes opened. I shall tell my children that the whites are as the leaves of the forest, and that to them we are but as the single berry left on the bush to wither and die in the winter. I shall tell them that the whites are our friends and will keep us and protect us, and that the white chief has given promise to do so."[42] Based on his extensive travels and many conversations with elite whites over his lifetime (especially after violent resistance did not seem to be a legitimate course of action going forward), Sitting Bull saw the writing on the wall. But did he actually believe that Lakota and other Indigenous peoples were simply a "single berry left on the bush," left to wither away? His statement was not simply one of despair. He realized that settler society did not care much for Indigenous peoples and that the settlers were determined to impose their own conception of civilization upon Lakota and other Indigenous communities by further stripping them of land and resources. But Sitting Bull shifted quickly, telling his audience that whites would protect his people. Although this statement was hopeful, it was also a common rhetorical strategy used by Indigenous people during that time. As historian C. Joseph Genetin-Pilawa observes, Indigenous diplomats witnessed "a sea of changes in U.S. Indian-relations" that would force them to "work within, as well as against, the contradictions constructed by the confinements of the process."[43] As demonstrated by Sitting Bull, even the realm of performance for settler audiences became a political site through which diplomacy could be articulated. With the intention of laying to rest white fears of Indigenous peoples, he told them what they wanted to hear: that Indigenous peoples would place their well-being in the hands of settlers.

Sitting Bull's time in Detroit seemed productive. He was able to make some money and push forward his agenda for Lakota rights. Yet the way in which Detroit citizens accepted him reveals the contradictions of living in a society that rapidly went from killing Indigenous people to memorializing them. On the one hand, they might have respected his past exploits as an "Indian brave," a common trope during the period. On the other hand, they may have respected him in the present, someone in whom they saw a great leader engaging with "civilization," while stubbornly resisting it at the same time. Regardless, these politicians parted with Sitting Bull having learned a lot about the man; the local newspapers, however, did not.

The Detroit newspapers also spent time discussing Sitting Bull. A newspaper column analyzed his performance in Buffalo Bill's Wild West show. While they appreciated his efforts, they were disappointed in what they did *not* see. The disappointment was not rooted in the performance; rather, it was based on what the writer believed was a lack of authenticity—or, the fact of Sitting Bull, the man, not fulfilling the settler imaginings of what the audience believed him to be. "Beyond doubt, Sitting Bull is brave and has the usual cunning of his race," read the column, "but there is another and truer side to his nature which all the feathers and other ornaments on earth cannot hide from the man who has been much in Indian country."[44] The article expressed disappointment that Sitting Bull did not fit settler conceptions of manhood. Settlers could remember their constricted idea of Indigenous manhood—as a warrior—but one that was no longer a threat to their civilization. At that moment, Sitting Bull, like others, ceased to be men, according to the logics of settler masculinity.

The writer was not satisfied with actual Indigenous peoples, wanting instead for Indigenous performers to meet the settler desires of authenticity. The writer desired the pristine scene of "squaws chopping wood" or "carrying buckets of water with a papoose or two" on their backs. Indeed, the performance would have met the gross desires of the settler imagination if Sitting

Bull himself had a "canoe paddle in one hand and a bottle of whiskey in the other."[45] Although the performance would not have been as entertaining, "the realism would have been there."[46] The symbolism of Sitting Bull, the perfect embodiment of a settler construction of Indigenous masculinity, paddling in a canoe with whiskey is very profound, reflecting the localized understanding of Indigenous stereotypes. Detroit's Indigenous history could not escape the actual presence of the Great Lakes waterways. The water perhaps signifying the inability of Indigenous people to move into modernity, especially in Detroit, where one could paddle in the canoe just outside the city but unable to get close enough. Indigenous people like Sitting Bull could live next to modernity, witness it, feel it, smell it, but could not partake in it.

It was not enough that so-called authentic Indigenous peoples participated in the performance and played Indian. Their physical bodies were only useful if they appealed to the ongoing imaginings of settlers. The white people looked at Sitting Bull through their own lens—the lens of whiteness, a masculine Victorian whiteness—which limits the ability of those in power to hold accurate conceptions of Indigenous peoples. This representation also showed the limits of performances as a way to challenge the settler gaze.[47]

Sitting Bull departed on September 5, 1885. Indian police killed him in 1890. However, nearly sixteen years later, Sitting Bull's name reappeared as a part of Buffalo Bill's Wild West performance in Detroit. Once more, perceptions of Sitting Bull were dominated by settler imaginations about their constructed character—not the actual person. An article reprinted in the *Detroit Free Press*, "Sitting Bull and Buffalo Bill: Latter's Big Show Will Exhibit at Detroit Tuesday Afternoon and Evening," showed the infamous picture of Sitting Bull in full regalia standing to the left of William F. Cody (Buffalo Bill). The tone of the article suggests that Native peoples were conquered and no longer presented a threat to settlers, or to U.S. progress, as Chiricahua Apache Geronimo and Lakota Red Cloud were. Geronimo was then a prisoner at Fort Sill; Red Cloud was confined to the Pine Ridge Reservation. Because they had been conquered, they no longer fit the settler masculine imagination. In contrast, "Sitting Bull was a warrior to his death." He died "as he had lived, the incarnation of red defiance and independence." The discourse about Sitting Bull was based on the history and valorization of Indigenous resistance through warfare. Unfortunately, it illustrated the *Detroit Free Press*'s idealized stories about Indigenous people. They could not appreciate other forms of resistance that had been building up during the last decade of the nineteenth century. Indigenous people's presence in Detroit, real or imagined, was largely based on the past—that is, on what settler imaginations wanted to remember.

The stories of Sitting Bull and Black Hawk in Detroit reveal the contradictions of dispossession and indigeneity in Detroit. Detroit citizens desired to connect to the infamous Indigenous men of the past in order to demonstrate what the citizens had overcome. The contradictions of an extant Indigenous presence in the city and settler imaginings of Indigenous history would continue, in parallel, throughout twentieth-century Detroit, especially in the case of Pontiac, who was and remains perhaps the most iconic Indigenous relic of Detroit's identity.

Pontiac's City

To local Detroiters and to people throughout the United States, the name Pontiac holds many meanings. Most know it as the now discontinued General Motors automobile model. A quick Google search of "Pontiac" reveals first the General Motors brand and then the city, Pontiac, Michigan. The third "Pontiac" subject in the search result is the Odawa war chief who helped stage an epic battle against the British in 1763. In the light of this, it is bizarre but necessary to state the obvious: Pontiac the man, the historical figure, preceded the vehicle and the city. On the eve of an auto revolution, Detroiters in the late nineteenth and early part of the twentieth century knew about Pontiac the historical figure, in the form of "Pontiac's Conspiracy."

In 1872, an article proclaimed that Pontiac "made himself so prominent that his name will be remembered by Detroiters for a hundred years to come."[48] Similarly, in 1899, one local wrote, "Before the white man's foot had trodden the wilderness where now stand thriving and populous cities and while the red man still held undisputed sway over the territory in the region the great lakes, the name Pontiac was a familiar and honored word."[49] An article in 1913 described Pontiac's importance to local Detroit legends: "A name, next to a mound of earth, is one of the most persistent things in the world."[50] Pontiac was an important part of Detroit's presence in the late nineteenth century and beyond. But now, Pontiac the man exists mostly as a ghost of Detroit's past. What accounts for this? Narrating dispossession at a moment in which Detroit was rapidly changing reveals the need to construct an origin story that was made in Detroit.

Pontiac and Detroit's Modernity

Elite white men like Clarence Burton and Silas Farmer were instrumental in creating a modern Detroit rooted in a deep sense of mythic histories and place. According to historian Karen Marrero, Burton "placed himself in the tracks of the original pioneers" and "fashioned a story of progress of the city from fur trading post to urban metropolis, defining a point from which the industrial development of Detroit could be traced."[51] Burton was a historian without portfolio, collecting what today is called the Burton Historical Collection—the basis of early Detroit and Midwestern history now held at the Detroit Public Library. Burton was born in 1853 and earned a law degree from the University of Michigan in 1874. He began practicing law shortly thereafter. While a student at the university, he developed an interest in the history of Detroit, and thus began a lifetime of collecting as much information as possible about Detroit's past. In 1908, he was named city historian; in 1913, he also served as the first president of the Detroit Historical Society. In addition, he translated Robert Navarre's journal, which was his account of Pontiac's "conspiracy."[52] Burton carefully and systematically curated what Detroit citizens would "know" about Detroit's history.

Silas Farmer was another prominent historian. Named city historian in 1882, he was the son of John Farmer, a well-known publisher of a map of Michigan. Silas died suddenly on December 28, 1902.[53] He was one of the city's most important historians, writing religiously about the history of Detroit, including, most notably, *All About Detroit: An Illustrated Guide, Map, and Historical Souvenir, with Local Stories* (1890) and *The History of Detroit and Michigan: Or, the Metropolis Illustrated* (1884).[54] His influence in shaping the history of Detroit was paramount, including serving as the lead editor of the book that documented the events of the 1901 Detroit Bicentennial.[55] Burton and Farmer, as city historians, constructed a city predicated on a certain narrative of progress that was easily accessible to a general audience. Local newspapers were also a tool for disseminating histories of Detroit, including that of Pontiac.

The concept of noble savagery is important in understanding the link between Pontiac and Detroit. Pontiac's name as a subject appears numerous times within local Detroit newspapers, many of which focus on what the historian Francis Parkman called at the time "Pontiac's Conspiracy."[56] On October 6, 1900, an anonymous person submitted a question to the editors of the *Detroit Free Press* through the "Letter Box" column. In order for a question to be published, it had to help clarify some "curious information" about Detroit or contemporary news around the city. The question read, "What connection has 'Pontiac's Tree' in Detroit with the celebrated Indian chief of that name?" The editor answered, "The tree is said to have been a silent witness of the battle of Bloody Bridge which occurred early in the morning of July 31, 1763, and which was one of the battles fought during the conspiracy of Pontiac."[57] Coincidentally, twenty years earlier, city historian Silas Farmer debunked such a myth in the same paper, stating that the tree may have been there when Pontiac attempted to seize the fort, "but if it was there then it had about as much to do with Pontiac, and he with it, as he had to do with any other tree in the vast forest of what was afterwards known as the Territory and the State of Michigan."[58] This question reveals, though, the importance of Pontiac in the minds of Detroit citizens, and what meaning Pontiac might have for them as they existed in the twentieth century.

According to the census records of the late nineteenth and early part of the twentieth centuries, Indigenous people were scarce in Detroit.[59] Although the census records are unreliable, as a source they are worth mentioning so that we can speculate about how dispossession narratives, including the census, are used as a method to demonstrate the dearth of Indigenous peoples in the area so that white settlers could claim the city as their own. Though the historical record does not reveal much about Indigenous people's contributions to Detroit's development, Pontiac's story remained in the city's collective consciousness, and white men were the key architects of it. They used Pontiac's image to construct Detroit as a modern American city.

Elite white men of Detroit were sincere in their efforts to construct a modern American city, and memorializing the defeat of Pontiac was key to their modernization project. On November 30, 1899, the Michigan Society of the Sons of the American Revolution and the Society of Colonial Wars held a joint dedication of the site upon which Pontiac first passed a gateway into Fort Detroit. A plaque celebrated his defeat.[60] Presiding over the affair was former senator Thomas Palmer, Mayor William C. Maybury, and Society of Colonial Wars president T. H. Eaton.[61] It is worth discussing Maybury briefly. He was a Democrat elected mayor in a state dominated by Republicans from 1897 to 1905. Prior to serving the city of Detroit as mayor, he served two terms in the forty-eighth and forty-ninth Congresses from 1883 to 1887. In 1900, he ran unsuccessfully for governor of Michigan. As mayor, Maybury oversaw significant changes in the city, especially the building of monuments and parks. Most notably, he created and oversaw a committee dedicated to celebrating Detroit's 1901 Bicentennial.[62] Finally, he was a close friend of

Henry Ford and the automobile industry.[63] As a leader of a developing city and monument making, Maybury, like Burton and Farmer, was a key figure in the mythmaking and uses of history in turn-of-the-century Detroit. The plaque, about the size of a small tablet, was located at the gate where Fort Detroit stood, circa 1763, near present-day East Jefferson Avenue.

Though small in size, the plaque should be read as a monument. In the words of historian Coll Thrush, monuments "mean both the happenstance detritus of colonialism's past and deliberate interventions in historical landscapes, all grounded in specificity of particular places."[64] This plaque was built to document the history of Detroit for its present citizens, but it reveals more, though, about white men's need to construct a sense of territoriality and remembering—a reminder that colonialism had been legitimated.

On the left side of the tablet is a tall Indian chief, wearing a headdress and looking stoic. He is holding a hatchet and a peace pipe. Apparently, it represents what Pontiac held while entering the fort. History has not revealed to us a legitimate portrait of Pontiac, the man. Instead, we have been left with the settler imagining of Pontiac. Apparently, an Indigenous woman made the plaque; for this, Senator Palmer encouraged the crowd to give "three cheers for the maiden."[65] After praising the work of this unnamed Indigenous woman, a cornet led the observing crowd in singing "America the Beautiful." The singing of "America the Beautiful" officially serenaded the memorialization of Pontiac by connecting the warding off of Pontiac's conspiracy as a uniquely American story, made in Detroit. This portrait represented a tall, stoic Indian—a stereotypical representation of indigeneity. Pontiac, standing erect, was just waiting to commit some "treachery," and yet the plaque also symbolized how white men had overcome the "savage" past. Not only did the British stand tall against his "crafty," "treacherous" nature, they also subsequently created a thriving city.

The plaque's dedication ceremony was not only to celebrate the past but also to narrate the progression of this place from a fort to a metropolis. Following the words of Senator Palmer, Mayor Maybury proclaimed, "One hundred and thirty-nine years ago, there stood two figures at the gate marked by this tablet. One was a white man carrying a rifle, a shovel, a hoe and an ax. The other was a red man, magnificent to look upon." The "red man" also carried a rifle, "but his face was scarred and he carried also a tomahawk and a scalping knife. He came no one knew whence. The red man knew no duty aside from absolute freedom. The white man was the representative of duty and he was present to perform that duty." Here, Maybury created a dichotomy between Indigenous masculinity and Detroit's version of colonial masculinity. For colonial masculinity, the ax and the hoe represent the narrative that white men were coming to work and transform the land—a key narrative used to dispossess Native people. White men had the discipline to work the land. In contrast, the "red man" was interested only in committing acts of violence; Native people did not have the discipline to transform the land because they could not control their innate nature to roam free—at least according to European standards. Here, Maybury justified Indigenous dispossession and, at the same time, asserted white men's relationship to place because they came with the intent of working the land, making it modern. This narrative was instructive for contemporary Detroiters because it suggested that hard work was the only way things changed, or became modern.

Anthropologist Scott Morgensen writes that two points undergird colonial masculinity's power. First, it "had to be invented." Second, it had to change to account for ever-changing conditions. Thus, masculinity in Detroit had to adapt to new conditions of rapid urbanization and change in the Motor City. While white men had already conquered Detroit, men like Maybury used this scenario to further cement their status as a group that was "indigenous" to the city. This narration provided, for a present audience, the construction of Indigenous masculinity and white masculinity. Although Maybury was speaking about the past, his discussion of white and Indigenous masculinity was designed for the present. The white man came upon the shore of a place occupied by "wild" savages; white men like Cadillac came and made something of the space. This is the narrative of progress. Native men had the ability to engage in warfare but not to work the land. Creating distinctions here was to divide masculinity. Morgensen argues that "this mode of gender arises across a boundary between the civilized and the primitive, and it functions to police that boundary: by defining them as separate, and by dividing and remaking peoples and lands."[66]

The plot in this narrative was also a sign of progress, designed to assert more broadly U.S. imperial ambitions, and masculinity played a role in it.[67] In the midst of becoming an imperial force internationally, local stories like this one arguably contributed to the shift to "civilizing" others abroad, something they had perfected with the Indigenous peoples, who they now could memorialize on plaques and statues.

The memorializing of Pontiac was not so much about "playing Indian" as it was about evoking indigeneity to consecrate white men's triumph from savagery to civilization. During the late nineteenth century, Detroiters spent much time trying to rid city politics of corruption and advocate for a pristine way of living that catered to a white protestant ethic and sense of morality.[68] Whereas whites use previous forms of noble savagery as a critique of and contrast to European society in the early modern period, the Detroit version was used to cement white men's connection to place.[69]

Former U.S. senator Thomas W. Palmer (1830–1913) was another example of white men asserting their claims to the city. He was an ardent admirer of Detroit's Indigenous past, especially the story of Pontiac. Born in Detroit on January 25, 1830, Palmer was the son of Thomas Palmer and cousin of Friend Palmer, a highly successful businessman who came to Detroit following the end of the War of 1812. He served as a Republican senator from 1883 through 1889. He engaged in a variety of activities, including serving as the president of Chicago's World Columbian Exposition in 1893. He was a generous benefactor to the city, helping erect the Michigan Soldiers and Sailors monument at Campus Martius Park. He was also one of the founders and the first president of the Detroit Museum of Art, now called the Detroit Institute of Arts. Palmer was dedicated to constructing Detroit as the epitome of modernity. According to a contemporary, Palmer "cherishes for Michigan a love approaching idolatry."[70]

It is not clear why Palmer was so fascinated by Pontiac. Yet he spent years of his life collecting artifacts and information on the Odawa chief. Palmer laboriously looked for Pontiac's actual burial place, even though he likely knew that Pontiac was killed near St. Louis. However, Palmer reasoned that Pontiac deserved to be memorialized like other well-known Indigenous warriors, including Tecumseh (Shawnee) and Black Hawk (Sauk). As an architect of pageants such as the Columbian Exposition, whose goal was to show to the world the U.S. progress as the premiere, modern nation-state, Palmer surely viewed himself as doing a similar thing at the local level. Palmer desired to show that Detroit was in fact a modern city similar to any in the world, and Detroit's modernity rested on the shift from savagery to civilization.

The erection of a grave-memorial represented a deeper link between dispossession in the past and the need to memorialize an already conquered Indigenous presence—Pontiac—a representative of the larger narrative of Indigenous removal from Detroit. Palmer took it upon himself to assemble an artificial grave in Pontiac's honor and, according to the *Detroit Free Press*, "Hence upon this farm, a few miles north of Detroit, he laid out a little plot of ground."[71] He surrounded the farm with an artistic iron fence to protect the grave. He also had a monument placed above it with "an inscription setting forth appropriate historical information concerning the first of Michigan's warriors and a tribute to his bravery and his virtues." Apparently, Pontiac's grave attracted numerous people, both from and in Detroit, for it became "one of the most interesting historical spots in Michigan."[72] At more than 140 acres, Palmer wanted the park to be "one of the finest in the world," a place where local Detroiters could "read, study and enjoy nature."[73] He also built a log cabin for his wife, Lizzie Merrill Palmer, there so that she could escape the high anxiety of urban life.[74] In this effort, he illustrated historian Philip Deloria's idea that "Americans wanted to feel a natural affinity with the continent, and it was Indians who could teach them such aboriginal closeness."[75] Pontiac's memorial would be built right in the heart of nature, where urban anxieties were no more and where Detroiters could be at peace and connect with nature—the original component of noble savagery.

Palmer's erection of Pontiac's grave is striking for a few reasons, including these two. First, it was general knowledge at the time that, following Pontiac's failed seizure of Detroit, he departed for Illinois country. Second, Pontiac was killed near St. Louis. Historian William Nester suggests that Pontiac, who died at the hands of a Peoria warrior near Cahokia, was buried near downtown St. Louis.[76] These two reasons alone would seem to discourage someone from creating a false burial. However, settlers use monuments in a particular place's past in order to move forward in their own narrative of progress. It is not enough for settlers to simply recount an Indigenous past—settlers need also the most barbaric, savage historical accounts possible to justify their own existence as modern subjects.[77] Pontiac's grave was not simply a reimagining of history; it also served as the local monument to connect settlers' present to their Indigenous past. Palmer's Pontiac grave was a site of dispossession. He used it as a symbol to legitimate white male possession of Detroit. It was an attempt to dramatize, in the words of critic Edward Said, "the distance between and difference between what is close to it and what is far away," which, in this case, was the Indigenous past and the settler present.[78] The use of a grave represented the finality—at least that is what they believed—of Indigenous presence in Detroit.

The burial of Pontiac's bones in a grave was not just a metaphor for dominating Indigenous male bodies. The use of a grave represented the finality of Indigenous dominance in the contemporary life of settlers. It helped foster—in a cultural-ideological way—elite white men's attempt to more clearly delineate modernity, or modern Detroit, from times past. Pontiac's story, one that had long dominated the local folklore of settlers' development, could be permanently buried, finally, where he once tried to recapture Indigenous land. The ghost of Pontiac, the personification of Indigenous manliness, was, once and for all, conquered by an elite white man. Creating Pontiac's grave was the manifestation of settler masculinity.

At the local level, the erection of Pontiac's grave illustrates how white men desired to have control over the idea of Indigenous male bodies in order to construct their own present. Making claim to Pontiac's metaphoric, memorialized grave and erecting a monument was an enactment of colonial masculinity. By acknowledging the Indigenous past through Pontiac and by entangling his imagining about Pontiac, the Indigenous warrior brave, and his own sense of a settler masculinity, Palmer was able to advance a certain narrative of progress in order to further solidify white men's claim to space and history.

Pontiac's name was a persistent force in areas around Detroit, too. Apple Island is a small island in the middle of Orchard Lake in Orchard Lake Village, Michigan, surrounded by present-day West Bloomfield Township in Oakland County. The West Bloomfield School District uses it today as a nature center. It is about thirty miles northeast of Detroit. There remains a legend that Pontiac was buried there. Despite the lack of evidence, local resident Henry Richmond defended the use of legends and their importance to constructing a local history connected to Pontiac in a *Detroit News Tribune* article.

Published on August 3, 1913, the headline of the article reads "Legends Concerning the Death and Burial of the Great Chief Who Once Terrorized All Michigan; The Sacred Burial Place of the Red Men; Is the Big Mound a Tomb?"[79] The story mentions briefly how Pontiac and his allies seized forts throughout the Great Lakes area. The author believed that the name of Pontiac served an important function in the local history. "Every great man, long dead, becomes rich in tombs," began Richmond. Just like Homer, "Such is the case with the greatest of Indian chieftains, Pontiac, the conspirator."[80] Richmond continued by describing that, while Pontiac was killed near St. Louis, his body was never recovered. A mound on the south side of the island where legend suggests Pontiac's body might be buried, argues Richmond, should be allowed to persist. The locals called it "Pontiac's Mound."

Richmond acknowledged that history disproves that Pontiac was buried there. "But why should one fight history with legend?" asked Richmond. Pontiac's relationship to the local history made Detroit a unique place, for white people could craft Pontiac's attempt to drive out the British as both a uniquely Detroit story and an American story of triumph. History had very little meaning for Richmond, for "where history babbles and conflicts, tradition sometimes continues to whisper and point, and one may sometimes turn away from history and listen to legend and learn."[81] Legends are useful within the settler narrative of dispossession for they explain domination and removal, but they also reveal ways we can uncover Indigenous histories in urban settings.

Richmond's goal was to preserve Pontiac's name in relation to the Detroit area for its contemporary residents—that is clear. However, read another way, Richmond's understanding of legend versus history opens up the possibility to unearth urban Indigenous histories. These legends, while based in white men's early twentieth-century desires to construct a narrative of progress, can be used to, in the words of Coll Thrush, "resurrect the actual roles of Indigenous people and places in the urban past, and to reclaim the concrete details of a new narrative of urban Indigenous history."[82] Pontiac's function within the context of Apple Island, for a moment, presents an opportunity for us to rethink how we understand the role of indigeneity in urban history and what it might do in the present. Moreover, for historians of modern Detroit, Richmond's article suggests that it is important to consider the many islands near the city proper as Indigenous spaces in order to reaffirm the importance of indigeneity in the construction of modern Detroit.

For the 211th celebration of Cadillac's landing near Detroit in 1912, Detroiters used Pontiac once more. Clarence Burton, unhappy with the lack of an authentic history put forth in the 1901 Bicentennial, helped construct this celebration. Two "tribes," "smeared with war paint, full fighting accoutrements, weird head-dress and tomahawks" were set to attack Detroit on the evening of April 23, 1912. Going down Woodward Avenue, these two "tribes," led by Pontiac, were to "menace Cadillac and his men until the man who is responsible for Detroit's existence succeeds in disarming them."[83] This was an obvious example of settler imaginings. They knew that Pontiac had nothing to do with Cadillac. But the Frenchman Cadillac represented the genesis of Detroit's progress as a city and Pontiac represented the last challenge to white men's progress.

It is important to note that this Indian "attack" was a part of Detroit's growth, in celebration of the city's automotive success. An estimated $25,000,000 worth of automobiles, close to 10,000 cars were going to be lined up on Woodward Avenue.[84] The city's elite utilized Pontiac to simultaneously authenticate themselves as "indigenous." Six floats were made, including one of Cadillac's landing and Pontiac's siege of Fort Detroit.[85]

Pontiac was resurrected yet again just several months removed from the U.S. entry into World War I. On December 9, 1917, Charles Ward, a writer for the *Detroit Free Press*, searching for an image to evoke the dynamism of the rapidly transforming city he saw growing around him, wrote an article titled "If Pontiac Should Come to Detroit in 1918." "The difference between the Detroit of 1763 and the Detroit of 1917," argued Ward, "is not to be measured by years."[86] Rather, the difference, Ward reasoned, was "between this idyll of the Old World transplanted in the new and the last world in the 20th century high pressure urban efficiency."[87] Ward's narrative presented to the Detroit public an idea that elements of the "Old World" remained. The major difference, though, was Detroit's rapid transformation into an urban area with all the problems of "modern" life. Ward continued, "Should we now return to the scene of his ambitious exploit he would find in the immediate locality of his long-protracted siege concentrated the nerve cells of the industrial activity of more English-speaking people than inhabited the whole American continent."[88] Detroit had surely changed. It became a place where Indigenous people could not exist because the city's landscape and demographics had changed.

Ward also spent significant time describing the differences in the physical landscape of the city—dichotomizing modern times from those of the past. "Should Pontiac and his warriors leave the Canadian shore today, as they left it that bright morning in May, 1763, in their flotilla of canoes, bound on the conquest of Detroit," wrote Ward, they would instead see that "a much different sky line on the Michigan shore would greet the aborigines."[89] Ward juxtaposed Indigenous histories with modernity, or urban space. While it is true that if Pontiac returned he would have noticed significant changes, so would anyone, including the French who had once lived in the area and the British who had taken over the fort later. Conversely, those living in the present would not recognize the Detroit of years past. Pontiac as a discourse marker was used to further authenticate Detroit's narrative of progress.

According to Ward, Pontiac would find some connections between past and present. These connections, though, would be in name only; "He could find a connecting link between his time and the present in the nomenclature of the numerous streets which bear the names of the landed proprietors of his day."[90] Ward continued, "Doubtless many of the councils which preceded sallies against the English garrison were held in the tall timber that then covered the financial district of the modern city, and painted red men squatted in circles about campfires on the present sites of imposing temples of commerce."[91] Beyond this, Pontiac would recognize the city streets, for they were based on trails created by Indigenous people; later, European Americans would adopt them as their first roads. The Sauk Trail became Michigan Avenue; Grand River Avenue had been the Grand River Trail; Fort Gratiot Trail became Gratiot Avenue. Finally, the Saginaw Trail would become the most important street in downtown Detroit, running north and south: Woodward Avenue.[92] These names served as a reminder that the roads of Detroit were created by Indigenous people and for their travel purposes. Indigeneity, in the form of Indigenous-created trails, remained—still remain—as the mechanism through which Detroit developed. The very streets on which motorists have driven and pedestrians have walked illustrate the imprint of colonialism.[93] In other words, though Detroit is inflicted with its colonial imprint, including the invisibility of Native people, forms of indigeneity remain.

White men in the late nineteenth and early part of the twentieth century used Pontiac's story as a mechanism to pitch Detroit as a modern American city. In a general sense, we can say that the use of Indigenous imagery for narrating Indigenous dispossession is as American as cherry pie, or, simply, a byproduct and demonstration of the persistence of settler colonialism. But Pontiac was a uniquely Detroit story. Pontiac, the historical figure, or at least white men's representation of him, was the original arsenal of democracy. Just as Detroit is not the Motor City without the automobile, neither is modern Detroit's development without its local Indigenous population.

Reclaiming Space

In the previous section, I discussed how elite white men constructed their own settler masculinity through various representations of Indigenous men. Now, I want to turn to how First Nations people, specifically from Walpole Island, challenged, disrupted, perpetuated, and capitalized on the white settler gaze. Walpole First Nations served as a mirror to settlers. The relationship between the Walpole First Nations and Detroit's white community represented the link between what one Indigenous studies scholar has called "playing Indian" and the reflexive power of whiteness—and how it served as a "playground for the imagination" of both Indigenous peoples and Euro-American Detroiters.

These encounters were also about mobility—travel by ships and canoes, as well as the politics of mobility—and who could travel across time and space. Both settlers and Indigenous peoples traveled back and forth, but how settlers viewed Indigenous travel was very different. When white Detroiters traveled to Walpole Island, they were traveling to see the noble savage in order to enjoy a past, to witness Indigenous peoples dancing, singing, and performing their "ancient" customs in an "authentic" way. They were traveling to be entertained and to escape the hustle and bustle of city life. When Indigenous people traveled to Detroit, however, they were traveling to a world where they were othered and where they weren't supposed to be. They were traveling to a "future" time and a "modern" place—Detroit. However, in their travels and engagement with the settler city, Indigenous people were often portrayed as deviants and as those who could live only outside of modernity.

On June 19, 1867, two years after the Civil War, people from the Walpole Island First Nations decided to hold a meeting on their land, a celebration that would invite settlers to come and see them perform. Around 7:00 A.M., about 500 people gathered at the ferry dock in Algonac, Michigan, approximately 50 miles (80 kilometers) northeast of Detroit. They slowly boarded the Morning Star Steamer, which left the dock around 8:00 A.M. Riding down the Detroit River, these settlers believed that they were going to a place of the past, where they could, in their present, enjoy the ancient Indigenous traditions and see up close "the sons of the forest." When they arrived, the visitors were greeted by Oshahwahnoo, whom they described as an "ancient Indian chief" who fought alongside Tecumseh, who gave a welcoming speech in Anishinaabemowin.[94]

The visitors enjoyed the festivities of games, dances, and Indigenous baskets, among other goods. At around 3:00 P.M., the visitors left the island and returned to Michigan, to go back into their supposed modern world. This action would foreshadow the hundreds of times settlers visited Walpole Island.

From an Indigenous perspective, Walpole Island should be considered a broader part of the discursive, ideological, and physical geography of Detroit. Walpole Island, or Bkejwanong, meaning "where the waters divide," is a First Nations reserve in southwestern Ontario, between Michigan and Ontario. It is about 75 miles (121 kilometers) from Windsor and 77 miles (124 kilometers) from Detroit. It consists of Potawatomi, Odawa, and Anishinaabe peoples, or what was known as the "Three Fires Confederacy."

It is an unceded territory, which means that a settler government claimed ownership, but Native people contest it. It is located in the mouth of the St. Clair River, which feeds into Lake St. Clair. It is important to identify Bkejwanong as a part of Detroit because it not only represents a reclamation of land but also asserts how local Indigenous people understood their relationship to place, demonstrating that land is a form of meaning-making. As Seneca feminist scholar Mishuana Goeman writes, "Indigenous peoples make place by relating both personal and communal experiences and histories to certain locations and landscapes—maintaining these spatial relationships is one of the most important components of politics and our identity."[95] The Three Fires Confederacy on Walpole understand that their relationship to one another is based on their relationship to this particular place, regardless of the presence of settlers.

In addition to shared histories, Goeman claims, "Indigenous Nations claim land through a discursive communal sharing, and land is not only given meaning through consensus of claiming territory but also through narrative practices."[96] One important point that Goeman makes is that land is not just material but also discursive, a symbol that holds meaning and allows Indigenous people to remember their histories, claim their cultures, and dream of their futures. Narratives provide another way for Indigenous peoples to make claim to land, especially if they are unable—at the time—to physically claim land. They maintain land through narratives and memory.

Between the late 1870s and the early part of the twentieth century, the *Detroit Free Press* featured a few dozen articles about Walpole First Nation members traveling to Detroit and their interaction with white people. These articles generally depicted Indigenous peoples as backward, as criminals and drunks, and as incapable of existing in modernity. The space between Detroit and Walpole Island, at least according to these dispossession narratives, represent a larger, ideological gulf that white settlers created between the noble savagery of the past and the modernity of white people and their urban space, Detroit. The challenges that Indigenous people offered to these dispossession narratives laid the foundations for how Indigenous people would formally challenge racist stereotypes later in the twentieth century.

The *Detroit Free Press* included several short descriptions, often just one or two sentences, of Native people selling handmade crafts in the city. For example, on September 13, 1874, one article stated, "Gentle Indian maidens sell pin cushions on the Campus Martius."[97] On December 9, a column titled "Sayings and Doings" offered one line about Native women, even commenting on their physical appearance. It read, "Indian maidens, pretty and otherwise, sell beaded ornaments to romantic curiosity seekers from the interior."[98] Another account, on June 2, 1875, read, "Indians from Canada with a goodly supply of baskets, bows, and arrows and bead work."[99] The importance of these examples is not to highlight that Indigenous people were doing ordinary things, but rather that the newspapers viewed their presence as unique; the Native people were in an unexpected place—Detroit—and it was outside the settler ideological belief in their rapid disappearance. Other encounters and observations of settlers and Indigenous people were more robust in explanation but were still rooted in the dichotomy of savagery and civilization.

In September 1895, George Stanley, a doctor, wrote about his and other Detroiters' travels to Walpole Island. Writing of the Walpole Island First Nation as if he were going to an ancient, unchanged space, Stanley wrote, "The Island is as secluded, and almost undisturbed by the white man as though still beyond the invasion of civilization." Stanley was traveling from Algonac, which is about 50 miles northwest of Detroit, on the other side of Lake St. Clair, near the banks of the St. Clair River; it is about eight miles from the heart of Walpole Island First Nation reserve. Stanley told a story of hereditary chief, Peter Wekeshig.

Wekeshig was eighty-seven years old at the time. The oldest resident on the island, he traveled to Britain in the 1860s to secure land for his people. Wekeshig told stories about the life that Native people used to live, but he told the visitors, "It's all gone now." Stanley also heard twenty-five Native schoolchildren sing songs in English, which very much impressed him. He was also so impressed by their behavior that he remarked, "It would be difficult to find a white school where the children behaved themselves nearly as well." Stanley was surely engaging in a narrative that celebrated the assimilation of these Indigenous youth. While Stanley's story was rooted in benevolent stereotypes, likely because Indigenous people were no longer a threat and he was in their own space. Newspapers produced other accounts of Native travelers as criminals and drunks who were incapable, because of their supposed deviance, of living a life inside the modern world.

On March 11, 1888, two Walpole First Nations men traveled from their reserve to Detroit. A *Detroit Free Press* column titled "Observations Around Town" highlighted important sightings in Detroit. These two men stuck out. Wearing racoon-skin hats with tails, they, according to the article, came to "see the sights of civilization." It is not clear for what other reason they may have come to Detroit, but they entered City Hall. Once in, they were invited to go into an elevator. The elevator conductor sent them up, and they were apparently frightened. Another headline read, "Squaws Detected in Shoplifting: Walpole Indians Cause Merchants Trouble—Two Believed Incendiary."

Another example involved nineteen-year-old Austin Beaver. He traveled to Detroit likely looking for work. The article stated that Beaver was inebriated. The story is filled with settler fantasies of Native warriors savagely attacking stagecoaches, something that they would not have been able to see as entertainment since the Wild West shows. Beaver boarded an electric car. The story suggests that upon entering the car, Beaver's presence "stirred the century-old unrest of the bosom of the visitor." The other passengers then mockingly referred to him as "Chief Beaver," who was a "tribeless but unafraid contestant of the white man's supremacy." Here, the article reveals how white people viewed themselves in juxtaposition to Native people: one being civilized and the other being uncivilized. Beaver left the car at the next stop and was then approached by a police officer, Thomas Creedon, who detained Beaver and took him to jail so that he could stand before a judge in the morning.[100]

While most Walpole Islanders were portrayed in stereotypical fashion, some attempted to discursively challenge their land dispossession. On April 8, 1906, Thomas Sands, from Walpole Island, sent a letter of protest to the *Detroit Free Press*, challenging white men's claim to Belle Isle. It is not clear what motivated him to send a letter, but the newspaper published it, mostly to mock Sands. The letter was not published in its entirety, but the newspaper used Sands's claims to Belle Isle to construct the dichotomy between savagery and civilization, between white modernity and Indigenous pre-modernity.

The article began with a series of rhetorical questions: "How would Detroit's pleasure-loving thousands like to see Belle Isle, the city's brightest playground, revert to its primal state of savagery?" and "What would all these young men and maidens to whom Belle Isle is the Mecca of their delight, and those older Detroiters to whom it is the one loved spot that my infancy knew, think of this bright particular star in the city's crown jewels should go into the possession of the descendants of its original Indian owners?"[101] The author clearly wanted to make a mockery of Sands. Yet, Sands's narrative presents a case for Indigenous ownership or, at the very least, for us historians to reconsider how we narrate the link between indigeneity and Detroit's twentieth-century history.

Sands argued that other Indigenous peoples called the Isle's occupants suhswajewononenewug, meaning "people owning and residing on the territory where the big waters are divided into small channels"; they were also called memeshawenenewug, or "people occupying and owning a number of islands." Sands further said that his people "used to fish and trap on the upper islands, but Belle Isle was our camping ground." In furthering his point, he stated, "We never have surrendered these islands to any government whatever. We can prove it without any difficulty and we intend by legal means to reoccupy those islands ourselves. And then the whole civilized world will know how shamefully we have been treated for many long years by people who call themselves Christians."[102]

Sands's claims were based on his interpretation of the 1807 Treaty of Detroit. "All the islands in St. Clair River and lake north of the east and west tribal boundary line, including Belle Isle, fell to our hands, and we, today, are the legal owners of those islands." This changed, he said, in 1823, when "some greedy white people moved the legal boundary line from the north channel to the south channel, thus swindling us out of our ownership of all the islands West of Walpole's Island." Clarence Burton refuted these claims, saying that there was clear evidence to show that white men legally purchased Belle Isle.[103] Sands's claim to Belle Isle, the playground of the white elite of Detroit, was a brief moment of reclamation. His conception of land remapped and reclaimed, briefly, Detroit for Indigenous people. Though nothing came of it, it does reveal the contradictions in settler ideas of progress and dispossession.

Native people could not utilize history and legends to affirm their sovereignty as, for instance, Cherokee and Creek leaders did in the nineteenth century.[104] Yet, this brief story does reveal the potential for Indigenous people to reinsert their narratives into contemporary Detroit. It is also about the contradictions embedded in settler imaginings of Detroit. While white men attempted to narrativize Indigenous people out of their land and history, Indigenous people like Sands used the discursive Indigenous claims to Detroit and hoped that it might bring a different future for the Indigenous community. Other newspaper accounts continue the narratives of dispossession by describing Walpole Indigenous peoples as outsiders to Detroit's modernity.

In Detroit, the bonds that tie Black and Indigenous history were slavery and many forms of subjugation. Whites manufactured Black and Indigenous people as deviant and, if not incapable of being citizens at all, deemed them no more than second-class citizens. When embodied together, along with gender, the relationship between blackness and indigeneity could be harsh in the urban terrain of Detroit.

Josephine Kidroe: A "Negro-Indian" Woman

The relationship between Black and Indigenous peoples in Detroit goes back into at least the eighteenth century. This relationship was built primarily within the contours of freedom and unfreedom. Black and Indigenous peoples worked together against European empires and, often, were in conflict. While many might know about the early days of Detroit as a place of fur trading and clashes between French, English, and British empires, it was also a place rooted in enslavement. Historian Tiya Miles notes, "Detroit was a place built not on tobacco, sugar, or cotton, but on the skins of animals often prepared and transported by slaves."[105] While there was the formation of an Afro-Native community during the eighteenth century, Native people did use the work of enslaved Africans to assist them in the fur trade. Returning to Miles, "The history of Detroit reveals long-term Indian bondage originating in Native American captive-taking practices that the French adopted and elaborated, as well as African bondage derived from French, British, and American norms."[106] Even while Indigenous dispossession and enslavement occurred, the bondage of Africans also existed. As demonstrated, there has been both tension and collaboration between Black and Indigenous peoples. However, freedom was precarious for people in both groups.

In Afro-Indigenous histories in urban contexts, the unique experiences of Afro-Indigenous women are rare, especially during the early twentieth century. I want to turn to the story of Josephine Kidroe, an Afro-Indigenous woman who died in Detroit on October 30, 1906. The *Detroit Free Press* article describes her and the space she lived in as unkempt: "In the little, ill-smelling room at 84 Clinton Street in which she had slept and cooked and ate and drank—for the last five years, the turbulent life of Josephine Kidroe, a half-breed negro-Indian woman with a police record probably longer than that of any other woman in Detroit, ended yesterday."[107] The article's description of Kidroe and her home is written to highlight her lack of civility. Because she is Black and Indigenous, she can never be "civilized" and cannot live a clean, healthy life. During this period, Black people in general, and likely Native people, were segregated into the worst type of housing because of racist laws and policies.[108] In addition, it is not likely that Kidroe could have had a stable job.

Kidroe's seemed to be a unique story for early twentieth-century Detroit because she was part Black and part Anishinaabe, from Walpole Island. She was born in 1862. Her death certificate read "colored" and that she died of alcoholism. There is no other information about her beyond this death certificate and a short newspaper article in the *Detroit Free Press*, which means she was infamous. It is difficult to know of her experience. However, I think it is important to speculate a bit.

Historian Richard Thomas notes that in nineteenth- and early twentieth-century Detroit the Black elite mingled as little as they could with the "lower class" of their race until well into the twentieth century.[109] We don't know how people from Walpole viewed Black folks at the turn of the twentieth century. Even if they weren't openly anti-Black, they were probably aware of Jim Crow racism and surely knew that they did not want to be treated as Black. The story of one Indigenous person traveling to Detroit might offer some insight.

Clarence Thomas came to Detroit to see a cowboy-and-Indian movie. While on a streetcar, he told a fellow passenger that he wanted to see a moving picture that had a fight between cowboys and Indians. The passenger became startled, and notified the traffic officer. The traffic officer took Thomas off the car and escorted him first to a detention center and then to the police headquarters. When he saw a Black male, he ran over to him and assaulted him. It is not known if he knew the man or if he just hated Black people. Someone simply stated, "His antipathy for negroes is rivaled only by his hatred for cowboys and policemen."[110] Again, we don't know why he attacked this Black man, but he allegedly explained to the officer that whenever he saw a Black person, a police officer, or a cowboy, he attacked them. Maybe others felt the same about Black people. Although this is likely an aberration, we do know that the pervasiveness of anti-Black racism during the Progressive Era was extreme.[111] Even the Native elite harbored anti-Black sentiments. Either way, Josephine Kidroe was alone.

What we do know is that Kidroe was Black *and* a descendant from Walpole Island and, because of her dual heritage, was likely marginalized by both of her communities. There were other mixed-heritage people of Black and Indigenous ancestry in Detroit, at least since the eighteenth century.[112]

The newspaper article frames Kidroe as a deviant. Historian Sarah Haley explains how the carceral state constructed Black women during Jim Crow as gendered subjects who could be exploited for their labor. These women were often described as deviant. As Haley notes, "Representations of black women reflect the gendered character of a popular antiblack discourse that permeated the Progressive Era from the 1890s to the 1910s."[113] We also know that the histories of women like Kidroe are not easily identifiable in the archive and remain elusive.[114] The article suggests that Kidroe was arrested numerous times and had a long criminal record, though the article does not say exactly what the record was. In fact, Kidroe was known throughout the city for her crimes.

The newspaper's construction of Kidroe as a deviant and as a Black and Indigenous woman, points to how the settler state constructed ideas of race, gender, and criminality in the early twentieth century.[115] Haley continues, "Carceral institutions shaped constructions of gender not merely by distinguishing women from men, but by sedimenting invented taxonomies of female subjects with race as the vestibule of absolute difference, a fixed dividing line that constructs gender."[116] The press can be an extension or even an example of carceral institutions. In addition, Kidroe's deviance might have been rooted in her being both Black and Indigenous. On the one hand, her being Indigenous disrupted the white-settler gaze because Indigenous people are not necessarily supposed to exist outside of a limited set of parameters within the white imagination; on the other hand, as a Black woman—having this dual identity rooted in the white imagination—she was considered a deviant who could be portrayed as such. In addition to being a deviant, Kidroe also represents what it meant to be Black and Indigenous at the turn of the twentieth century. She represents a queer subject—as a nonnormative person caught between the white supremacist and settler patriarchy gaze of modernity.[117] Reading between the lines suggests she was also a sex worker.

The newspaper article does not explicitly state that Kidroe was a sex worker. However, it does say that she was well known for her crimes. According to public intellectual Melissa Harris-Perry, "The promiscuity myth has roots in Southern slaveholding society, which operated by a gendered social and moral code. The Victorian ideal of true womanhood required strict adherence to a code of piety, purity, submissiveness, and domesticity—virtues believed to be inherent in feminine nature."[118] However, Black women were not afforded such a distinction. Harris-Perry continues, "The myth of black women as lasciviousness, seductive, and insatiable was a way of reconciling the forced public exposure and commoditization of black women's bodies with the Victorian ideals of women's modesty and fragility."[119] The news articles seemed to be commenting on Kidroe's sexuality. Women during the early part of the twentieth century in Detroit were not afforded the same opportunities as white people and Black men. Some had to work in the informal economy, or a means to make money outside of the limited jobs that existed for Black women during the time period, in order to survive and make a living, though they often found agency with their assertion of their own reasons for engaging in that work.[120]

Harris-Perry's formulation offers a truth for Kidroe and women like her in the early part of the twentieth century: They didn't belong, and, if they were known, they could only be known through the eyes of settler, white-supremacist patriarchy, to be abused and commodified within the white imagination as a foil to white women's chastity. To return to Haley, Kidroe's brief story is about how Black and Indigenous women—or this Black Indigenous woman—are constantly incarcerated within the white-male imagination, both in the media and in popular culture.

Finally, Kidroe's story represents a Black Indigenous woman's geography. Settler archives did not leave much information about her beyond a death certificate and a newspaper account. However, her story left an imprint on Detroit's geography. While we don't know much about her social life and history, her story still matters and demonstrates "that black lives are necessarily geographic, but also struggle with discourses that erase and despatialize their sense of place."[121] While we don't exactly know what she did, she made sure that her relationship to Detroit was known; and perhaps she was able to carve out a brief sense of freedom and belonging in a rapidly changing city, as a Black Indigenous woman.

* * *

To fulfill the first order of dispossession, the French occupied Detroit, also changing its name. The United States brokered treaties with Native people in order to make a profit and to expand the nation. Elite white men used narratives of the past and memorializations to construct their own sense of masculinity and to further relegate Indigenous men to the past. Indigenous people resisted on their own terms. The roots of dispossession in Detroit required white men to create narratives of dispossession to cement their own place in the future of the city. As the twentieth century dawned, white men would use one especially notable spectacle as another key site of dispossession.

CHAPTER 2

Performing Dispossession: Detroit's 1901 Bicentenary

On July 13, 1901, two weeks before the start of Detroit's bicentennial celebration, George Cortelyou, a writer for the *Detroit Free Press*, wrote with excitement about the imminent arrival of between 50 and 100 Indigenous people in Detroit to partake in the celebration. These were not ordinary Native people; they were performers coming from the Pan-American Exposition in Buffalo, New York. Cortelyou was most excited about seeing the Chiricahua Apache Geronimo: "The celebrated Indian chief Geronimo, the greatest red man alive to-day, will lead the delegation of Indians."[1] A white man's looking forward to Geronimo's coming to town was ironic. Indeed, only a decade earlier, seeing or even imagining that Geronimo was coming one's way conjured up fear in white America. Yet, after surrendering to General Nelson Miles, Geronimo was no longer a threat. Although Geronimo did not attend the event,[2] other Indigenous people did come to Detroit as a part of the 1901 bicentennial.

In many ways, the spectacle of the Detroit bicentennial inaugurated the twentieth-century culture of dispossession in Detroit. Elite white men of the city used the bicentennial as a performance to help further the white settlers' claims to Detroit, allowing them to move further away from Native claims to the space. Importantly, racial ideologies are constructed not only through the possession of property and ideas of citizenship and belonging but also through performances.[3] The performance of dispossession does at least two things. First, the bicentennial planners—elite white government officials and businessmen—used the celebration to cast Detroit as the epitome of modernity and, through performance, cement themselves as "indigenous" people of Detroit. "Central to all of this," observes White Earth Anishinaabe historian Jean O'Brien, "is the construction of an origin myth that assigns primacy to non-Indians who settled the region in a benign process involving righteous relations with Indians . . . that led to an inevitable and . . . lamentable Indian extinction."[4] Through the legacy of the Frenchman Cadillac, their European forefather, elite white men constructed for themselves and Detroit citizens, a direct historical lineage from Cadillac, the "founder" of Detroit in 1701 to the celebration in 1901. In order to construct themselves as "indigenous" to the city, however, they used actual Indigenous performers as a mechanism to legitimize white Detroiters' claims to Detroit. Second, elite white men used memorialization and pageantry to promote narratives of dispossession. The 1901 bicentennial ushered in what political theorist Kevin Bruyneel calls "settler memory." Bruyneel writes, "Settler memory refers to the mnemonics—that is, the functions, practices, and products of memory—of colonialist dispossession and settlement that shape settler subjectivity and governmentality in liberal colonial contexts such as the USA."[5] For my purposes, white men in Detroit used settler memory to fashion themselves as the new occupiers of the city and to project a future for the city, a process whereby they wrested Detroit from an uncivilized and untamed geographic space occupied by the Indigenous past into the future of a civilized and modern city now.

These settler memories, through performance, were used to usher in a collective (Detroit) identity of self. They combined the ideas of whiteness and masculinity into the central components of a Detroit identity. Elite white men were not the only ones to construct a sense of belonging in Detroit. Black Americans, reacting to white supremacy and the loss of political power, also attempted to make a place for themselves in Detroit's settler memory. Competing for their own place in Detroit's past and its present, but, more importantly, manufacturing the city's future, Black folks sought to control how they would participate in the celebration. As a result, the ways in which Black Americans sought to create their path as participants in Detroit's bicentennial or in the larger project of U.S. democracy, unfortunately relied on Indigenous erasure, a major component of dispossession.

In settler states around the world, and especially in the United States, expositions, pageants, and world's fairs were an important way to cement settler control of history and place, as well as to serve as a transmitter for U.S. empire and imperialism.[6] Indeed, as urban studies scholar Jane Jacobs writes, "Imperialism lingers in the present as the idea of empire itself, as a trace which is memorialised, celebrated, mourned and despised."[7] Detroit became a spectacle, a place to behold. The grand scale of the performance offers a critical insight into the larger processes of empire, gender and racial formations, and historical memory. It demonstrates how memorialization and pageants are central to the cultural performance of dispossession.

Detroit was not a unique city in memorializing its past. These local celebrations had occurred in other places, including Chicago. However, in Detroit, the elites celebrated their progress and modernity through the calculated performance of colonization. It was not just about celebrating empire and progress, though that was a part of it; it was about cementing white men's place in the historical reimaging of Detroit by asserting themselves as the original inhabitants.

Detroit in 1901 was quickly becoming the Motor City. Five years earlier, Charles Brady King drove the city's first gasoline-powered car down Woodward Avenue. Three months later, Henry Ford test drove his first car. By 1901, Ransom E. Olds, founder of Oldsmobile, produced the first car for everyday people. It traveled 18 miles per hour and cost around $650.[8] The production of automobiles would change Detroit and the United States forever, especially after Henry Ford created the Model T. Detroit quickly became the archetype of modernity and progress in the early part of the twentieth century. It is within this context that the elite of Detroit began to not only seek to modernize itself but also to make itself a uniquely American city. However, dispossession requires a performative component in order to codify the relationship white people had with Detroit and to assure the public that Native people were no more.

On February 21, 1901, Mayor William Maybury called together Detroit's most prominent white men to discuss the possibility of having a grand arrangement to celebrate the 200th anniversary of the founding of Detroit. The mayor, known as a politician of the people, sent out a special invitation to dozens of the city's most prominent citizens to begin planning for what would be one of the city's most important moments. To assist in the planning of such an extraordinary event, he enlisted the services of one of Detroit's most important citizens, former senator Thomas W. Palmer.

At the first meeting, held February 28, the mayor opened his address by outlining his goals and suggestions for hosting such an event. At the behest of Reverend C. L. Arnold, they decided to create an executive committee that would be responsible for the plans.[9] Others agreed, and this ended the first meeting. At the second meeting, held on March 4, they announced the executive committee; on March 11, the Common Council allocated $25,000 for the program, which is about $790,000 today.[10]

On March 19, the executive committee reported to the rest of the group a plan about how to move forward to celebrate the city's founding. The committee members suggested the dates of Wednesday, July 24, through Thursday, July 25. They also recommended certain guests who should be invited, including "all the descendants that can be found of those who were the first settlers of Detroit."[11] In addition to the first settler families, they also believed it to be a good idea to invite President William McKinley and his cabinet; governors from Indiana, Ohio, Illinois, Minnesota, Iowa, Missouri, Wisconsin and Michigan; the governor general of Canada; the mayors of Quebec and Montreal; and other Canadian city officials who preside over cities within close proximity to Michigan. McKinley did not attend.

The executive committee met weekly from February to May 1901. In the bicentennial's initial plans, there was a desire to have some "authentic" Indigenous representation. The committee members also believed that they could get at least "100 Indians of different tribes to be present on the occasion" because the "government has agreed to the transportation of 600 Indians to Buffalo, where they will be encamped at this time."[12] These performers would come from the Pan-American Exposition in Buffalo, New York. And the committee members believed that "no difficulty will be found in having a detachment here to take their part in this celebration."[13]

Likely fascinated by the spectacle of colonialism, Mayor Maybury and a delegation traveled to Buffalo, New York, to see the Pan-American Exposition and the performances of the Indigenous people. There, they met Colonel Fred Cummins. Cummins was in charge of the Indigenous people who were there to perform at the Pan-American Exposition. The Detroit bicentennial committee paid Cummins $1,000 for the services of his performers, though it is not clear whether Cummins paid the Indigenous performers. Maybury had a meeting with Cummins and at that moment Cummins agreed to release fifty Indigenous performers to attend the Detroit bicentennial. The details of conversations about why Detroit's executive committee sought out those performers are difficult to capture. However, we do know that Maybury and a delegation went to Buffalo in early June to seek out Indigenous performers.[14] Perhaps Maybury and the delegation also wanted to experience and take notes on the grand structure of the Pan-American Exposition. Whatever these men discussed, Cummins agreed, and on July 22, 1901, Cummins and fifty Indigenous performers began their journey on the train from Buffalo to Detroit.

Black Citizens and the Planning of the Bicentennial

A major part of the bicentennial celebration was the Parade of Nations. Chaired by A. M. Seymour, elite white men used the bicentennial to usher in a collective, multicultural, inclusive view of Detroit. Though the city still dealt with the racial fault lines between Black and white and between white ethnic groups during hardening color lines caused by Jim Crow, and especially during moments of pageantry, elite white men could create a brief moment of inclusivity that celebrated all nations in Detroit. Their idea was to have each European nation represented, as well as Indigenous people, in hopes of illustrating to the world the inclusive nature of Detroit. This made sense, for, in 1900, nearly 12 percent of Detroit's population spoke no English, which was the highest non-English-speaking population of any city in the nation.[15] Seeking multicultural inclusion, elites desired to illustrate that, when it came to race relations, Detroit was modern and accepting. In this regard, the elites even included Black Americans, who held a precarious position within the settler memory/origin story. Yet Black Americans held a vexed position, if not simply because of their difficult relationship in a settler society but especially because of Jim Crow segregation. According to scholar Khalil G. Muhammad, Black Americans across the United States began to be criminalized more aggressively. For white Americans in the United States and in Detroit, "African American criminality became one of the most widely accepted bases for justifying prejudicial thinking, discriminatory treatment, and/or acceptance of racial violence as an instrument of public safety."[16] Furthermore, by 1901, they had been shut out of city politics; this would last until 1930. Having long been involved in antislavery and suffrage movements, Black Detroiters were shocked to be excluded from city politics, which further tethered their already nebulous relationship within Detroit's racialized political arena.

Thus, Black citizens advocating for themselves to be included in the bicentenary affairs was not just for representation. The political landscape had changed dramatically. Two years before the *Plessy v. Ferguson* Supreme Court decision (1896), in which the U.S. Supreme Court ushered in Jim Crow segregation, William Ferguson was elected to the lower House of the State Legislature. He was a lawyer and had graduated from Detroit City College. He would be the last Black city official elected. It was under Mayor Hazen Pingree that these changes occurred. Remembered as one of the best mayors in the city's history, Pingree was anti-immigrant and wanted to restore "Anglo-Saxon rule" in Detroit. He also helped facilitate, through his advocacy of the primary system in the state of Michigan, the elimination of "non-Anglo Saxons" from state political offices. This had the consequence of removing Black Americans from office.[17] The combination of increased racism based on criminality and exclusion from city politics explains, in part, the importance Detroit's African American elite placed in respectability politics and why they pushed for representation at the bicentennial.

The bicentennial planners constructed the Parade of Nations so that each nation would be represented in the order of their arrival in Detroit. Each nation would have at least twenty-four representatives. Indigenous people would lead the parade because they were the first Americans. It was an extraordinary affair. The *Detroit Free Press* observed that it "would be the greatest pageant ever held in the two hundred years of Detroit's existence."[18] Indigenous people would wear war paint; Swedes would wear brown coats with red sleeves, loose red trousers trimmed with gold, and black riding boots; Polish would be adorned with a uniform from the time of Gustavus Adolphus.

The position of Black Americans and their arrival in the city and how they would be portrayed within the settler memory was difficult because, quite simply, they were not white and not "vanishing"; they were caught in a "settler regime." By "settler regime," I mean the construction of race in the United States predicated on both white supremacy and settler colonialism. Although they go hand in hand, they, at particular moments, operate differently for Black Americans and Indigenous people, even though both groups are impacted by the same social structure. Within Detroit's settler memory, Black peoples' precarious belonging to a colonialist and racialized city was magnified. In the early 1900s, Black Americans understood political involvement in any form, including in the bicentennial planning, as an exemplar of their ability to be first-class citizens.[19]

The bicentenary executive committee invited Detroit's Black elite to participate in the planning of the celebration, hoping to highlight Black peoples' unique contribution to the city's history. According to historian Richard Thomas, many members of the Black community migrated from Virginia, from cities such as Fredericksburg, Petersburg, and Richmond, in the 1830s and 1840s, though people of African descent had been in Detroit in the eighteenth century because of French colonization.[20] The majority of these migrants were mechanics and tradesmen who sought to escape from the increasingly harsh realities of Black Codes in Virginia. Many of the free Blacks would go on to become active in the abolitionist movements in mid-nineteenth century Detroit. For example, William Webb's home was the venue for the meeting between Frederick Douglass and John Brown on March 12, 1859.[21] By the 1890s, Detroit's Black community, which had enjoyed a bit of political power, no longer had the political clout it once enjoyed.[22]

Black people came to Detroit long before the Great Migration of the twentieth century. In 1890, Detroit's Black population was 3,431; by 1900, it had increased to 4,111. As a key site for Black freedom during the Underground Railroad because of its close proximity to Canada, Detroit became a haven for free Black people, though they continued to experience white racism. Still, in the 1850s and 1860s, Black people celebrated diasporic Black freedom, including the abolishment of slavery in the British West Indies, which occurred on August 1, 1834. The free Black community also celebrated the Emancipation Proclamation, as well as the ratification of the Fifteenth Amendment. However, the Black elite, tired of the celebrations in their desire to be considered more American and to assimilate.[23] The Black elite looked down on the Black working class, especially recent southern migrants. However, by the 1880s, the emerging Black middle class, like the larger Progressive Era movement, began to focus on racial uplift. As Thomas remarks, "Racial solidarity and self-help were, therefore, the philosophical pillars of the new black middle-class mode of community building that emerged between 1870 and 1900."[24] The Black community created churches and fraternal organizations. For the elites, the dispossession of formal political power in the city was especially frustrating.

Though the bicentennial executive committee invited the Black community to participate, the Black community wanted to participate in a way that avoided the resultant problems of Jim Crow segregation: the drawing of the color line. They sought to challenge ideas of citizenship and belonging. Importantly, though working on behalf of themselves, they also participated in the larger settler historical memory, subjugating Indigenous people within their historical imagination. For example, members of the Union League, an elite group of Black men, protested, and desired nothing more than to be treated as U.S. citizens, without their color being a barrier for protest. Their demand to be treated as American citizens was rooted in late nineteenth-century politics when Black folks were increasingly under pressure to conform to the barriers of white racism. Writing on the rapidly changing conditions of Detroit's Black community in the late nineteenth century, sociologist Forrester Washington observed, "Beginning with 1890, there developed an increasing rift of cordial relations which had existed in the white and colored races in Detroit."[25] According to Washington, what caused the change in social relations was the increasing number of Black folks migrating to the state. Still, the Black community met several times during the month leading up to the bicentennial.

The first meeting was held on May 19 at Cole's Hall on Gratiot Avenue. It was here where they planned exactly how they would participate so as not to be subjugated to the color line. After the meeting, members decided that they would not participate in the parade of nations program. A. W. Hill, president of the Union League, stated, "It is not that we do not want to partake in the celebration." Rather, "we do not want wish to countenance the drawing of the color line."[26] By May 22, the Union League members decided that they would refuse the executive committee's invitation to participate. Upon hearing the news, A. M. Seymour, chair of the Parade of Nations, responded by explaining the logic behind the structure of Black Americans in the event: "They were told that they would be assigned to the place in line that belonged to them; corresponding to the date of their coming to Detroit."[27] The Black community protested this characterization. From their perspective, creating a scenario in which they were told by a white man exactly where they were to line up must have been troubling, if not outright disrespectful, especially because the event was premised on the idea of inclusion—not segregation. Seymour continued his justification, stating, "The French and then the English. Others have not objected because their race was given its appropriate place in the line, and if any of the peoples object to taking the place where they belong in their chronological order they can stay out of the line."[28] Seymour's version of historical memory was rooted in the ideas of colonization and empire.

While Hill disagreed with Seymour, he inserted his own version of history, one rooted within the confines of settler memory. "If the French and Indians are to be kept separate, I suppose our objection will hardly hold good," stated Hill.[29] He further commented, "We ought to be classed as citizens of Detroit and not as colored people."[30] Hill's memory of Detroit's early history represents how racialization and settler memory worked in early twentieth-century Detroit. He understood that Indigenous people and the French co-created Detroit, but he also understood Indigenous history only within the confines of settler colonialism. Hill continued his comments within the Detroit Black perspective that desired inclusion within the American mainstream. "We came here long before there were any American born people on the ground," he said, "and are as much American citizens as they are."[31] It is unclear as to who were the "American born" people. Hill, though, seems to suggest that whiteness, likely English or French whiteness, is equated with Americanness.

Another reading of Hill's comment suggests that Indigenous people were not a part of his conception of the original Americans. Hill participated in the erasure of Indigenous histories. Hill ended his comment, stating, "When they divide the Irish and the French, and the Germans, then we will be willing to be separated from others, but until then we want to be considered as citizens of Detroit."[32] This passage points to the complications that the Parade of Nations caused for Detroit's history and the elite settlers. In an attempt to create a sense of belonging to the city's past, especially within the context of their removal from city politics, Black Detroiters also participated in the erasure of Indigenous peoples.

This problem was resolved. On May 25, Mayor Maybury invited Union League members to his office in order to discuss the issue, and to clarify to them what their role in the bicentennial would be.[33] He explained his vision for the bicentennial and the role that Black Americans could play in it. The mayor was successful, and he convinced his Black citizens that they were indeed a part of Detroit's past, present, and future.

The last records of Black participation were the memorial plaques that were subsequently erected. Black citizens wanted to structure their participation in a way that highlighted the community's achievements in art, literature, and national affairs. They commemorated two important sites. The first site was William Webb's house; the second was where white abolitionist Seymour Finney had his barn, which served as a key site for Blacks escaping slavery in the South.[34]

Black people protesting their place within the bicentennial celebration was important because they had long sought respect and inclusion as citizens and as a free Black community, and they wanted to end their precariousness as citizens of Detroit. They had celebrated triumphs over their subjugation (i.e., an end to slavery and the passing of the fifteenth amendment) for decades prior to the bicentennial. On the one hand, celebrating special occasions of modernity were important. On the other hand, they no longer desired to be excluded from the political culture of the city. They simply wanted to belong. However, elite white men, having sought to make themselves the "indigenous" population through narratives of dispossession, did not want to share their stage of modernity. To be a Detroiter and to have a stake in the future of the city rested on what it meant to be human or on a developing whiteness. That future could not also hold blackness.

Blacks' participation in the planning of the bicentennial, or at least their protesting their position in the Parade of Nations, is a simple act but an important one. While they found themselves in an impossible position because of Jim Crow, Black people made it known that they did not want to be subjugated to the effects of white racism. Still, though careful to protect themselves as best they could, Indigenous histories of Detroit were necessary only to the extent that those stories allowed them to construct their own niche in the racial regime of Detroit. It remains difficult to know how much Black Americans in Detroit accepted the larger narrative of Indigenous people as a "vanishing race." While Black Americans dismissed Indigenous histories, whites wanted to make claim to Detroit through Indigenous peoples—using their supposed disappearance to authenticate their claims to Detroit.

Cementing Dispossession at the Bicentennial

Leaving Buffalo, New York, on Monday evening, July 22, 1901, the Indigenous performers sang songs all night, enjoying each other's company, and even keeping up their fellow passengers on the train. At least eleven tribal communities came to Detroit, mostly Dakotas and Lakotas, as well as a few Blackfeet, Crows, Winnebagos, and Arapahoes. They arrived on July 24, at 6:00 A.M., pulling into the Wabash Depot station, and were greeted by Mayor Maybury. The mayor stated with pride that "Noble Order of Red Men are always welcome" in his city. Following this very brief introduction, the Indigenous performers loaded onto two local streetcars, and a Walpole Indigenous person transported them to Palmer Park, which is about nine miles from downtown Detroit.[35]

Dr. Daniel LaFerté, a prominent surgeon in Detroit, performed the role of Antoine de la Mothe Cadillac. He was to lead a group of men and paddle down the Detroit River onto the banks of Detroit—a reenactment of that which occurred in 1701; this was the first act of the bicentennial celebration. At sunrise on July 24, those performing the roles of Cadillac and his party traveled down from Peche Island. Peche Island is one of many islands in the Detroit River at its opening in Lake St. Clair, a little more than a mile east of Belle Isle. In this part of the program, the Detroit presses emphasized the authentic version of everything. Unlike the 1701 landing, Cadillac would see the changes in land, from a virgin soil to a thriving, modern metropolis.

An article in the *Detroit News-Tribune* remarked that Cadillac and his party "beheld the grandeur that nature has there prepared and which civilization has now utilized for an outing place for the tired and weary toilers of the city which Cadillac founded."[36] As he paddled down the river, Cadillac was paddling from the pre-modern, where Indigenous people would meet him on the shore. He would pass the "arches of the bridge at Belle Isle, where civilization has replaced the wild beauty with beautiful clubhouses."[37] Cadillac would no longer see the river lined with trees; he would no longer see the possibility of land—a potential rooted in colonization of Indigenous land and bodies. He would see the complete change in the landscape, including yachts moving on the river. He would even hear "huge steamers laden with the products of the great northwest" that "would plow by on the opposite side of the river."[38] Upon reaching the shore, Cadillac would be met by the Indigenous performers, who would "again rush down to see the visitors and the guides will jabber to them in their wild tongue, but the scene will be far from real."[39]

Cadillac and his party also landed on Belle Isle. The planting of a cross symbolically placed the origins of the city within the broader narrative of Christian origins of the United States. More than this, the planting of the cross was a sacrament designed to reclaim Detroit as a Christian space—a space now devoid of its "pagan," "savage" past, but civilized and dominated by Christian, white men. This performance segment of the bicentennial represented the movement of time and space, though it was not "authentic" because "years ago those dusky warriors were driven away from their lands by Cadillac and those who followed him until the few now in Detroit are among the last of the fast fading race."[40] The history presented here of Cadillac's landing and domination of Detroit is curious, especially given the fact that Cadillac beckoned several Indigenous groups to live by him for protection and survival. As historian Helen Hornbeck Tanner has noted, "Knowing that his isolated fort was insecure without Indian allies, Cadillac issued an invitation for midwestern tribes to settle in Detroit."[41] The reenactment of Cadillac's landing assured the citizens of Detroit that the initial founding of their city fit into the American settler narrative of founding a place with sheer determination, and one in which Indigenous people played only a minor role.

After getting out of the boat, Cadillac and his party, led by the Indigenous performers, marched down Woodward Avenue. With Chief Long Horse at the head, the Indigenous performers led the march. They adorned their faces with war paint. The newspaper observed that they walked stoically and paid close attention to the crowd.[42] The parade began at Atwater Street, then proceeded west to Woodward Avenue, ending at Jefferson. Two marshals mounted on horses, escorted Cadillac up Woodward Avenue and ended at the Russell House, then Detroit's most prestigious hotel, across from Campus

Martius Park, giving the 1901 Cadillac the keys to the city, Mayor Maybury made a speech. made speeches.

In dramatic fashion, Cadillac drew his sword from its holster, hoisted it up to the sky, and stated, "In the name of the King of France, I take possession of this land."[43] He also planted the French flag, symbolizing the colonization of the land. After Cadillac had done his duty of colonization, Mayor Maybury gave a speech that authenticated the history of the area, wedding both French and U.S. colonization together, a moment of uniting racialization, masculinity, and colonialism. "One other evidence remains to remind you of the past in the presence of children of the forest," remarked Maybury, "and who have come to salute you as their ancestors did of yore."[44] Yet, Maybury quickly turned to the Progressive Era belief of the "vanishing Indian," stating, "but we grieve to say that they are a sad remnant of the powerful race that first extended to you a friendly hand, and then the sole and undisputed owners of the soil."[45] He began to explain to "Cadillac" what happened to the Indigenous people, ironically ignoring the Indigenous population(s) that remained in Michigan:

> They have followed the course of the sun westward, and as its rays of brightness fade at its decline, so are they fading from the land where once they ruled. Your first welcome was by comparatively few, but now you are welcomed by many. Your first welcome was by one race of people only, while those who welcome you to-day hail from every clime and creed and nation. We beg you to tarry with us as our honored guests, while we manifest in every progress of the centuries, coupled with our delight at your return. We would have you believe that we have not been unfaithful stewards of the trust committed to our care, and that our endeavor is to be patriotic, progressive and peaceful. Again I greet you and extend to you a cordial welcome.[46]

Mayor Maybury's speech was an important moment in which racial formation, settler memory, and masculinity collided. Elite white men were in a quest to define masculinity and reenact historical memory by showing how one man was able to define and found a city with such sheer force. And, for a brief moment, the differences between white ethnic communities could be subjugated simply because settler memory needs a collective founding of a place, especially when dispossessing Indigenous people from both land and its historical memory. This speech illustrates that Maybury used indigeneity to construct Detroit as a white masculine space.

Mayor Maybury gave Cadillac the keys to the city so that Cadillac could "resume again his rule over the city [he] founded."[47] Maybury overstated Cadillac's founding of Detroit. However, the mayor's presentation of Detroit's history to the public allowed for the collective history of the area—one with little Indigenous contribution—to be "authentic." Cadillac also gave a speech, which further authenticated the history of the area. His contribution was to explain the connection between the past and the present, something that Cadillac of 1901 could appreciate:

> This village of Detroit, Mr. Mayor, has undergone a marvelous transformation. Were it not for its natural surroundings on land and water, while time has not changed their original outlines—the stream through which flow the waters of the great lakes above on their way to Lake Erie and the Atlantic Ocean; the shores and islands, rendered, perhaps, still more attractive during the progress of civilization, and the beautiful bay on whose western shore the modern city has been built—we should have had some doubts that we should have reached the locality we sought.[48]

Here, Cadillac made the link between geography and modernity. The original French settlers came to Detroit because of its proximity to waterways. The landscape was a virgin soil capable of change only when white men came to settle it. Indeed, as gender scholar Anne McClintock writes, "By flamboyantly naming 'new' lands, male imperials mark them as their own, guaranteeing, thereby . . . a privileged relation to origins."[49] The city and this celebration was a monument, a myth, a ritual, that allowed the ideas of memory and colonization, constructed through white male origin myths, to circulate.[50] To further engage in the celebration and ideological processes of settler memory and implementation of settler masculinity, they also dedicated a chair in Cadillac's honor.

Cadillac's Chair and Settler Origins

The second act of the bicentennial celebration was the dedication of Cadillac's chair. Called the stone chair of justice, it was unveiled at Cadillac Square. The chair was symbolic for many reasons. Though city historians had told Cadillac's story for some time, the dedication of Cadillac's chair, and the surrounding performance symbolically affirmed white men's masculine origins in Detroit. They desired to cement dispossession through performance and memorialization.

Silas Farmer, during the unveiling of the chair, proclaimed, "A chair is a place in which to sit—it suggests occupancy." Farmer continued, explaining the importance of a chair dedicated to Cadillac, the founder of Detroit: "When Cadillac and his colonists seated themselves here, the settlement—the colony of Detroit—began."[51] But in Farmer's re-remembering of the past for this broad audience, he asserted historical inaccuracies to usher in a collective sense of unity for Detroit: "It is especially appropriate that a memorial to Cadillac be erected on the square named in his honor, and it is singular coincidence that in this year, when for the first time, we have 'one-man' boards in several city departments, we should dedicate this chair to the memory of the founder of the city who most emphatically illustrated 'one-man's rule.' Louis XIV, who then held the scepter of France, said: 'I am the state.' He was absolute in France; Cadillac so at Detroit."[52] Farmer overstated Cadillac's absolute rule over Detroit. But he was reflecting a white masculine perspective, an ideology that could insert a historical narrative of white male origins. Farmer continued, though, commenting on the absolute rule of Cadillac, stating, "Let us imagine in his chair of justice two hundred years ago. He had the power of life and death. Practically the only restriction upon his acts was the fact that harsh treatment would weaken the settlement and thus injure himself."[53] Farmer's rendition of Cadillac's power in Detroit was futile at best. Cadillac used gender ideologies in order to appeal to the French head of state during his time. Cadillac, although a leader, had to rely on French-Indigenous families in order for Fort Detroit to operate.[54]

The chair served as a symbolic marker of erasure. It illustrated that Cadillac created the colony but with little help from Indigenous people. The seat meant that the land was unoccupied, ready to be settled, only giving birth because, after all, civilization began when white men turned a virgin soil into something that could be built upon. As literary scholar Anne McClintock argues, "Imperial men reinvent a moment of pure (male) origin and mark it visibly with one of Europe's fetishes: a flag, a name on a map, a stone, or later perhaps, a monument."[55] The narrative of Cadillac founding Detroit without Indigenous people dismissed the role of Indigenous people and allowed for Detroit's 1901 citizens to be ushered into a collective form of modernity, one in which both masculinity and whiteness—not yet fully formed—could thrive.[56]

Giving Cadillac "keys to the city" and dedicating the stone chair were symbolic of settler masculinity. They were important gestures that represented

Figure 1. Cadillac's Chair, dedicated during the 1901 Detroit Bicentennial. Drawing by Liseth Amaya.

the necessity of performing colonialism in a way that validated white men's claim to space. Elite white men used Detroit's bicentennial as a mechanism to clearly demarcate savagery from civilization. Perhaps most important, though, as seen through the two aforementioned acts, was the authentication of settler masculine origins in Detroit. By reconstructing this memory, connecting Cadillac from the past and reenacting (and overstating) his role in the present, Detroit's elite not only could gloat and imagine what they had done but also could think about what they wanted to do in the future. Unfortunately, history does not reveal to us what the Indigenous performers thought about the entire processional. Perhaps they wondered among themselves about the performance of this history. Though it is not known what they thought about these two acts, they did engage in their own performances at Palmer Park in which they had more control over their representation, albeit on a limited basis.

Ironically, the symbolic importance of the chair waned quickly. Formerly a symbol of the city's performance of dispossession, it became a resting place for unhoused people. By 1905, city officials believed that it was no longer an aesthetic work of art and needed to be removed.[57] By 1921, the *Detroit Free Press* remarked, "Once upon a time the chair stood for a great deal in Detroit." However, although it cost the city $2,500 to make at the time, now "it looks more like 30 cents."[58] In 1941, the chair was removed and was alleged to have been stored at the Detroit Institute of Arts, though, in 1972, no record of it could be found.[59]

The Allegorical Parade and Pontiac's Return

The last event of the bicentennial celebration was held on Friday, July 26, around 8:15 P.M. It was an allegorical parade. Covering some sixteen miles, the newspapers said that it would "surpass anything of the kind ever given in this country."[60] The article expressed the unique function of parading through history at the local level. Parades serve as a form of public spectacle and political acts that illustrate social relations.[61] A part of settler memory, the parade floats allowed for the citizens of Detroit to see the development of Detroit's history, and how indigeneity was erased from that history. The twenty floats represented the past, present, and future of Detroit. The floats were brightly erected on electric motor cars.

The floats were a panorama of Detroit's history. Once more, Pontiac's attempted seizure of Fort Detroit was a recounted event. Float 7, labeled "Conspiring Pontiac," showed Pontiac holding council with his followers, encouraging them to rebel against British occupation. It is there that Pontiac revealed his plans to take over Fort Detroit; this float was a continuation of elite white men demonstrating the shift from savagery to civilization, in an attempt to construct their sense of a masculine self, as I documented in Chapter 1. Perhaps the most important float to demonstrate the settler memory of Detroit, also showcasing the settler origins of Detroit, was Float 18.

Three flags illustrated both settler origins and settler memory, as well as how the elites erased indigenous history. The float carried the British, French, and U.S. flags. These flags represented both the narrative of white settler origins and the colonization of the area. It also offered a misleading view of Detroit's history, one in which Indigenous people played very little part. Indeed, once Pontiac failed to capture Fort Detroit, indigeneity was no longer necessary—at least, that is how the story was portrayed. Yet the last float, titled "Future of Detroit, 2001," pointed to how elite white men wanted to see the future of the city: "As an appropriate ending to this magnificent parade, the last float represented a beautiful triumphal arch, illustrative of the industrial progress of the city. Statues representing Detroit, Art, Science, and commerce were seen at one end, and one industry at the other."[62]

Mayor Maybury thought that the bicentennial was a great success. Speaking to the City Common Council, Maybury remarked, "In the last year the celebration of the founding of the city in its two hundredth anniversary was carried out in a manner which I believe met the commendation of all."[63] For Maybury, though, the best cultural artifact left by the bicentennial was the book, edited by Silas Farmer, "With the completion of the official book . . . this pleasant event will take its place in the history of the ongoing of our city." The book, as a cultural artifact, was important because it could further allow the future citizens of Detroit an opportunity to go back in time and recount a moment when settlers were able to celebrate the official history of the city, when it was on the brink of greatness. In fact, they even set a box which would not be opened again until 2001.[64]

Following the bicentennial, Silas Farmer wrote, "If any city on the American continent deserved an elaborate memorial on reaching its bicentenary, Detroit is that city. He further explained, "Its history in many particulars is so unique, its age for an American city so remarkable," that no other city deserved to be celebrated in such a magnificent way."[65] He was correct.

On Friday, July 26, the Indigenous performers began to board the train that would take them back to Buffalo, New York. Following the celebration, only a few people mentioned the experience of the Indigenous people. One stated that the "Indians ate up $142 worth of victuals during their stay in the city."[66] The other encounter occurred between Indigenous men and white women while the few Indigenous women who attended the celebration were loading everyone's belongings onto the train so that they could prepare for their journey.

As these white men demonstrated, performing colonialism was central to the construction of modern Detroit. The celebration and the subsequent publication of a book that documented the entire scene illustrated how indigeneity was a lever to bolster both white masculinity and ideas of their relationship to Detroit. In the posthumously published book, the importance of the celebration was summarized for the city residents in this way: "Those days of celebration were crowded with the events of two centuries of the city's life. Like a panorama the two hundred years sped by, and all their varied history was told again and most vividly reproduced. It is a privilege to claim citizenship in Detroit in this beginning of a new century of the world and of our city's life, and certainly this generation of our citizens has the highest inspiration to civic pride in the worthy celebration of the city's birthday, in the midst of her greatest glory of natural beauty and civil prosperity."[67] The city's elite white men had reason to be optimistic, for they were on the verge of a great technological breakthrough with the coming of the soon-to-be-booming car industry. The bicentennial heralded this coming modernity. White men were not only able to reimagine the past for Detroit's contemporary citizens, but they also could reflect on their present condition and imagine where they wanted to go. The contradictions embedded in settler memory were not easily overcome, however. Elite white men constructed settler memory through indigenous histories in order to erase an actual Indigenous presence in the area—and they could imagine the city's future using indigeneity as the mechanism to construct their future, again, first by narrating out Indigenous histories and then without an actual Indigenous presence. The city elite actively advertised their idea of dispossession: that Indigenous peoples had no future in the city and that African Americans were a part of the future only to the extent that they accepted their limited role. Black Americans sought to assert their presence in Detroit's constructed historical memory, but they did so at the expense of Indigenous people and their role in Detroit's history.

CHAPTER 3

Reclaiming Detroit: Blackness and Indigeneity During the Age of Fordism

Perhaps nothing defined Detroit's modernity and white men's possession of the city more than the automobile industry. Even today, the general public views Detroit as a place of car manufacturing. The city is, after all, referred to as the Motor City. By the 1920s, Detroit's automobile manufacturing had fundamentally changed the methods of production. Fordism, a term coined by Italian theorist Antonio Gramsci, describes the combination of the assembly line and the mechanization of mass production; the use of machines and specialized labor and skilled, efficient workers; and the creation of a living wage. Hegemonic in nature, according to Gramsci, Fordism and its creator, Henry Ford, were deeply invested in union busting and helping the capitalist class exercise influence over the private lives of workers.[1]

As geographer David Harvey explains it, Ford sent social workers into the homes of workers to ensure that his employees were living a moral life and actively becoming American.[2] He also created the Ford English School so that European immigrants could learn English. Thus, while earning their wages through their labor, they had to transform their lives from European to American.[3] Making workers learn English as part of the assimilation process was similar to the experiences of Native American youth during the boarding-school era, where they were forced to drop their native tongue in order to learn labor and American values.[4]

In 1914, Henry Ford's introduction of the $5-a-day wage, in addition to the start of World War I, helped create the first Great African American migration to northern and western U.S. cities. This chapter analyzes briefly the experiences of Black migrants to Detroit during the age of Fordism, especially the challenges they faced, including housing insecurity and a lack of employment. It also highlights Detroit's Indigenous population—namely, through the experience of the Society of American Indians' meeting in the city and the life and times of Charles Eastman. Both demonstrate that Native people began to assert their presence in the city, a small but important step in directly challenging a decades-long attempt by white men to erase them from Detroit's modernity. This focus on Black migration and Indigenous presence foreshadows how Black and Indigenous peoples experienced the city, and also how they would later challenge their respective dispossessions in the post–World War II era.

Detroit's African American population blossomed from nearly 6,000 in 1910 to nearly 41,000 in 1920. It was the largest growth for any major city during the period. By 1930, that number would swell to 120,000.[5] In addition to the boll weevil nearly decimating the southern cotton industry, a major reason that Black people migrated from the south to the north was rooted in dispossession.[6] Many could never own land in the South. They were forced to take on a massive amount of debt through sharecropping, and Black women especially did not hold autonomy over their own bodies. Even before they moved to the north, as historian Sarah Haley explains, Black women "represented a cultural battleground in a contest over gendered and racial constructions of humanity."[7] The south was a violent place, and that violence was rooted in gender.

Yet, Black people who migrated from the South to the North did so for a variety of reasons. While the typical narrative of the Black male migrating from the South to the North in order to work in the factories between 1915 and 1945 has dominated previous scholarship, Black women also migrated, and for their own reasons. As historian Darlene Clark Hine notes, Black women, in addition to economic motivations, had numerous reasons for leaving the South, including their desire to have bodily autonomy and freedom from sexual exploitation from white and Black men. They worked in the most undesirable jobs and often performed labor that was similar to what they had previously done in the South, such as domestic work.[8] Some educated Black women who had worked as teachers had to switch to domestic work when they moved to the North because that was the only work available.[9] Even being educated did not significantly assist Black women in obtaining better employment.

Those who left the South faced another form of dispossession in the North: They could hardly find adequate housing. Ulysses S. Boykin, an editor for the *Detroit Chronicle*, a Black newspaper, conducted a history and sociological study of Black Detroit, and he found that a lack of decent housing was a major issue for recent arrivals. "Many of the Negro's shortcomings,"

Boykin wrote, "can be traced to the bad housing conditions under which he was forced to live." For those who did find a rental, they lived in rat-infested housing, and they paid high rent. On the east side of the city, where the majority of Black folks lived, 76 percent of all the homes were considered substandard; 50 percent of the Black population lived in those homes. Home ownership was another issue. In 1910, Black people owned one home for every forty-five people.[10] Black migrants also struggled with adjusting to the city, frequently considered outsiders by the Black elite and whites. As a result of a lack of housing security and of stable employment, some turned to the informal economy, or illegal activities in order to make a living so that they could supplement inadequate wages or because they were excluded from the job market due to racist and/or sexist discrimination.

Black migrants who could not find employment often participated in gambling, playing the numbers, sex work, and, during Prohibition, bootlegging. Black people were arrested for gambling more than white people. For instance, in 1939, there were 2,557 males arrested for gambling; 1,191 were Black and 1,366 were white. Black women were arrested for sex work 51 percent more often than were white women. According to Boykin, in addition to the lack of adequate wages, a major reason Black people were arrested "has been attributed to more stringent enforcements and closer surveillance of Negroes by law enforcement officials than of other groups."[11] Many recent migrants subsidized their meager wages with work in the informal economy. Others found that informal work gave them more money. Still, as historian Victoria Wolcott explains, "The informal economic world . . . was not a pre-modern 'moral economy' but was (and is) an integral part of a larger capitalist economy."[12] Even before Black migrants headed to the North could set foot firmly in Detroit, they already began to experience the consequences of dispossession. While some were able to benefit from working in the factories, many migrants suffered under the challenges of racism, and whites sought to keep them outside of modernity. Economic dispossession was a fact of life for Black people. Those middle-class Black people who were fortunate enough to work for others challenged the economic dispossession by forming Black Nationalist organizations that responded to the economic plight of their community.

One group that formed to address the plight of Black Detroiters and to articulate a broader message of social belonging was the Housewives League of Detroit. The League was a group of Black women who dedicated themselves to uplifting their race through educating the community about economic self-determination. As Clark Hine notes, the Detroit Housewives League "developed a communal womanist consciousness that enabled them to fight one struggle on many different fronts, using strategies according to their effectiveness in a given space and time."[13] Black women founded the League not only because they struggled to find employment due to race and gender discrimination, but also because they supported economic self-determination. The Housewives League began with a group of 50 and it grew to 10,000 in just four years. It expanded to 16 neighborhoods throughout the city, and, in just over a decade, Housewives Leagues were formed in more than twenty-five cities.[14]

The "Declaration of Principles," jointly written by the Booker T. Washington Trade Association and the Housewives League, offered ten principles by which the League would operate. The tenth principle was particularly significant. Here they outlined the importance of the economic significance of Black housewives. "We recognize the economic power that is resident in the hands of the housewife. We believe that she, more largely than anyone else, holds the key to the locked door of opportunity for us, and we are appealing to her throughout our city and nation to join with us in a sincere effort to patronize the business and professional men and women of our group." These women cleverly understood that in order to take care of their entire race, they had to engage in economic nationalism.

From the 1880s until the 1920s, Indigenous peoples had experienced their own form of dispossession through assimilation.[15] They were erased and marginalized in the popular imagination. The U.S. government's dispossession campaign during this period was to remove them from the land and eradicate Indigenous peoples' identity as Native people. They used boarding schools to do so. Perhaps nothing sums up the U.S. goal in dispossessing the whole of Native people more than Richard Henry Pratt, the founder of the Carlisle Indian Industrial School, who infamously stated, "Kill the Indian in him, and save the man."[16] Government officials removed children from their home communities on reservations. Indigenous dispossession in this context forced many to adapt to rapidly changing circumstances. My great-great-grandmother, Eliza Silas, attended the Mount Pleasant Indian Industrial Boarding School. The school opened in 1893 and closed in 1934, and had an average of 300 Indigenous students per year, from ages as young as five to young adults. Students performed hard labor, including laundry, farming, and domestic work; they also engaged in remedial study. Each morning, students recited a prayer,

Now I get me up to work,
I pray Thee Lord, I may not shirk;
If I should die before tonight,
I pray Thee Lord my work's all right.[17]

Eliza wrote a letter to her mother, updating her on what she and her brother Thomas had been doing:

> Dear Mother,
>
> I am well. I hope you are the same. This is the last letter home until after vacation. I am not going home. Maybe Thomas will go home. I must work. I am in second grade. My brother is in third grade. I like to play with girls. Do you know Nancy? She is going to school too. I will have fun. The Band is playing here. We are going to school pretty soon. So good by.[18]

Eliza must have written this early in the morning in her shared room. She tried to keep her mother abreast of when they would come home. This letter also suggests that her first language was Anishinaabemowin, and she was learning English. These letters were an important point of literary expression and, in some ways, some of the only connection they had with family members.[19] While boarding schools were meant to erase Indigenous cultures, what emerged were individuals, who, though suffering from the effects of the boarding schools, were a generation of people who fought for recognition and visibility in the United States as modern people who respected the ways of their ancestors and desired to be sovereign and respected as people. Meanwhile, groups like the Society of American Indians (SAI) and individuals like Charles Eastman, while rooted in the racial uplift discourse of the era, also sought greater sovereignty for Native nations.[20]

The SAI is one of the most analyzed organizations in studies of Progressive Era U.S. Indigenous history.[21] Previous scholarship has identified the SAI as an assimilationist organization that was focused on helping Indigenous people integrate into U.S. society. However, that perspective ignores how Native people dealt with the rapidly changing environment around them. While they were indeed the boarding-school generation—this was often forced upon many of them—they did their best to leave a legacy of fighting on behalf of Indigenous people. As historian Philip Deloria argues, "Understanding this generation has meant mobilizing a set of now familiar words . . . to describe practices that are difficult to grasp, much less communicate." Deloria goes on to note terms like "complexity" and "cultural hybridity," even "syncretism" and "synthesis." Scholars have tried to understand the SAI in a variety of ways: "They 'talked back' to civilization. And they pursued something called citizenship and reform. They created new culture, performed to others' expectations, even while they resisted American ideologies. And more."[22]

The Society of American Indians was a prominent American Indian organization that emerged during the Progressive Era. Though general histories suggest that it was conceptualized at the first meeting in October 1911, other evidence suggests that conversations began much earlier. For example, on January 9, 1904, Fayette McKenzie, a white ally of Indigenous rights, wrote with enthusiasm to W. E. B. Du Bois about forming an all-Indigenous political organization. McKenzie believed that if he "could persuade 50 to 100 or 200 Indians to combine for the good of their race into an association which stood for the unity and solidarity, the intelligence and progress," those American Indian intellectuals would "guide the whole race to a higher civilization." It is not known whether Du Bois took active steps to assist McKenzie in any significant way. However, seven days later, Du Bois replied to McKenzie with a short response, endorsing the plan: "Dear Sir: I think your plan most excellent," he wrote, and "[I] would be glad to aid it in any way." He further stressed, "The uplift must always come from the top and the training and unification of leaders is a great thing."[23] The SAI emerged during the era of racial uplift. Within the African American context, this meant, in the words of historian Kevin Gaines, that educated African Americans "sought to refute the view that African Americans were biologically inferior and unassimilable by incorporating 'the race' into ostensibly universal but deeply racialized ideological categories of Western progress and civilization."[24] One of the challenges with racial uplift was the class elitism and stratification it reproduced. Still, the Indigenous elite believed in a similar ideology. Like the Black elite's view of racial uplift as a mechanism to ending the worst of white racism, Native people also believed that if they garnered the respect of white America, they could demonstrate that they were worthy of modernity. Thus, like African American racial-uplift organizations, the Society of American Indian members believed they could create a future for Native people.

Related to this, sovereignty was also important to the Society of American Indians. Following the passage of the Dawes Act of 1887, the United States rapidly dispossessed Native people of land. By 1932, they had lost two-thirds of the 138 million acres they had held prior to the passing of the act. In this context, they wanted at the very least to halt the loss of more land.

It was within this context that the SAI met in Columbus, Ohio, October 12–15, 1911. Many notable Native leaders attended, including Laura Cornelius Kellogg (Oneida), Charles Eastman (Dakota), Carlos Montezuma (Yavapai Apache), Arthur Parker (Seneca), Sherman Coolidge (Arapaho), Zitkala Sa (Lakota), and many more. They came together because they wanted to solve the "Indian problem" as educated, Native people. Their approach was informed by their relationship with the white world. Their experiences included being students at boarding schools, which also resulted in the formation of a common lingua franca (English) and a common identity that shifted from individual tribal nation identity to a collective, Indigenous identity.

The SAI shared a broad desire to be the leading voice for all Indigenous nations in the United States. A major part of its platform was to protect Indigenous lands and to advocate for U.S. citizenship. Historian Frederick Hoxie argues that early members of the SAI believed that "securing U.S. citizenship for all Indians would empower their members to become forceful actors in the nation's democracy."[25] They strategically framed themselves as immigrants so that they could create scenarios of resistance for their larger goal of sovereignty.[26] They were also concerned about what they perceived as the dictatorial nature of the Bureau of Indian Affairs (BIA). The SAI and other groups believed that they should govern their own affairs and viewed the BIA as an impediment to their progress.[27] Thus, the SAI desired to be the preeminent group that would represent all of the Indigenous nations.

The original executive board members were Sherman Coolidge, Thomas Sloan, Hiram Chase, Henry Standing Bear, Lauren Cornelius Kellogg, and Arthur Parker. Working diligently, these board members drafted a platform from which they would create change for the future of all Native people. In the first adopted constitution, the SAI used the rhetoric of the time, including the Progressive Era language of enlightenment and evolution:

1. To promote and co-operate with all efforts looking to the advancement of the Indian enlightenment which leaves him free as a man to develop according to the natural laws of social evolution.
2. To provide, through our open conference, the means for a free discussion on all subjects bearing on the welfare of the race.

3. To present in a just light a true history of the race, to preserve its records and to emulate its distinguishing virtues.
4. To promote citizenship among Indians and obtain the rights thereof.
5. To establish a legal department to investigate Indian problems, and suggest and obtain remedies.
6. To exercise the right to oppose any movement which may be detrimental to the race.
7. To direct its energies exclusively to general principles and universal interest, and not allow itself to be used for any personal or private interest.[28]

The SAI's platform signified two core expressions of Indigenous political thought during the Progressive Era. First, it defined Native people as a racial group. During this time, other social groups, including the National Association for the Advancement of Colored People (NAACP) formed in order to combat racial injustice through the courts. While it is not known whether the SAI based any of its formation on the NAACP, surely, they knew the NAACP existed. Indeed, W. E. B. Du Bois, a co-founder of the Niagara Movement, which would morph into the NAACP, became an associate member.[29]

They also understood the nature of Progressive Era politics and that of Jim Crow racism. They spoke of race in terms of a "race consciousness and the emergence of "race leader"; of the interests of Indians as both a race and a collection of individuals; of racial characteristics that might be detrimental to full engagement with modernity; of the relationship between racial and national (that is, American) advancement."[30] Though leaders identified with their individual Indigenous nations, they also understood the importance of a broad identity, one that would make it legible to European Americans. Thus, they utilized a nationalist racial rhetoric, one that focused on their common struggle—most common, their fight to maintain their land and customs without government interference.

Second, they realized they had to dismantle the image of Native people as "savage" warmongers in the minds of European Americans. It was not that long ago when whites believed Native people to be a threat to U.S. progress. The fear of the "savage warrior" was not lost on European Americans by the turn of the twentieth century. In order to manufacture a broad appeal in their fight for U.S. citizenship, they knew they had to create alternative propaganda of the "authentic" view of Native people so that their appeals for U.S. citizenship would not fall on deaf ears. Education in the white world, based on their own experiences, would be paramount in their struggle for Indigenous rights. Yet, these individuals within the SAI were not concerned solely with the myopic idea of assimilating into mainstream U.S. culture. They wanted to challenge the representation of Indigenous people in mainstream popular culture, and to abolish the Bureau of Indian Affairs.

According to the U.S. Census, Detroit's interwar Indigenous population was 350 in 1930 and 434 in 1940. Interwar Detroit was filled with racial turmoil and strife. The city's elite promoted what historian Karen R. Miller describes as "Northern racial liberalism." This political ideology, which rhetorically eschewed racial segregation while upholding structural racism, suggests that "all Americans, regardless of race, should be politically equal, but that the state cannot and indeed should not enforce racial equality by interfering with the existing social or economic order."[31] This racial idea shaped social relations in a demographically changing city. Thus, when the SAI members came to Detroit, they entered a political situation in which they could be embraced by the political elites of the city and still be treated as pre-modern subjects. Here I argue that the SAI meeting in Detroit was part of Indigenous peoples' traveling to Detroit in order, even if only momentarily, to demonstrate that they could be mobile in modernity and engage in different forms of struggle outside of the reservation space and could challenge the expectations of white settlers.

By the time the Society of American Indians came to Detroit in October 1921, the group was near the end of its existence. Membership had been declining for years; political differences regarding how much the organization should engage with the BIA and if it should support the Peyote movement, a religious movement that used the psychedelic peyote plant for ceremonies that existed among the Native American Church, were just a few of the major problems.[32] Yet, the remaining members came to Detroit in order to continue their mission of challenging the idea of Native invisibility and their perceived "savagery." It is not known why they chose Detroit as a meeting place, though it is not surprising. Seeking to avoid the stigma attached to holding a meeting on a reservation, urban spaces (or at least those not on reservations) allowed for them to present themselves as modern people. As Philip Deloria argues, "The organizers insistently urban vision . . . grasped modernity, in part, through cities and their large numbers of people."[33] The SAI members wanted to ensure their audiences that Native people and urban spaces were not incompatible.

Local advertisements suggested that it was to be an international affair. "Every tribe of Indians in America, from Alaska to the Mexican border, will be represented at the national convention of the Society of American Indians." The historical record does not indicate how international the event was, or if people from Mexico came. Yet, people did come from multiple organizations, including fraternal organizations, such as the Tipi Order of America, the Society of Native Alaskans, and the Mission Field Indians of California.[34]

The SAI's decision to hold a meeting in Detroit is significant because the group consisted of some of the most important Indigenous activists and intellectuals in the early part of the twentieth century. Indeed, this was the first time since the 1901 bicentennial celebration that a significant group of Native people came to Detroit. A major reason for this conference was to challenge the idea that Native people were a dying race. However, they were also contending with the end of World War I.

Following World War I, the Allied powers convened in Paris for the Paris Peace Conference in 1919. Zitkala Sa remarked, "Paris, for the moment, has become the center of the world's thought" and the "world is to be made better as a result of these stirring times." However, she also understood this to be a moment that Indigenous people needed to capitalize on in order to advocate for Indigenous citizenship in the United States. "There never was a time more opportune than now for America to enfranchise the Red Man." Thus, she asked, "Who shall represent [the Indigenous] cause at the World's Peace Conference?"[35]

The SAI convention began on Monday, October 24, 1921. The group held the event at the downtown Detroit YMCA. The local newspapers documented the group's arrival. "The continent's foremost survivors of the ancient tribes," read the article, "including prominent attorneys, the physicians and churchmen," would attend or be speakers. The attendance was low. Attendees included: Thomas Sloan, Carlos Montezuma, Sherman Coolidge, Thomas Bishops, and Reverend S. A. Bingham, a pastor of the Episcopal Church on Walpole Island, a First Nation not that far from Detroit. Members of the SAI invited President Warren G. Harding to appear, however, he declined, stating, "I want your organization to know of my strong and continuing interest in the Indians and their full rights and immunities."[36] Even First Nations people attended, including members of the League of Indians of Canada. Frederick Ogilvie Loft, a Mohawk from Six Nations of the Grand River Reserve and a World War I veteran, founded the League of Indians of Canada in 1919 as a response to the unfair treatment of First Nations communities following World War I.

The local media made a mockery of Native people coming to Detroit, likely because they did not fit the stereotypical image in the white imagination. Someone submitted an anonymous poem to the *Detroit News*:

The Indian, the Indian,
Convening in Detroit,
Sees with dismay the movie play
His noble race exploit.
The tommyhawk, the tommyhawk
No longer does he wield,
But doth assert he turns the dirt
And plows the fertile land
The whoop of war, the whoop of war
No more it sounds in dread,
But sweet refrains and jazzy strains
He uttereth instead
The Indian, the Indian,
He once was nature's child,
But now he gets a grouch and frets
When someone calls him wild.[37]

The poem mocks Native people. It also represents the larger ideology of European Americans at the time. When Indigenous people tried to create an alternative, modern vision of Native people, they ran into a wall. Even though they faced these seemingly insurmountable challenges in altering settler imaginings of Native people, members like Carlos Montezuma, who had long fought against racist stereotypes of Indigenous people, continued struggling in the vineyards.

The convention began with a pipe-smoking ceremony with James "Jim" Couzens. Couzens rose to fame in Detroit because of the enormous wealth he gained after investing in Henry Ford's Motor Company, where he was also second in command. Couzens served as Detroit's mayor from 1919 to 1922 and would later serve as the Republican senator from Michigan for a fourteen-year period, following his resignation as mayor. He was apparently one of the more well-regarded mayors in the city's history, advocating for honestly run political machines. One of his claims to fame in office was gaining municipal ownership of the electric railway.

Couzens was ecstatic to have the SAI hold its convention in the city. "The citizens of Detroit, always alert for advanced ideas in sociology and the betterment of the citizens of the entire nation" said Couzens. "We welcome you."[38] He noted that this was the first time Detroit had officially welcomed a large group of Indigenous people.

The first item on the SAI's agenda was to challenge the portrayal of Indigenous people in mainstream representations. For example, Carlos Montezuma stated that "the general public is indifferent as to Indians." He continued, "They are more versed in the blood-curdling stories they have read. They can tell you what they saw in the movies. An Indian took revenge upon a white man who did him wrong many years before, or attacked some innocent people in a regular Fenimore Cooper stockade."[39] Montezuma understood that key to challenging settler imaginings of Native people was to create an alternative vision of Native people. He, and the SAI during this time, believed that challenging centuries-old stereotypes about the wild "savage" Native would hopefully alter settler views of them. Montezuma continued, "We do not eat people. We have no tomahawk concealed under our coat. We do not hold a scalping knife between our teeth."[40] Besides making this speech, Montezuma and other members of the SAI planned to run a national campaign and send pamphlets to both "Indians and friends." Montezuma understood that by changing the perception in the popular imagination, they could halt the continued dispossession of Indigenous peoples. Unfortunately, the campaign did not take off.[41] While unable to alter mainstream perceptions of Indigenous people, the SAI maintained its consistent desire to advocate for something that appealed to all its members: an end to the colonial bureaucracy of the U.S. government. In this regard, Thomas Sloan, a founding member of the SAI, offered his thoughts about ending the Bureau of Indian Affairs' grip on Indigenous communities.

Sloan gave an impassioned speech, calling for an end to the Bureau of Indian Affairs. "The Indian is under a double government that has developed every autocratic symptom present in Russia under the rule of the Czar," he said. He then shifted to advocating for Indigenous citizenship. "There should be no reason why an Indian, whose land was taken in the first place by the white men who now thrive on it," he said, "should not be granted the privileges of citizenship which are granted within five years to any foreigner who came to our shores." Sloan used familiar xenophobic language to convince his audience that Native people deserved citizenship.

Sloan continued, arguing that President Warren G. Harding was "given as great an opportunity in establishing the Indians on the rightful basis of citizenship that is theirs, as Lincoln was given when he freed the slaves." Sloan continued speaking in hyperbole, though believing that "the plight of the Indian is the same, for he is the slave of the Indian Bureau." He ended his speech suggesting that the "Indian reservations must be abolished and an equal citizenship must be established."[42] Sloan argued that the connections between U.S. modernity and Indigenous futures required that reservations be abolished and the United States grant Indigenous people citizenship.

It appears that some white Detroiters were proponents of Indigenous people becoming U.S. citizens, something that the SAI had advocated for years, and which would eventually happen when Congress passed the Indian Citizenship Act of 1924. "The wiser course, it would appear, would be for the government to make citizenship easier for the advanced individual and continue its policy of encouraging assimilation into the white man's social order."[43] The author advocated for citizenship as long as it did not interfere with a complete overhaul of the "white man's image" of Native people. "As to the incidental contention of Indian spokesmen that the traditional picture of the noble redskin should be erased from the American consciousness," argued the author, "we are not prepared to endorse it."[44] This comment illustrates the nature of Native people in European America's psyche: Indigenous could assimilate, but only as long as they maintained their status, in some form, as "noble savages"—no longer dangerous but legible to settler fantasies. The author continued: "The virtues of the aborigine are celebrated in American fable and song and constitute one of our choice legendary possessions. To attempt to destroy that picture is to strike at one of our prize sentimentalities. Let us have the tomahawking braves as we have coon-skinned frontiersman, as romantic reminders of a robust past."[45] Native people in the European American imagination are central to American identities. As Philip Deloria argues, "Indians, it is clear, are not simply useful symbols of the love-hate ambivalence of civilization and savagery. Rather, the contradictions embedded in noble savagery have themselves been the precondition of the formation of American identities."[46] Constructing American identities through Indigenous people or, rather, European American men's conception of Native people is a U.S. practice as old as the country itself. Even the Society of American Indians found it impossible to dent the armor of the settler gaze, despite all efforts to create alternative discourses and images.

Some European Americans did, however, believe that assimilation, as citizenship, the way some were discussing it, would not be ideal for Indigenous people.

Dr. Frederick M. Smith, president of the Reorganized Church of Jesus Christ of Latter-day Saints, from Kansas City, Missouri, gave a speech in front of the convention. His speech centered on the training of both white men and Native men, which, he deemed bad for white men and worse for Native people. "They do not train the future citizens into a consciousness of his responsibility toward the state and his fellow men," contended Smith.[47] He continued his criticism of assimilation and white society, and how it did not benefit Native people: "The young Indian is taken from the reservation and given the training that fails to make the white child a good citizen." It is difficult to tell exactly who should bear the brunt of his criticism; however, we can assume that he was likely referring to the processes of settler colonialism. That is, how colonialism created who could be a citizen (white) and who was a non-citizen (Indigenous). "The primitive man," he said, "has suffered through assimilation of the white race's vices enough."[48] Smith did not provide much of an alternative as to how best to deal with the "Indian question." However, it at least illustrates that not all white supporters were uncritically invested in the idea of assimilation.

The rest of the convention was not well documented, and it is difficult to glean what impact, if any, the convention had on the city of Detroit. By 1924, the U.S. government granted Native people U.S. citizenship. However, after 1924, historian Fred Hoxie argues that Native people were unsatisfied with the idea of citizenship: "Few activists now imagined that extending U.S. citizenship to Indians would empower Native people. The implementation of the Dawes allotment law over the previous three decades had extended citizenship to more than half of the American Indian population, but the recipients of this new status were so hampered by poverty and overawed by the power of the federal supervisors that their lives had changed very little."[49]

Only two years later, the SAI was dismantled. As scholar K. Tsianina Lomawaima contends regarding their legacy, "Their work was not in vain, but citizenship and the ability to file claims materialized in circumscribed forms." These forms included Congress passing the Citizenship Act in 1924 and, in 1946, establishing an Indian Claims Commission, at which successful claims could only result in monetary compensation, not in regained lands.[50]

The legacy of the Society of American Indians is complicated and is still couched in dichotomized terms of assimilation versus resistance. Its legacy for the history of Detroit should be acknowledged for its peculiarity and for the fact that, tangentially, it served as an early illustration of Indigenous political formations in the Motor City. In the next section, I illustrate the important role Charles Eastman played in challenging white masculinity.

The Life and Times of Charles Eastman

In 1911, Fayette McKenzie, a white supporter of Black and Indigenous educational issues, who would go on to become president of Fisk University in 1915, wrote that Charles Eastman was "the best known Indian in the country."[51] This is quite a title but certainly deserving. Numerous books, articles, and essays have been written about Eastman. None of them, however, documents his life in Detroit. Though sources are fragmented, even scarce, they reveal some insight into one of the most important Indigenous intellectuals in the twentieth century "by virtue of his Indian ethic, his indigenous experiences, and his native eloquence," as American Indian studies scholar David Martinez argues.[52] He was also an important but forgotten figure in Detroit's Indigenous history.

Scholars depict Eastman as someone who walked among his people and worked within the white world in order to gain respect for Native people. In his time, he believed that a major problem between whites and Native people was misunderstanding. Eastman lived during a period of great change in the United States. He and other Natives had to contend with the omnipotent discourse of the "disappearing Indian." Still, the importance of unpacking Eastman's role in Detroit is also to acknowledge his pivotal role, among many, in reshaping the image of Native people. If settlers designed dispossession to erase Native people's sense of self, reclaiming Detroit as an Indigenous space through the life of Charles Eastman is one avenue through which Native people have challenged dispossession.

Settler assaults on Indigenous gender and sexualities have been central to Indigenous dispossession.[53] In Detroit, as I argued in Chapter 1, white men created the Pontiac brand based on the historical figure, and they turned it into a Detroit and American icon of modernity with the creation of the Pontiac vehicle. The performance of white, Victorian manhood during the Progressive Era can be summed up in this poem published in the *Detroit Free Press*. Titled "Manhood," it reads:

He stands the test where souls are tried
And trust honor finds,
Who conquers, manfully the pride
That rules in feebler minds.
Who seeks not rest in life's career,
Nor yet beyond the grave.
Whose heaven is duty's noblest sphere—
Not that which idler's crave.
Once on the plow his hand he lays,
His eye ne'er backward turns;
Fortune he seeks in virtue's ways,
Ill-bought success he spurns
Looking his fellow in the face
He sees God's image there;
Whate'er may help to lift the race,
His hand is quick to share.[54]

Victorian, white manhood was rooted in labor, piety, and dedication. Eastman tried to produce an alternative, Indigenous masculinity. According to Indigenous studies scholar Brendan Hokowhitu, masculinity "does not exist, other than through historically constructed performance."[55] In this vein, Eastman sought to reconstruct an Indigenous masculinity through his public performances and engagement with the YMCA.

Eastman was born Ohiyesa near present-day Redwood Falls, Minnesota, on February 19, 1858. He initially grew up without his father, Many Lightnings, after being separated during the Dakota War of 1862. He lived in Manitoba for a time with his maternal grandmother. As a teenager, he reunited in South Dakota with his father, who had converted to Christianity and adopted the name Jacob Eastman. The young Ohiyesa, following the advice of his father and after adopting Christianity, took the name Charles Alexander Eastman. His father believed strongly in education and encouraged Charles and his older brother, John (who would go on to become a minister), to attend White American schools.

Eastman attended Beloit and Knox Colleges, before finally graduating from Dartmouth College in 1887; he would later attend medical school at Boston University where he would earn a medical degree in 1890. Following graduation from Boston University, he took a post as a physician for the Bureau of Indian Affairs at the Pine Ridge Reservation in South Dakota. It was there, on December 29, 1890, that he witnessed the Wounded Knee Massacre—the deadliest in U.S. history—where more than 150 men, women, and children were killed by the U.S. 7th Cavalry. This had a profound effect on Eastman. Despite this atrocity, he would go on to be known for his career as a prolific lecturer and writer.

Eastman authored numerous books, which toggled between telling the story of his life and the life of his people, the Dakota; and his struggle with living in a world in which whites actively sought to destroy Native people and their ways of living. He also actively created histories through his writing for European American eyes, something that they could digest, in order to create a more humane picture of Dakota in particular and Native people more generally.

A part of Eastman's life goal was to create an alternative vision of Indigenous humanity through lecturing. His lectures served as a corrective to the idea that Native people were incapable of living in modern times. Importantly, it was not just an attempt to illustrate to European Americans that Native people could assimilate into mainstream U.S. society; that narrative perpetuates a deficit perspective on Native peoples' ability to understand their particular circumstances and find creative ways to respond in what they considered to be the most appropriate way, based on their particular experience. The irony of Eastman's life and his lecturing and writing presents the conundrum of being an Indigenous public figure in the United States during the late nineteenth and early twentieth centuries. On the one hand, such figures made money by "playing Indian" and catering to white-constructed beliefs about Native people. At the same time, he was making a way for Native people after him to live as they actually existed, in hopes of creating a path for Indigenous people of the future.

Eastman lectured throughout the United States and the world. Perhaps most notably, he shared a platform with a Black American intellectual who was certainly his equal, W. E. B. Du Bois. Eastman presented a paper on the "North American Indian" and Du Bois presented a paper on the condition of Black Americans at the Universal Races Congress in London in July 1911.[56] Thousands of people from all over the world attended this meeting in hopes of discussing the issue of race, colonialism, and imperialism in the world; unfortunately, because of World War I, the second meeting never happened. Still, it is notable that Eastman shared a stage with some of the most important intellectuals in the world. Eastman dedicated his life to both asserting Indigenous peoples' humanity and educating an ignorant, even racist view of

Native people: "My chief object has been, not to entertain, but to present the American Indian in his true character before Americans. The barbarous and atrocious character commonly attributed to him [was] dated from the transition period, when the strong drink, powerful temptations, and commercialism of the white man led to deep demoralization. Really it was a campaign of education on the Indian and his true place in American history."[57] Eastman's goal was to engage in reeducating European Americans about Indigenous peoples' history, and give them a seat at the table within U.S. history. In other words, Eastman's life goal was to assert present Indigenous people as modern subjects to the European American public. Still, his major contribution was as a founding member of the Society of American Indians.

Though Eastman was a founding member of the SAI, he was not an active participant for the first seven years. He kept in contact with his peers, and, in 1918, members of the SAI voted him president. Eastman was reluctant to accept the position, mostly because he had not formally participated in the SAI. Yet, he appreciated his peers' vote of confidence and ultimately reasoned that joining the SAI, even for a brief moment, would be advantageous both to him and to his career. Eastman's speech dovetailed with his belief in the ability of Indigenous people to contribute to an idea of modernity, and it served as a prelude to his contributions to Detroit.

The SAI held its eighth official meeting in 1919 in Minneapolis, Minnesota. Eastman began his speech by offering an apology for not attending the previous meetings, suggesting that he was busy doing other work and caring for his growing family. Throughout his speech, Eastman connected Native peoples' sense of belonging as a fundamental part of the U.S. nation-state. Eastman believed that the U.S. sense of indigeneity, as the stewards of this land, meant very little without Indigenous peoples' contribution to U.S. development.

Eastman discussed the core elements of Indigenous peoples' humanity as they related to U.S. democracy, equality, and freedom. His first discursive move was to place Native people within the formation of U.S. democratic practice. "We Indians started the whole basis of Americanism," said Eastman.[58] He continued, "We are a part of this great Nation and we must be some good to this country." Eastman straddled the fence of asserting Native peoples' relationship to U.S. ideologies but also made sure to illustrate that Native people, who white Americans considered a dying race, would have a seat at the table. "The day an Indian becomes leader of this country will be the day when civilization may come on a more stable foundation." Here, Eastman used a discursive, cyclical move, arguing that when the United States acknowledged the original Americans, and one became a leader of the country, then U.S. democracy would finally live up to its ideals.

It is important to note that Eastman gave his speech within the context of World War I. Therefore, a part of his speech asserted Native peoples' contributions to the U.S. war effort, but he pitted their contributions against those of white ethnic groups—namely, immigrants. "During this terrible time of the last three or four years, the American Indian is the only one who has not been challenged for seditious work against the government or in spy work in favor of the enemy across."[59] Eastman's comment was uncritical at best, and xenophobic at its worst. But he carefully returned to Native people serving their country, arguing, "The Indians stand, and when he was called to arms in defense of this country our boys, like fathers, needed no urging. They knew their patriotism and they did their work because they loved their country."[60] At the turn of the twentieth century, European Americans were terrified of Native people. However, with the end of the "Indian wars" and the belief that Native people were dying off, it was important for Eastman to strategically use language that did not alarm European America's lingering belief in the "savage Indian" who only knew destruction and warfare.

An important part of this speech was Eastman's discussion of the links between patriotism and masculinity, especially constructing an alternative vision of Indigenous masculinity. This is not surprising. Though he wanted to present an alternative view of Indigenous peoples to the U.S. public, he also wanted to resurrect Indigenous manhood. His activities throughout his life give credence to this point. In *Indian Boyhood* (1911), Eastman spent considerable time analyzing what it was like growing into manhood as a Dakota man. According to historian Gail Bederman, during the Progressive Era, "just as manliness was the highest form of manhood, so civilization was the highest form of humanity."[61] Moreover, "Manliness was the achievement of a perfect man, just as civilization was the achievement of a perfect race." Eastman discussed masculinity within the Victorian idea of masculinity; one in which being civilized and racialized were intimately connected.

Warfare was one way in which Native men were able to construct a part of their masculine identity. "Warfare we regarded as an institution of the 'Great Mystery,'" wrote Eastman, "an organized tournament of trial courage and skill, with elaborate rules and counts for the coveted honor of the eagle feather."[62] He continued, saying that warfare was "held to develop the quality of manliness, and its motive was chivalric or patriotic, but never the desire for territorial aggrandizement or the overthrow of a brother nation."[63] His conception of indigenous masculinity was a direct critique of U.S. (Anglo) masculinity, and the masculine character of warfare for territorial gain. Eastman placed Native people on a higher moral ground in order to assert their humanity.

Eastman continued describing Native masculinity. "His own conception of bravery makes of it a high moral virtue," wrote Eastman, "for to him it consists not so much in aggressive self-assertion as in absolute self-control." Controlling one's emotions, for Eastman, was the epitome of masculinity and represented "the heights of chivalry, patriotism, and real heroism."[64] Returning to his speech, he distinguished Indigenous masculinity from white masculinity. "Indians have never hated any race," stated Eastman, unlike white men, who hated each other. "We could fight because the next time we met, we would give each other everything we had, we would take the shirt from our back and hand it to our brother enemy. This was the habit and characteristics of our ancestors—manliness."[65]

Eastman's version of Indigenous masculinity as juxtaposed with white masculinity shifted the gaze of settler imaginings from one myopically focused on Indigenous "barbarism" and "savagery" to one of compassion and love. Eastman did not tie modern Indigenous masculinity to colonialism, even as it is through that historical process from which it emerged. He sought to assert Indigenous people as modern subjects. Indigenous masculinity was fluid enough to be its own thing and coexist (and, at times, preempt) white masculinity. It is important not to romanticize Eastman's conception of masculinity. He was not immune to, at times, reproducing Victorian ideas of masculinity. Indeed, he, as a cis-heteropatriarchal man, and although a colonized subject, in the words of Brendan Hokowhitu, "willingly enjoyed a dividend through association with dominant forms of colonising subjectivities."[66]

Toward the end of his speech, Eastman implored his audience to be proud. "You, an Indian, be proud!" he stated. "It was our fathers who faced the elements, slept in the snow, on the ground, we stood on our merit, we were men, we were what the world honors now, the world respects, we were that original American character."[67]

Eastman's speech was a prelude to his later work in Detroit, where he would move part time in 1928. Eastman resigned from his post as president of the SAI in 1919, two years before the Society of American Indians meeting in Detroit, which he did not attend. He engaged in numerous activities following his resignation. For instance, in 1921 through 1923, he served as Indian Inspector for the Bureau of Indian Affairs. He traveled to several reservations to inspect the state of the people. He visited seventeen in the Western part of the United States and in the Midwest, including the Sault Ste. Marie reservation in Michigan's Upper Peninsula, near Mackinac. There, Eastman investigated charges against the superintendent, whom the Indigenous community had accused of mistreating them and dealing dishonestly with them with regard to allotments, even illegally allowing a lumber company to enter Indigenous land. Eastman investigated these claims and, after three weeks, found they had no basis, and the charges were dropped.[68] Nineteen twenty-one was also the year that Eastman and his wife, Elaine Goodale Eastman, permanently separated; they would never see one another again.[69]

Eastman invested much effort in discussing the role that Native people played in U.S. history, and why they should be considered modern subjects. More than this, Eastman's work in Detroit set the tone for how other Native people in Detroit would do the same later in the postwar era.

Ohiyesa in Waawayeyaattanong

The Detroit newspapers began documenting Charles Eastman's life as early as 1891. Written on the front page of the *Detroit Free Press,* one headline read, "Unison of the Races: The Coming Marriage of Dr. Eastman and Miss Goodale, of Pine Ridge Agency." The article documented the biographies of the soon-to-be-wed couple, where the wedding would take place, and where they would end up. Other mentions of Eastman, scattered in newspapers throughout the early part of the twentieth century, made mention of his books, especially those dealing with boyhood.

For instance, at Detroit's Russell House on October 6, 1905, Eastman gave a lecture to the Cosmopolitan Club, a social club of which many of the city's elite were members. He gave lectures on the topics of boyhood development and Native "folklore," both of which stemmed from books that were often tailored to settler fantasies about "authentic" Indigenous life. Those books included *Indian Boyhood* and *Red Hunters and Animal People.*

On April 8, 1906, Eastman wrote an opinion piece that was published in the *Detroit Free Press* on his role in creating anglicized names for Lakota and Dakota people as a part of his job in the Bureau of Indian Affairs.[70] The Detroit newspapers documented instances such as these throughout Eastman's life. It reveals, more than anything, his public persona and foreshadowed his importance to Detroit and Michigan.

By 1928, Eastman made Detroit his part-time home, living with his only son, Charles Eastman Jr. (called "Ohi"). Ohi was an appliance salesman.[71] The elder Ohiyesa built a cabin on the western shore of Lake Huron near Sault Ste. Marie so that he could spend his summers on the lake. From 1929 until his death in 1939, Eastman split his time between both places.

During his time in Detroit, Eastman was an active participant in the community. He held a membership at the Detroit Public Library. One of the most important parts of his Detroit life was his lecturing and engagement with the Young Men's Christian Association (YMCA).

There is very little known about Eastman's life after 1928.[72] However, Detroit newspapers followed his life in spurts, suggesting that the person whom Fayatte McKenzie called "the best known Indian in the country" maintained his status even in Detroit. His presence in the city was not important simply because he represented a link to the white constructed past but because his body, his message, and his activities presented an alternative version of indigeneity in Detroit even as the city was rapidly changing. While the local media wrote of Eastman from the perspective of their settler imagination, Eastman challenged those settler constructions with everyday forms of resistance and subtlety, in various ways in Detroit.

Camp Ohiyesa: Charles Eastman and the Detroit YMCA

The Detroit YMCA was founded in 1852, eight years after the first one was founded in 1844 in London, England. Perhaps the most important mentions of Eastman centered on his role with the development of boyhood culture in general and his influence (though tangential) on the development of the camping and recreational component of the YMCA of Detroit, especially camp Ohiyesa, named after Eastman. It is interesting to note that in spite of Eastman's involvement with the YMCA, the organization excluded African Americans. Even so, African Americans continued to participate in the YMCA. In 1853, with no assistance from the central committee of the Y, Anthony Bowen, who was formerly enslaved in Maryland, founded the first African American YMCA.[73] Still, they had no building; they met on Sundays in Bowen's home. By the 1860s, Black communities had built YMCAs in Charleston, South Carolina, and Philadelphia, Pennsylvania. In 1888, the Black community formed a YMCA in Norfolk, Virginia. William Hunton became its first paid Black director. In 1890, the YMCA formed a "Colored Men's Department," and Hunton, who was born in Canada to a formerly enslaved father and a free Black mother, was assigned as the secretary until 1916. Hunton was aided by Jesse Moorland, whom he had hired in 1889. Moorland was born in Ohio in September 1863 to free parents. His grandparents instilled pride and patriotism in him, telling him that his family had fought in the American Revolution, Black Hawk's War, and the Civil War. Apparently, his family also participated in the Underground Railroad and at least one more relative settled in the African American colony of Liberia.[74] He helped launch fundraisers to assist in building Black YMCAs.[75] By the 1920s, Black folks had formed over fifty YMCAs throughout the United States. By 1946, the National Council ended its racist and segregationist policies.[76] Still, the YMCA was a key site through which to understand the connections to masculinity and how white men and Eastman used it to construct ideas of masculinity in the early part of the twentieth century. As a cultural institution, these buildings were also designed to take up a certain type of space, representing modern manhood. Eastman's ability to work within this context demonstrates how, when white men wanted to construct their own sense of modernity, they used their ideologically constructed image of Indigenous men.

In the first official history of the YMCA, titled *One Hundred Years with Youth: The Story of the Detroit YMCA, 1852–1952*, written by Adolph G. Struder, who served as the general secretary of the Detroit YMCA for fifty-five years,[77] wrote a hundred-year history of the YMCA in Detroit. In describing the history and importance of the YMCA, Struder began with a familiar history of Cadillac:

> Detroit, founded by Cadillac on July 24, 1701, attracted thousands of young men from the east and also from overseas, seeking adventure and fortune in this richly endowed section of America. The influx of this large group presented many difficult problems. Discipline was lax, there were no wholesome recreational activities for the leisure time of these young people and the brothel and saloon attracted them in large numbers, which resulted in a great increase of crime of all kinds. Like any other settlement of a semi-military character, the morals of Detroit, almost from the first, was one of its greatest problems.[78]

Struder's use of Cadillac's settlement of Detroit falls in line with the longer history of settler memory in Detroit.[79] White men constructed their origins from the Frenchman Cadillac, creating a lineage of settler origins. Thus, Struder constructed the YMCA as an institution rooted in modernity and settler manhood. Like those before him, Struder used Cadillac's settlement as a mechanism to describe the necessity of a Young Men's Christian Association for mid-nineteenth-century Detroiters. Thus, the YMCA, as an institution, was also an "indigenous" institution of Detroit; "indigenous" here meaning that the institution was a major part of Detroit's development, at least according to Struder. Just like Cadillac had founded Detroit for it to be developed into a space occupied by white men, so, too, was the YMCA founded in order to give Detroit's young white men the discipline to be worthy citizens, and men, of Detroit, nearly 150 years later. On June 1, 1884, Eastman became the Indian secretary of the International Committee. He resigned four years later, seven years before William Hunton was appointed as the first Black American secretary to work on the International Committee.[80]

The early churches of Detroit sought to meet the needs of youth in the city. However, according to Struder, they did not meet with much success.[81] On September 27, 1852, at the Young Men's Hall, elite white men—including one president, Edward C. Walker, and five vice presidents, all of different religious affiliations—formed the YMCA. After some financial difficulties in the first decade, Silas Farmer, who would later become city historiographer and a key architect of constructing Detroit's history, attended the Eighth International Convention of the YMCA held June 4-7, 1863, in Chicago, Illinois. He was appointed the corresponding member of the Executive Committee for Michigan. Several months after his return to Detroit, he helped call a meeting of members of various religious affiliations, and, on July 28, 1864, a general meeting was held, during which they re-adopted a constitution and elected officials. They also solicited funds and secured the third floor of the Merrill Block, located at the northeast corner of Woodward and Jefferson Avenues.[82] The YMCA fundamentally constructed a Christian masculinity built on being hardworking, religious, and physically fit. These were the core philosophies of being a man in the late nineteenth and early twentieth centuries in Detroit.

Men like Joseph L. Hudson, founder of the Hudson's department store, were also deeply invested in the development of Detroit's idea of masculinity. Hudson became chairman of the Finance Committee and, later, both the chairman of the Board of Trustees and chairman of the Building Campaign. In 1906, during his time as chairman of the Building Campaign, Hudson helped raise $423,179.25 in twenty-three days.[83]

The YMCA buildings, as social spaces, were instrumental in constructing social relations and ideologies, especially as they related to manhood, in the late nineteenth and early part of the twentieth centuries. As landscape architecture historian Paula Lupkin argues, "The YMCA building, with its leisure spaces, dormitory rooms, and educational facilities was a key element of a complex spatially segmented system of class, race, ethnicity, age, *and* gender identity that helped define and maintain a culture of corporate capitalism."[84] These buildings were also instrumental in constructing an idea of modernity as well. "Conception, design, construction and reception of a YMCA building," continues Lupkin, "were important processes in the development of a new physical and social order for modernity."[85]

In 1900, Lake Orion, approximately thirty-five miles northeast of Detroit, became the first permanent boys camp. In 1902, the YMCA purchased a three-acre island on the lake. Other camps followed. In 1918, the Metropolitan Boy's Work Committee found a spot on Fish Lake, near Holly, Michigan, about 50 miles northwest of Detroit. Harry B. Earhart, purchased the one-hundred-acre property for about $4,500 and presented it to the YMCA Board of Directors for the following purposes:

> 1. To provide a camp for:
>   a. The boy who can afford to pay a moderate fee.
>   b. The underprivileged boy; the cost of his period at camp to be contributed by interested men and organizations.
> 2. To provide for a short-term period of ten days to two weeks; ten days for underprivileged boys and two weeks' period for the regular camper. The short-term camp permits the Association to give a larger number of boys the benefits of camping.
> 3. To provide after the close of the regular camping period of facilities for week-end gathers of Association, church, and other groups to hold conferences for religious and educational purposes, and the training of leaders.[86]

Camp Earhart was supposed to be the name of the camp. However, Harry Earhart declined, and it appears the board chose Eastman's Dakota name, Ohiyesa, which means "always wins." Apparently, the board chose Ohiyesa because of the meaning of the name and because it represented the "three requirements for an Indian runner to win; namely: patience, courage and endurance."[87] Struder also noted that Eastman was a famous "Sioux Indian leader," doctor, and author.[88] If Struder knew of Eastman's accolades as a doctor and author, he surely knew of Eastman's role in establishing more than two dozen YMCAs throughout Indian Country.[89]

If, according to Lupkin, "the grand central YMCA buildings in the nation's cities were aimed primarily at bolstering the hegemony of middle-class Protestant men,"[90] so, too, were the camps in the woods. These camps were designed to further bolster urban masculinity through their relationship to nature or their perceived notion of Indigenous masculinity.

At Camp Ohiyesa, young men could learn about Christian values, about nature, and about how to "play Indian." Indeed, in May 1931, Eastman spoke to three hundred young men, ages ten to twelve, at a meeting, which the media labeled an "inter-branch pow-wow."[91] Charles Eastman catered to white men's fantasies by making numerous appearances at the Detroit YMCA in the 1920s and 1930s. He appeared in Detroit to give numerous talks on boyhood development, including giving a lecture as a part of the city's "Father-and-Son Observances" week in February 1930.[92] At the sixty-sixth anniversary dinner celebration of the founding of the Detroit YMCA, which was held at the Masonic Temple, Eastman attended and dressed up as an "Indian." It was noted that Eastman would appear in "costume" at the dinner.[93]

In 1932, 781 young men attended Camp Ohiyesa. During "Dad's Week," more than one-hundred families drove to the camp to see the annual pageant titled "The Decline of the Red Man."[94] The content of what these camps consisted of is difficult to surmise, though there seemed to be Indian play at the camps. And there is reason to believe that Eastman contributed, in part, to this particular version of playing Indian at the camp bearing his name.

On July 17, 1932, Eastman spent time at Camp Oahe in New Hampshire, which he created in 1916 in order to educate young white women, for he and his wife believed that they would educate the next generation of children. He did his best to include Dakota cultures and customs into the camp activities.[95] He spoke to nearly a dozen young white women. The women, dressed in Plains Indian costume, lived in wigwams, answered to "Indian names," and lived under tribal organization." The young women sat eagerly at Eastman's feet, listening to him tell stories. "Man is a part of nature. He springs from Mother Earth and belongs to her. The Indian realized therefore that he must attune himself to nature, study nature's laws and obey them." Eastman appealed to the young women's belief that in order to enter the stage of the ideal version of European American womanhood, they had to connect to the idea of the authentic, noble savage. Historian Philip Deloria argues that "the ways people construct authenticity depend upon both the traumas that define the maligned inauthentic and upon the received heritage as defined by the authentic past."[96] Searching for this authenticity requires an "Other." This "other" can be "coded in terms of time (nostalgia or archaism), place (the small town), or culture (Indianness)." The desire for the authentic "has often been played out in the contradictions surrounding America's long ambivalent engagement with Indianness."[97] Eastman was aware of how European Americans required these connections; however, he also used moments like these to critique mainstream society as well. He stated in front of the young women, "While I have learned much from civilization, I have never lost my Indian sense of right and justice."[98]

It is not surprising that Eastman dedicated his life to the education of young men and women. He wrote *Indian Scout Talks* (1914) and dedicated it to the Boy Scouts of America and the Camp Fire Girls of America. In this book, he argued that living for a time in nature could sharpen young peoples' senses, including the building of the self. "In civilization there are many deaf ears and blind eyes," wrote Eastman. He continued, because the "average boy in the town has been deprived of close contact and intimacy with nature, what he has learned from books he soon forgets, or is unable to apply. All learning is a dead language to him who gets it second hand."[99] Eastman's work with the Camp Fire Girls had its limits. On August 25, 1918, the Camp Fire Girls of Harbor Springs, at a resort in Harbor Point, did a dance "to music of red men." At the event, titled "America," the girls participated in Indian play. Celebrating the shift from savagery to civilization, the first part of the play required them to dance to drums and participate in an Indian ceremony "when the last of the harvest is brought as a sacrifice to the Great Spirit for the rain and sunshine which made it possible." The play consisted of "mist maidens, trees and pioneers who overcame the wilderness." In the last part of the play, the girls demonstrated the importance of civilization, showing American education, art, music, and Christianity as key signifiers of modern civilization."[100] The Camp Fire Girls' performance demonstrates the limits of Eastman's efforts. In an attempt to show settlers a humanistic side of Native people, that their spirituality was similar to Christianity, he opened up Pandora's box and, in some ways, furthered racist stereotypes when it was taken out of context.

Eastman frequently visited YMCAs to talk with young people connected to the Detroit YMCA. For instance, Eastman attended the opening of Camp

Ohiyesa on June 22, 1936. According to the newspaper, he would "wear the white buckskin, bead-trimmed Indian dress, complete with feathered war bonnet."[101] At times, Eastman did wear such attire, but whether he did for this occasion is unknown. He did attend Camp Ohiyesa, a year earlier, dressed in full "Indian regalia."[102]

In addition to lecturing to young people at the YMCA, Eastman would give talks to Detroit adults. For instance, in May 1938, he gave a lecture to the Aboriginal Research Club on the topic "Michigan Indians Before the Coming of the French Settlers."[103] In late December 1939, less than a month before Eastman's death, he visited a local branch of the YMCA. The newspaper article headline read, "Chief Ohiyesa Visits Detroit." Jackson D. Haag, the author of that article, wrote: "The distinctive full blood American Indian will in a comparatively few years be a rarity."[104] Eastman's comments were apparently brief, but they were pessimistic at best. He contended that the "Indian lore, traditions," and "handicraft" were "passing." But he did, one more time, challenge the idea that Native people were inept. In this case, he responded to the idea that they were more prone to being drunk and lazy. "Some drink" and "some are lazy," but "show me a race that doesn't produce such [people]."[105] He ended by mentioning that he was an active member of the YMCA and the Boy Scouts of America.

Thus, the fact that Eastman, in his old age, was visiting the YMCA, was less about Eastman's visit than about the assumed coming demise of Native people in general. Eastman may have been old in age, but it had more to do with the changing of the guard, so to speak, in Indigenous cultural practices, where some had to yield to the conscience of European Americans.

The Death of Ohiyesa

On January 7, 1939, Eastman entered Grace Hospital after suffering cardiac arrest. Several hours later, he became comatose; he died the next day at the age of 80.[106] Having covered Eastman's life since the beginning of his public persona over four decades, the newspapers covered his death in a long obituary. "Dr. Charles Eastman, a noted Indian lecturer, and under his Sioux name of Chief Ohiyesa, international writer on Indian life and customs, died Sunday afternoon in Grace Hospital. He was 80 years old." Dead was the longtime Dakota activist and intellectual, who had, for his entire life, attempted to help shape settler imaginings about Indigenous people and to assert Indigenous humanity by establishing, through stories about his own people, Indigenous peoples' modernity.

It is difficult to surmise Eastman's possible impact on the rest of Detroit's citizens, especially the other Indigenous folks living there. Eastman's meaning to Detroit as a major intellectual and political activist should not be understated. After all, he was an Indigenous person in an unexpected place and should be recognized as a key contributor not only to Indigenous studies but also to histories of Detroit.

Shortly after Eastman's death, Indigenous political resurgence in Detroit began. Even as Indigenous people fought to assert their humanity, they continued to have to deal with the challenges of living in a settler city, where Native people were not supposed to be. Eastman's time in Detroit reflects the complicated nature of being an Indigenous political figure in the first half of the twentieth century. He seemed torn between continuing to educate the general public and offering an "accurate" glimpse into past Indigenous life, while also finding solace in living in nature. Indeed, as David Martinez writes, "When one looks at the details of Eastman's work, a different picture begins to emerge, a complicated hybrid of both Dakota and American values but with priority placed on the Dakota tradition."[107]

In spite of Eastman's lifelong attempt to portray Indigenous people of the past and his contemporaries in the present as complex human beings who also contributed to U.S. culture, he could not ultimately completely change the cultural hegemony of settler imaginings. Though Eastman at times "played Indian," he also tried to shape how indigeneity would be deployed and understood by mainstream society. Unfortunately, the currents of settler colonialism's waves were too strong, and even as a person as gifted as Eastman, who dedicated his life to Indigenous uplift, he could not change much.

In order for white men to produce dispossession, they require specific places and ideological constructions. Places like the YMCA, rooted in American manhood and modernity, were important sites for Eastman to also attempt to reshape the meanings of modernity for Indigenous manhood and challenge the ideas of their supposed, inevitable disappearance. As far as Eastman's relationship to Detroit, it is largely in retrospect where we can discuss his impact on Indigenous thought and Detroit. He had an impact. He was an Indian in an unexpected place, and he challenged and contributed to settler expectations of how Native people are supposed to be. He participated in modernity and produced Native ideas of modernity; that is his impact.[108]

Eastman should be lauded as a person who contributed, in part, to Detroit's Indigenous modernity. While he and the SAI laid the groundwork for Indigenous political activism and, during a moment, to create their own ideas of modernity and masculinity, they were moving in a world that continued to dispossess African Americans. This dispossession would continue from the 1940s onward, further illustrating that, while, for a moment, Native people could be visible to Detroit politicians, and while they could have their own agendas, they engaged with people who were clearly racist.

CHAPTER 4

Citizenship and Sovereignty: Black Nationalism and Indigenous Self-Determination

Black Americans and Indigenous peoples have used ideas of nationalism and self-determination as central mechanisms to challenge white racism and dispossession. According to political scientist Michael Dawson, Black Nationalism is the second-oldest political ideology among Black people. Black Nationalism is a response to racial oppression and assumes that white racism is the fundamental reason for the oppression of Black people. As a result of racial oppression, Black Nationalists use race as an essential organizing tool in order to organize against their racial subjugation. Because America is fundamentally racist, Black people must create alternative institutions.[1]

In Detroit, the principles of Black Nationalism varied. They included a focus on economic and political self-determination, religious nationalism, Black international feminism, and even alliances with non-Black people.[2] Black Nationalism in Detroit during the early part of the twentieth century was largely in response to political and economic deprivation and segregation, all under the umbrella of white racism. Many attempted to create what a political scientist has called a "Black utopia."[3] The formation of the Moorish Science Temple (MST) and the subsequent creation of the Nation of Islam were central to the development of Black Nationalism in the city.

During the early 1930s, W. D. Fard founded the Nation of Islam, which would go on to become one of the most influential Black Nationalist organizations of the twentieth century. Fard claimed to have been born in Mecca in August 1877 to a Black man from the tribe of Shabazz and to a white mother. He is said to have arrived in Detroit during the early 1930s in order to rescue the "so-called Negro" from the pits of Christianity and to share his divine message of deliverance so that Black people would take their righteous place as Allah's chosen people. According to historian Judith Weisenfeld, Fard was born in Afghanistan or New Zealand in the 1890s and traveled to Portland, Oregon, in 1913. By 1917, he had relocated to Los Angeles. Convicted of drug crimes in 1926, he spent three years in San Quentin State Prison. After he completed his sentence, Fard traveled east, likely spending time in Chicago before eventually settling in Detroit.[4] Fard was influenced by the Moorish Science Temple's founder, Noble Drew Ali. Ali, who was born Thomas in Virginia in 1886, moved to Chicago in the 1920s where he founded the MST. The official MST documentation states that he was born in North Carolina and was part Cherokee and Moroccan; it is likely he included this information to demonstrate his indigenous roots in Africa and the United States. He died in Chicago in 1929.[5] Fard was expelled from Detroit sometime around 1934, never to be seen again. His disappearance left vacant leadership duties with Elijah Muhammad, an ardent follower of Fard. The founding of the Nation of Islam, the Moorish Science Temple of America before it, and other religious-racial groups during the early twentieth century were a key part of the city's identity. According to Weisenfeld, religious nationalism was just as central to the development of the Black self and community as other forms of Black Nationalism.[6]

During and immediately after World War II, African Americans worked in greater numbers in factories, but they were given the worst jobs and were also denied adequate housing. Most of all, the dispossession that African Americans experienced centered on federal laws in housing discrimination and segregation. Thus, they required a more confrontational politics rooted in nationalism. As historian Beth Bates argues, "The politics of self-determination was part of a larger, long-term goal to remove vestiges of inferior status embedded in a system that was still coming to terms with accepting black Americans as first-class citizens."[7] Before Detroit turned into the "arsenal of democracy," the city was a hub of Black Nationalism and self-determination.

Native people also asserted forms of Indigenous nationalism and self-determination. Their use of Indigenous nationalism and self-determination consisted of creating cultural institutions, a conscious manufacturing of a pan-Indigenous identity across tribal nations with the goal of exhibiting some forms of sovereignty, and the development of an explicitly urban Indigenous identity.[8] Their forms of resistance centered on their desire to establish associations, such as the North American Indian Association (NAIA), that would now be able to take care of their own people. As more Native people began to repopulate Detroit and other cities during and after World War II, they found it imperative to sustain themselves and to create broader definitions of what it meant to be Indigenous as a political and cultural unit in an urban space.

Within the confines of Detroit, Black and Indigenous peoples constructed ideas of nationalism and self-determination in order to respond to the changing political climate in the United States. African Americans in Detroit, in addition to the racial-uplift organizations such as the NAACP and the Detroit Urban League, produced Black Nationalist organizations that desired more immediate and radical transformations in society, done without the necessity of white people. Although Native people developed a separate but parallel ideology of self-determination, that ideology was not based on uprooting the capitalist order. They desired and produced cultural sovereignty through the formation of political clubs whose goal was to support Native people and, in some ways, earn visibility and respect in the Motor City. I now want to briefly document some of the activism of Black folks prior to World War II that laid the groundwork for the postwar radicalism of the 1960s.

While middle-class organizations like the Detroit NAACP, which, by World War II, had become the largest chapter in the country, other Black Nationalist and class-based organizations emerged.[9] Organizations such as the Universal Negro Improvement Association (UNIA), National Negro Congress (NNC), the Detroit Civil Rights Congress (CRC), and the Nat Turner Organization were all rooted in the idea of Black self-determination—a political ideology designed to respond directly to white people exploiting them, rendering them second-class citizens, trying to coopt their movements, and generally disrupting their ability to live free as human beings.[10] While organizations like the Detroit UNIA was a hub for diasporic, Pan-African ideology in response to white supremacy, which lasted well into the era of African decolonization, they often exhibited Victorian ideas of masculinity, thus subjugating Black women, even as they were central to the founding and running of Black Nationalist organizations.[11]

Prior to World War II, Detroit was a prominent hub for Black Nationalism and a prominent place for activism, seeking what A. Phillip Randolph called "economic citizenship."[12] The U.S. entry into the war changed the course of action for African Americans. The African American newspaper the *Pittsburgh Courier* popularized the Double V concept. On February 7, 1942, Arthur Huff Fauset, an activist writer, argued that the Double V campaign meant that "the first V is for victory over our enemies from without, the second V for victories over our enemies from within."[13] The campaign took off. A month later, the *Pittsburgh Courier* featured on the front page of the paper the myriad of inquires its readers sent in to clarify the meaning of the campaign. While there existed some uncertainty among white America about Black peoples' desire to be patriotic and volunteer to serve in the military, the *Pittsburgh Courier* responded in no uncertain terms that, "'Double V' is a victory slogan adopted by Negro America as an expression of its traditional patriotism" and it stood for "victory against the enemies abroad [*sic*] against the forces at home who would deny the Negro full and free participation in every phase of national life."[14] Native people also participated in the war, at a rate higher than any other group, and some believed that they were fighting for their tribal sovereignty at home and against the spread of evil abroad.[15]

Detroit became a hub for wartime machine manufacturing. Before the end of World War II, Detroit produced almost 30 percent of the war machinery needed to defeat the Axis powers. With the heads of Chrysler, Ford, and General Motors opening their factories during the war, they produced tanks, airplanes, boats, other vehicles, and weapons to aid the war effort.[16] This boom in military production caused more Black Americans to migrate to Detroit in search of a better life.

From the 1940s until the 1960s, more than three million Black Americans migrated to northern and western cities as a part of what historians call the Second Great Migration.[17] The end of World War II had many global repercussions. It was the beginning of the Cold War, and there were increased efforts of so-called Third World countries in Africa and Asia to liberate themselves from the colonization of European powers; and the United Nations was created. Human rights discourse became a staple of post–World War II activism around the world. However, African American soldiers fighting at home and abroad did not end racism. White conservatism increased during and after the war. As a result, Black folks increased their militancy during and after the war by creating Black radical groups in order to advocate for more radical changes.[18]

For Black and Indigenous peoples, World War II and the subsequent years played out differently. Although some had the chance to gain steady employment, whites actively contained African Americans to certain parts of the city. They reasoned that integration "would threaten their status, their pocketbooks, and ultimately their way of life."[19] Furthermore, according to historian David Freund, whites were irrationally "threatened by the continual expansion of urban black communities and by black people's willingness to challenge their second-class status publicly by moving into white neighborhoods, protesting against discrimination, and using public spaces once the exclusive preserve of white people."[20] Native people who migrated to the city in order to work in the factories were finally able to gain some visibility in the city, and they began to form political organizations.

Indigenous Migrations and Cultural Formations

Native people moved to cities in great numbers during World War II. According to the 1940 U.S. Census, there were 434 Native people living in Detroit; by 1950, that number had increased to 730. Most Native people who migrated to Detroit came to the Cass Corridor area. It is not clear if whites actively segregated them as systematically as they did Black folks.[21] They created what historian Kent Blansett has called an Indian City.[22] It is important to remember that the Anishinaabe, the local Indigenous population, had been traveling back and forth to Detroit at least since the modern reservation system began in Michigan, from reservations in both Michigan and Canada, as I documented in Chapter 1. What was different during and after World War II was the migration of tribal communities from across the United States and Canada; I will explain the reasons later. I want to pause here and offer a brief story of my great-grandmother who was part of a wave of Native people who came to Detroit just prior to World War II.

Esther Shawboose was born on May 3, 1924, to Westbrook Shawboose and Eliza Silas. She was born a month before Congress passed the Indian Citizenship Act, which granted citizenship to "all non-citizen Indians born within the territorial limits of the United States."[23] Shawboose was my great-grandmother. In discussions with family, we don't know very much about her life before her time in Detroit besides her briefly attending boarding school. We aren't even sure why she came to Detroit. But we do know that she arrived in the winter or spring of 1940 and, on May 8, 1940, she married Robert Isiah Mays, a Black American, who was born in Detroit in 1918. How they met or why they married is still a mystery. If they did not know each other beforehand, she was likely looking for some security, as finding employment would have been difficult for a Native woman. Esther and Robert began to have children, and like other Native people, she quickly desired to help construct spaces where her children could grow up in the city that had culturally and educationally relevant institutions for the future of Native people. Though her particular experience is unique, her finding community with the Native population was not.

In the late 1930s, Native people began to organize social clubs. These social clubs were made up of a variety of Native people from across the United States and Canada. The clubs were an incubator for the development of a unique, pan-Indigenous identity, which was crucial for later resistance to dispossession. Native people formed the Indian Fireside Council of Detroit, a social club designed to help Native people from different tribes come together. The club lasted from 1935 to 1937.[24] The first permanent organization that Native people set up was the North American Indian Club. These social clubs were important, as they marked the initial spark in Indigenous self-determination, even as they were originally designed to be social organizations.[25] It is important to recognize that the coming together of these Indigenous communities was an early form of Indigenous nationalism. The individual people represented hundreds of tribal nations with different languages, customs, and traditions, although their major connections were that of dispossession and they found common ground as Native people. These Native organizations were not just a response to the necessity of meeting with people of similar backgrounds, they were also an attempt at forming a forged consciousness, which a previous generation had begun to do. Only this time, they formed it in an urban space. These organizations became the foundation for later, more radical attempts at resisting dispossession.

Detroit is fundamentally a colonial space. And when Black and Indigenous migrants came to Detroit, they were walking on the trails of Anishinaabe peoples who had created them long ago. The imprint of colonialism is illustrated by the very streets on which motorists drove their cars and where pedestrians walked. And yet these streets exist because Indigenous people made them. Though Detroit is inflicted with its colonial imprint, including the invisibility of Indigenous people, an Indigenous presence has remained, occupying the streets, as an invisible entity. Like other cities—Chicago, for example—Detroit's modern streets are based on Indigenous-created trails.[26] For instance, the main street, Woodward Avenue, which goes north and south, was based on the Saginaw Trail. Michigan Avenue was the Sauk Trail, and Grand River Avenue was the Grand River Trail.[27] These same streets were used to help clear out African Americans with the creation of the Chrysler Freeways. By 1950, Detroit was home to nearly two million people.

Typical newspaper accounts of Indigenous people included descriptions of cultural expression, the public "adoptions" of government and public officials by Native people into their community as honorary members, and celebrations at pow-wows. These were largely centered on the broader discussion of Indigenous pre-modernity and the ability of Indigenous people to be modern people. For example, on April 5, 1948, the *Detroit Free Press* headline read "Indians in City Hold Old-Style Pow-Wow." Staff writer George S. Bush proclaimed, "Big City Indians are no different from other people, most of the time, that is." "But every once in a while they get together for a pow-wow" and this allows them to "keep alive their ancient rituals and traditions."[28] The rest of the article centered on the familiar idea of the vanishing Indian and his lack of authenticity. "Most of Detroit's Indians," he wrote, "are not redmen anymore" because "they have as much Caucasian blood in them as Indian."[29] While the Indigenous youth would root for the cowboys instead of the Indians and speak English instead of their "ancestors' tongues," they were caught between having to perform being Indigenous for the white gaze versus being Detroit people, in search of recognition in the Motor City.

Three years later, Detroit's Indigenous community came together to form the North American Indian Club (in 1966, they changed the name to the North American Indian Association). In the original constitution, the purpose of the NAIC was to create a cultural hub for Native people to be able to interact with others who shared similar experiences coming to the city and intertribal cultural experiences across tribes from Canada and the United States.[30] Because of Detroit's close proximity to Canada, right across the water, and the free-flowing travels of people across the border, it is not surprising that First Nations people came from various parts of Ontario, Canada, which unfortunately has been disrupted. The constitution was important because it also illustrated the tension that existed between First Nations in Canada and Indigenous people in the United States.

Ralph West, a Creek Indian from Oklahoma, came to Detroit in 1939 to study law. He had graduated from Haskell Institute, a boarding school in Lawrence, Kansas, and, in 1929, upon graduating, he enlisted in the U.S. Marine Corps. In 1933, he was honorably discharged. He then attended Grinnell College in Iowa, where, in 1938, he earned a Bachelor of Arts degree in history, with a minor in political science. The following year, he came to Detroit to study law at what was then called Wayne University, working also during the day at the Ford Motor Company. When the United States entered World War II, West enlisted, and served with the infantry in the South Pacific. Following an honorable discharge, he enrolled in Wayne University, seeking a Master's of Art in sociology.

He believed that there was no racial discrimination in Detroit that hindered the progress of Indigenous people. "On the whole, the Indian on coming to live in Detroit has improved his economic status," wrote West, "but he has not improved himself socially because of the persistence of his "Indian" attitudes and behavior, basic to which is a sense of inferiority generated by reservation living." It is difficult to decipher what exactly West meant by "socially," but he does present a negative attitude toward Native people who had come from the reservation. It is not known whether this was a common belief among "elite" Native people. Regardless, Native people needed a place to come together, and the NAIC served that purpose.

On September 19, 1940, about twenty-five Native Americans attended the first meeting of the North American Indian Club at the Central Young Women's Christian Association (YWCA) of Metropolitan Detroit, at Witherell and Montcalm. The club's main purpose was to create an intertribal meeting space for Native people, where they could come together, enjoy each other's company, and meet other Native people. By 1943, there were 175 paid members. Although they did not explicitly restrict membership to Indigenous people only, it seemed to happen by default. They met every first and second Sunday.

Each meeting began with a meal, which was followed by business and then entertainment. It was to be a cultural hub, a space where Indigenous peoples could meet outside of the bars. Throughout the 1940s, members of the NAIC participated in a variety of recreational activities, including playing on organized basketball and baseball teams in the Detroit Parks and Recreation Leagues. Many also enjoyed going to the bars between Second Avenue and Sixth Street, turning these spaces into "Indian bars."[31] The club also honored the Native World War II veterans.

In the early 1940s, the club was social in nature. Perhaps aware of the brewing racial tensions, which resulted in the 1943 race riot, Indigenous people stayed in the background. In addition, at an annual dinner at the YWCA, they inducted Miss Charlotte E. Townsend, who worked as the executive in the Business and Industrial Department of the YMCA, as an honorary member. They gave her a beaded headdress and the name Bee Guan-Bei-Quah, which meant "Lady Who Sits in Front," honoring her for her contributions to the success of the NAIC.[32] During World War II, they illustrated their patriotism. On September 2, 1943, nearly three months removed from the race riots in the city, which caused thirty-four deaths, the NAIC recognized its veterans.[33]

The primary goal of the NAIC was to bring the Indigenous community together. It allowed for Indigenous people to meet one another, share stories, and find some sense of community for those who were removed from their own, usually reservation communities. They also received some recognition from the local newspapers, albeit mostly in ways that fed into the white imagination.

For instance, in January 1947, members of the North American Indian Association challenged racist representations of Native women—in particular, the use of "squaw." White people have used this term as an epithet against Indigenous women since the early stages of colonization. White men often use it to describe Indigenous women as sexualized and less than human, in opposition to white womanhood.[34] They sought a resolution that would end the use of the slur. Not much is known about the source of this resolution or what impact it had, but it does demonstrate that Indigenous people were advocating for discursive changes in their representation in the media.[35] In this way, as Indigenous people sought recognition, and to challenge the decades' worth of Indigenous stereotypes, the NAIC allowed for them to form a sense of community, prepping them to begin the fight for relevance in the Motor City.

Post-World War II Detroit consisted of three worlds differentiated by race and class. In 1952, Arthur Kornhauser, a professor at Wayne State University, published a short book on Detroit citizens' views of the city they called home. He interviewed 593 people from May through August 1951, during the same year as Detroit's 250th birthday. His study illustrates that people did not view racial divides equally. In the data, 65 percent of Detroiters believed that it was a good place to raise a family; 85 percent said they were "proud of Detroit"; and 82 percent said they were unwilling to leave Detroit.[36] According to the survey results, two of Detroit's biggest problems in 1951 were the lack of housing and Black and white relations. While Blacks viewed race relations as getting better, more than half of "all white Detroiters are against treating Negroes as citizens with full and equal rights." Kornhauser's study suggested that race relations would likely improve in the long run with young people. That turned out to be naïve at best.

His belief in Detroit's race relations improving was rooted in a certain idealism, based in part on data but also, it seems, on the belief that race relations simply had to improve. This survey reveals the further erasure of Indigenous people from Detroit. It also serves as a prelude to the shifting nature of how indigeneity began to function. That is, during the first half of the twentieth century, European Americans began to claim Detroit as their own almost exclusively; by 1951, due in large part to Black migration to Detroit during World War II, Black Americans began to assert their presence in Detroit at a much more rapid pace.

By the 1950s, the newspapers began to document Native peoples' challenges to racism. Perhaps a major reason was the preparation for Detroit's 250th birthday celebration. In a book titled *Then and Now: Detroit's 250th Birthday, 1701–1951,* F. E. Bange penciled sketches of Detroit's transformation from a fort to a major U.S. city. Each sketch was juxtaposed one to another, usually with how the city looked in the past to how it looked in 1951. These white-settler representations illustrated the transformation of Detroit from a French fort to a burgeoning metropolis.

In the introduction to *Then and Now*, Robert E. Palmer, the president of the Detroit Historical Society of that time, wrote, "Led by the same dreams that bring men to Detroit today, Cadillac founded Detroit on the morning of July 24, 1701." What were those dreams that connect Cadillac and apparently white men in 1951? Palmer does not describe them in detail, but he does end this short statement, arguing Detroit's importance for creating industry and solving social issues of its time. "The world fame of their names and of later names like Chrysler," wrote Palmer, "point out Detroit's success in both war and peace in mass production technique." Furthermore, names such as Henry Ford II, Walter Reuther, and Ralph Bunche show that Detroit in meeting today's social problems may again change the world's pattern of life." The discourse surrounding the 1951 celebration differed from the 1901 version in that city officials were surer in 1951 of the city's ability to help shape United States society at large, and they used it as a time to reflect on the past.

Bange's first sketch illustrated the first encounter between Cadillac and his company, and unnamed Indigenous people, and an aerial shot of the 1950, skyline of downtown Detroit. The caption reads, "On the morning of July 24, 1701, Antoine de La Mothe Cadillac landed and started to construct the fort at Detroit." Here, Bange presents a narrative history that links direct moments of white men's creation, in order to establish, for contemporary Detroiters, an origin narrative that connects them to the city's founding. This genealogical creation allows for the possibility of whites to imagine a future without Indigenous people. Cadillac and his men are in a flotilla, just a few feet away from the shore, where three Native men, with menacing looks—one holding a spear, another holding a bow, and the third crouched down. Cadillac, with a smile on his face, extends his hand to his new neighbors. Immediately behind Cadillac are two men, one holding a flag and the other, a Jesuit priest, holding a cross in his hand. The others in the flotilla are paddling. This represents the idea that Cadillac's settlement, or, more precisely, colonization, was a cordial encounter between Indigenous folks and the French. It also illustrates the twin tools of Indigenous dispossession: violence and religion. Indigenous Detroiters not only had to deal with stereotypes but also with possible termination.

Following World War II, the U.S. government sought ways to cut expenses. One way they did this was to stop giving aid to tribal nations, which they believed was no longer necessary. The government had retreated on the preceding twenty years' worth of legislation that had been put in place to maintain Indigenous cultural ways. Now, the legislators turned back the clock and returned to the late nineteenth-century ideology of assimilation, which they believed would help modernize Native people; as a result, Native people were encouraged to come to urban areas. For instance, in 1956, Congress passed the Indian Relocation Act, which was intended to help adult Native people ages 18–35 secure vocational training in order to assimilate into mainstream culture. However, it was actually designed to move Native people from the reservation and to get them to leave their cultures behind.

Some historians have narrowly framed the urban Indigenous experience, as if their living in cities was entirely outside of their cultures. Historian Donald Fixico writes, "Many Indian relocates did not leave their country, but, rather, left the center of their culture and beliefs."[37] Assuming that Native people and cities were incompatible, he continues, "In the cities, their beliefs in communal lifestyles and their intolerance of close encounters with other people were misunderstood by the mainstream society." While this might be true in certain cases, in Detroit, Native people found a variety of ways to be both Indigenous and urban. Or, more precisely, to produce an identity that was Indigenous and directly influenced by those Indian cultures. As historian Douglas K. Miller has remarked, "Native people bent relocation to their own purposes and influenced its outcomes in unpredictable ways."[38] It is worth noting that the Bureau of Indian Affairs vetted Detroit's Native community to see if they would support the legislation; they resoundingly said no. They said no because they did not want to participate in the termination of Native tribes and they considered what impact the legislation might have on their community.

In 1956, the Bureau of Indian Affairs tried to persuade some Native people to support the termination bill. Tribes such as the Saginaw Chippewa initially supported the bill, believing that it would help protect their land from further expropriation. The bill was designed to "provide for the termination of Federal supervision over the property of Indian tribes, bands, and groups, and individual Indians in Michigan, and for other purposes." In reality, though, the bill terminated Michigan's tribal nations by allowing for individual members to sell land. A key component of this proposed legislation was to quickly restrict who would be able to claim Indigenous ancestry. In Section 3 of the bill, each tribe would have only six months to prepare and submit the proposed roll of members, which would be published in a federal register. If the tribe failed to submit such a roll, the secretary would be able to create a registry that would then be used. And if a person believed that he or she had been left off of a roll, that person could dispute it, but that must be done within ninety days. The secretary would then be able to determine whether said person had a case.

A report authored by Olin Hatfield Chilson, under secretary of the Interior, further supported this legislation in Michigan. It was fundamentally based on the belief in Indigenous integration into the U.S. political system. Chilson reasoned that people were misunderstanding Indian relationships to local, state, and national governments. While acknowledging that Native people had the same rights as other U.S. citizens because they consented like them, he also believed that Native nations therefore had no basis on which to claim self-determination because that right "has no application to any minority group of United States citizens. No minority ethnic group has the right to determine that it shall not be subject to our Federal-State constitution." Of course, he did not mention that the concepts of self-government and self-determination were quite different for tribal communities. Fortunately, Detroit's native community vociferously balked at termination. People like Hannah Aikens, a Delaware Indian from Canada, opposed termination, stating that it would "mean a great hardship for our people."[39]

In addition to opposing termination, Detroit's Indigenous community continued to participate in cultural activities in the city. In February 1951, the movie *Tomahawk* premiered in the city at the lobby of the Palms Theater. Detroit's Indigenous community came to meet some of the actors who were a part of the movie. It is interesting that the newspaper documented the most infamous Indigenous names possible, including Sitting Bull. The North American Indian Club brought beadwork and baskets, as well as war bonnets and other such items, that appealed to the settler imagination.[40] Another reading suggests that the community believed it important to try to challenge stereotypes every step of the way. In a quest for relevancy and an attempt to dismantle centuries-long, systematic erasure, participating in such events and having actual Indigenous people show up was important, a necessary act for asserting Indigenous humanity. There was a variety of Native people in Detroit at the time who were not "indigenous" to the area. Nevertheless, they experienced other forms of dispossession, so they created organizations and staged performances to challenge their dispossession. At the same time, Black Detroiters were experiencing their own form of dispossession through urban renewal.

Urban Renewal as Black Dispossession

During an oral history for the *Eyes on the Prize* documentary, Helen Kelley, a Black woman and resident of Detroit, reflected on her experience with urban renewal. She and her neighbors had been discussing the coming of the Chrysler Expressway for months. She stated that her family didn't want to leave. One morning, she woke up and "the bricks started coming through the window and I know we had to leave from there." She said she "was still in bed" and jumped up, only to find out "they was tearing the building down next-door."[41] This sort of dispossession and forced removal was not new in U.S. history. Yet, the cruelty with which the overseers of highway construction dealt with Black citizens demonstrates the vulnerability that working-class Black people felt. One day they could be living their life as normal, and the next day they could be forcibly displaced.

Commenting on the controversies of urban renewal in the 1960s, noted Black author James Baldwin stated, "Urban renewal means Negro removal."[42] "Negro removal," or Black dispossession, also happened in Detroit. In retelling this story, I want to move beyond the simple narrative about removal as racism. The elite white men of Detroit, in conjunction with some Black elite, in an attempt to create an ideal city, sought to clear slums in order to dispossess poor and working-class Black folks from the place they called home. Despite the rhetoric of building new homes, the city elite were invested in confining Black people to particular areas of the city.

In 1930, Detroit's population was about 1.5 million people; Black Americans were about 9 percent of that population, or just over 149,000 people. The majority of Black Americans lived on the east side, in Paradise Valley and Black Bottom. The "First Annual Report of the Detroit Housing Commission" offered a brief history of the Black population. The report commented on the great migration of Black folks who came to Detroit before World War I from the south in order to work in the factories. It also documented the lack of housing for Black folks and the racist practices that kept them confined.

Overcrowding created higher rents and kept people who could afford to move into white neighborhoods economically constrained as they had to pay higher rents.[43] Black people were forced to live in these areas because of racial capitalism. Black organizations had documented the lack of adequate housing for Black folks since the early part of the century. And yet, those who owned the homes made a profit. They could easily obtain mortgages, and they built homes elsewhere, creating more slums.

Because of segregation, Black folks were confined to those areas, often with multiple families living in dilapidated buildings. Black homes were filled with disease and infant mortality. According to a study conducted by the Detroit City Planning Commission, the crime rate in those areas was 7.5 times higher than in the rest of Detroit; juvenile delinquency was 10.4 times higher. Disease was another issue. Residents of this part of the city suffered from tuberculosis at a rate 6.5 times higher than in other parts of the city; pneumonia, 8 times higher; and infant mortality, 1.5 times higher.[44] The housing was terrible. Sixty-four percent of the dwellings were considered unfit for human habitation.[45] In the executive summary, the report stated, "Today, these areas present Detroit with a financial, economic and social problem beyond remedy of individual initiative, beyond the reach of private rehabilitation."[46]

The Detroit Housing Commission (DHC) emerged because the Federal Emergency Housing Corporation gave the city of Detroit a $3.2 million grant in November 1933 for slum clearance and for the development of low-income housing.[47] While Blacks continued to live in terrible conditions, the DHC began to advocate for slum clearance during and after World War II. Thus, Black dispossession began to rapidly happen.

In 1940, Blacks covered only 6.3 percent of the total city area. By 1950, they covered 13.2 percent.[48] A combination of mortgage bankers, real estate boards, builders, and neighborhood associations prevented Black people from moving into different neighborhoods.[49] Those who have power, including a combination of government policies and racist landlords, not only "confine those who have *no* power" but also "perpetuate their powerlessness."[50] They lived in internal colonies.

The Federal Housing Act (FHA) of 1949 helped accelerate Black dispossession. The federal government in concert with cities across the United States, under the guise of bettering their city infrastructure, wanted to eradicate dilapidated housing. By eradicating rundown housing, filled with poor, Black residents, urban planners and governments believed that they could increase tax revenue by bringing new businesses into the city. According to geographer Joe Darden, Title I of the FHA sought only to reduce the supply of housing. The language of the law was vague enough to legally allow cities to eliminate slums and to build up convention centers, luxury housing, and offices.[51] Government officials did not care much to account for the displacing of Black residents. This form of dispossession is an extension of settler colonialism, where the goal is to acquire land and eliminate the "indigenous" population.[52]

The redevelopment policies of Detroit were similar to those in other cities during the 1940s and onward. What was unusual in this context was that there was not a strong public and private relationship between city officials and the business elite.[53] Although the policies of slum clearance were terrible, the stories of those impacted reveal the challenges people faced in real time. A series of articles in the *Detroit Free Press* documented the challenges that Black families faced during slum clearances. An article titled "Racial Bars Complicate Slum Crisis" stated: "One of the major problems in connection with Detroit's slum areas is the difficulty faced by the non-white population in gaining access to better residential areas."[54] They highlighted the story of Elizabeth Barney, a Black mother of five. She lived in dilapidated housing on the city's east side for fifteen years. Her house was filled with rats, and the infestation forced her to keep tins over the holes in the walls and on the floor. Her efforts didn't stop a rat from biting one of her children. One of her brothers died of pneumonia there, and her sister died of tuberculosis. She attributed their deaths to the condition of the housing in which they lived. Barney applied for low-income housing and was eligible, but she had only a 1-in-700 chance of getting it. From 1946 to 1956, Detroit built a total of 100,000 new houses. However, only 2,000 were built for Black people. In addition to discriminatory practices around mortgage lending and a lack of financial resources, white racism constrained the Black working class and poor to the slums of Detroit.

Mrs. Barney was one of many Black women looking for low-income housing in the 1950s in a place that hardly had any.[55] In the post–World War II era, property ownership was a key sign of citizenship and belonging.[56] That meant the converse was true: Without housing, Black people living in slums were the dispossessed. Interestingly enough, Black elite organizations such as the Detroit Urban League, were proponents of slum clearance and urban renewal. As they noted in one report, "The realization of this objective will enable the city of Detroit to undergird its tax base, avoid the increasing expense of supplying services to slum areas, as well as provide community environments which will be less conducive to the attrition of the human personality."[57]

Detroit was considered the epitome of urban development innovation. One pamphlet, written to discuss the importance of city development, stated, "In the evolution of Western civilization, the city has always been the center of development." In 1941, city officials and urban planners created the "Detroit Master Plan." The plan included land use, slum clearance, and expressway and thoroughfare routes, as well as new sites for recreation, schools, and public-service buildings. Within the context of the master plan, another important example of Black dispossession was the Gratiot Redevelopment Project.

City planners proposed the Gratiot Redevelopment project in 1946 as a slum-clearance program, which was a foundational part of the Detroit Master Plan. It was furthered by the passing of the federal Housing Act of 1949, which granted assistance to city governments to clear out slums and redevelop them.[58] With his upset victory over George Edwards in the 1950 mayoral election, Albert Cobo accelerated the process. Cobo supported restricted covenants, which allowed white neighborhoods to prevent Black families from moving in. Edwards's campaign tried to convince the white working class that Cobo was a part of the business elite. On November 5, 1949, in a debate at St. Andrews Hall, he correctly outlined Cobo's plan for slum clearance: "My opponent's plan is all right if you're a member of a real-estate corporation as he is, but to the people who need low-rent housing it is a fraud on their basic rights."[59] For Cobo, slum clearance would eliminate excessive costs in policing and the city paying for the welfare of its most vulnerable.[60] The white working class supported Cobo, and he won in a landslide. This election represented the early roots of white America's conservatism in the postwar era.[61] After he won the election, Cobo argued with the Housing director, James H. Inglis on Inglis's proposed housing program. Inglis wanted the new housing built first and then the slum clearance to occur. Cobo insisted that the slum clearance occur immediately.[62] Cobo got his wish. In September 1950, city officials relocated nearly 2,000 families. By 1951, the city had acquired all forty-three blocks.

The Gratiot Redevelopment Project consisted of the bounded area of Lafayette, Hastings, Gratiot, and Dequindre. There were 958 buildings, with about 1,550 dwelling units. About 1,050, or two-thirds, were considered substandard. More than 1,000 of the dwellings were dilapidated or had no running water. By 1952, of the 1,564 families that had been relocated, the whereabouts of 64 could not be traced. It is as if they disappeared. By 1953, the Housing Corporation of America purchased 47 acres for $1,266,000.[63] Harold Norris, a lawyer from Detroit, and architect of the Michigan Bill of Rights, was an opponent of Mayor Cobo's slum-clearance project. [64] Speaking to the Greater

Detroit Public Housing Tenants Council in 1952, he aptly described the dispossession logic that undergirded Cobo's policies: The "purpose for this removal program is to clear the land and permit the private development of housing."[65]

How elite white men applied the logic of dispossession to Black people was not far removed from the process of dispossession of Indigenous people. The logics of settler dispossession are a combination of discourse and representation, government policy, removal, and displacement and disappearing. For instance, in the dispossession and removal of Indigenous people, settlers create narratives for the public to make them believe that something is wrong with the people in need of dispossession. Then a government entity creates a policy legitimating removal, followed by the actual removal. In this way, the population is displaced and, later, no longer exists in the public imagination. This process further cements the government's control over the now "abundant" land. The aftermath includes the accepted history of removal and the changing of the land. The people no longer matter and those in power are in control of the land and benefit from it.

The development by private companies was one of the first of its kind. Joseph Kanter, president of the Housing Corporation of America, noted the "purchase of this property by Housing Corporation of America, under the provisions of the Urban Redevelopment Act, is the first attempt by private enterprise to develop large-scale housing in slum clearance areas." Finally, Kanter boasted, "It is a pilot project and a model for changing the face of urban America." Detroit was chosen because of the "progressive efforts of the Detroit Housing Commission in completely demolishing all buildings on the site." Indeed, slum clearance, backed by federal legislation, was a precursor to public-private interests in urban planning and housing development.[66]

Slum clearance and urban development as dispossession cannot be understood outside of its relationship to suburbanization. With investors, insurance companies, bank and mortgage lenders all concerned with the downtown core and city planning, they were deeply invested in redevelopment for their own financial interests. Even as African Americans tried to protest and resist their own dispossession, as historian Thomas Sugrue remarks, "They faced one of the most powerful, well-organized political movements in Detroit's history, a grassroots movement that had as its primary purpose the maintenance of Detroit's racial boundaries."[67] Moreover, Detroit's liberal politicians also were directly implicated in Black dispossession, including Democratic politician

Thomas Poindexter, who founded the Greater Detroit Homeowners' Association Council in 1962, which was designed to keep neighborhoods white and to avoid mixed-race housing.[68]

The legacy of urban renewal, restricted covenants, slum clearance, and other forms of racial segregation in urban America has been well documented.[69] It negatively impacted the life chances of the city's Black working-class population, furthering the notion that Black people were second-class citizens and were the most vulnerable to dispossession. Highway construction not only dislocated hundreds of families, it also helped pave the way for white flight so that white people could more easily move to the suburbs and travel between the suburbs and the city. While urban renewal was "supposed to stimulate the rise and expansion of crucial institutions and the revitalization of residential neighborhoods," African Americans experienced financial woes and emotional agony. They were dispossessed of their homes and unable to secure adequate housing.[70]

The discourse of urban renewal was new in practice—that is, its focus on clearing out Black folks during a particular historical moment—but it was part of the larger historical pattern of dispossession. White people viewed Black peoples' relationship to space as always in doubt. In this regard, the history of dispossession goes back to the shores of the African continent, when European colonizers forcibly stole Africans from their indigenous lands. The enslavers further solidified Black dispossession on the plantation, exploiting Black labor and controlling the movement of Black people, even as enslaved Africans used everyday acts of resistance to challenge their exploitation. The plantation was a place of both violence and community building. From the plantation of the nineteenth century to the cities in the twentieth century, Black life was a part of the U.S. agenda of controlling Black people. Urban renewal was part of a larger genealogy of Black subjugation, but it was also an extension of settler logics of colonization.

When placed within the context of longer histories of Indigenous dispossession, urban renewal is part of a historical pattern of clearing space and people, designing the space for a certain populace to settle, and then a few profiting off it. As legal critical race scholar Cheryl Harris has contended, from the founding of the United States, elite white men developed ideas of race and property within the American democratic project through the expropriation of Indigenous land and African labor.[71] Whether on the plantation, in which whites controlled Black people and exploited their labor, or in urban renewal planning, we can see that racial capitalism required the removal *and* exploitation of people. Urban renewal and the construction of highways that have displaced people of color throughout urban America was as American as cherry pie.

Reframing urban renewal as dispossession, and placing it as an extension of settler colonial logics does a few things. First, it demonstrates the ongoing nature of settler colonialism. That is, though a policy might not necessarily impact a particular place's Indigenous population, European American elites often implement policies in order to secure similar conclusions: land and power. Second, with all of the contemporary discourses about gentrification and land use in Detroit, we still need to discuss race. As Aileen Moreton-Robinson notes, "Whiteness is the invisible measure of who can hold possession."[72] Power is crucial. The ability to control and determine the fate of the city's Black population, in spite of the rhetoric of help, is crucial for thinking through how Black dispossession occurs. In the city of dispossession, both white conservatives and white liberals actively tried to control Black people, allowing them to exist within the city as long as they were powerless. One way for white people to do this was to displace Black people, as they had done a century before in dispossessing Indigenous people.

By the mid-1960s, the status of housing for Blacks changed slightly, but not necessarily for the better. As scholar Keeanga-Yamahtta Taylor observes: "Racism, and the economic exploitation of African Americans was the glue that held the American housing market together."[73] Meager gains in real estate coincided with the rapid exodus of white people. While Black populations increased, white exodus increased as well, leaving Black folks concentrated at increasingly higher rates than before. They also continued paying higher rent rates than white people did, and tensions remained intact between middle- and working-class Blacks and poor Blacks.[74]

It is not surprising that Mayor Cobo was an advocate of slum clearance. He was a product of a long lineage of settler memory. Indeed, in 1955, he posed in a picture during the celebration of Cadillac's landing. He, like other elite white men of the city, was dedicated not only to dispossessing Black people but also to reconnecting with the white settler past.

* * *

The legacy of Cobo is troubling. But while he was advancing the idea of Black dispossession, both Black and Indigenous peoples in the city began organizing themselves to create cohesion within the urban context. In the next chapter, I highlight Black and Indigenous resistance to dispossession, during the era of Black and Red Power. For Black folks, it was an extension of their long engagement with radical activism. For Native folks, influenced by their calls for sovereignty and Black radicalism, it was the beginning of their demand not only for visibility but also for sovereignty and justice.

CHAPTER 5

Black Indigeneity and Urban Indigenous Feminism in Postwar Detroit

In June 1976, Louis Cook, a writer for the *Detroit Free Press*, published an article for the *North American Indian Association Newsletter*, a local Detroit Indigenous newsletter. In the article, titled "Detroit's Forgotten People—American Indians," he wrote of the invisibility that Native people continued to experience in the city. "Being a stranger in one's own land is hard to bear," he wrote. He contended that Detroiters had found "black power, brown power, and even a little yellow power," but Native people were "still looking for red power."[1] The irony, of course, is that in Detroit Indigenous people, especially women, had been organizing and making waves, they just weren't as visible in the public eye as were African Americans.

In the postwar era, the experiences of African Americans and Indigenous peoples were similar in some ways but signified very different realities. Both groups sought to transform American society through protest, increasing calls to nationalism and increasing the desire to assert their humanity within urban contexts. However, to the mainstream public, African Americans began to increasingly demand change, whereas Native people continued under the veil of invisibility, even as they too protested in urban areas.

For instance, in June 1961, Native people gathered in Chicago for a conference at the University of Chicago organized by Sol Tax, an anthropologist. Hundreds of Indigenous peoples came together, and after a week of discussion they produced the "Declaration of Indian Purpose." This document did not repudiate American capitalism and colonialism as some documents would later. The conference participants simply wanted the United States to revoke the House Concurrent Resolution 108, also called the termination policy. This policy, a key source of Indigenous dispossession, sought to eradicate tribal nations and call for greater assimilation. They also wanted more education for Native people. This era marked the beginning of Indigenous self-determination.[2] While Native people called for greater attention to their plight and the need for greater control over their affairs, African Americans used more direct approaches to social change.

Within the context of radical activism, Black people sought to assert their belonging through what I call "Black indigeneity" and Indigenous people created alternative institutions in order to further cement their place in urban spaces where they were often invisible to the rest of society. With a focus on Indigenous women, I explore their role in asserting self-determination through what I call "urban Indigenous feminism."

This chapter explores how African Americans asserted their relationship to owning Detroit, as a physical space and as a political machine, through the lens of radical, masculine politics. Black activists had long organized against dispossession in Detroit through Black Nationalism. In a moment of radical calls for Black ownership of land, they began to more erroneously assert Black indigeneity. I define Black indigeneity as an assertion of Black belonging and making claim to a particular space, a call for self-determination, with the hope of securing Black futures. It differs from Black Nationalism because activists actively construct their own sense of place and belonging by relying on their perception of Indigenous dispossession, or the settler colonial idea that Indigenous people had disappeared entirely. Indeed, Black indigeneity becomes a problem when Black people, through their desire for freedom and because they have labored in the nation-state, erase Indigenous claims to space.[3]

Urban Indigenous feminism is a political ideology and practice that emerged in response to various forms of dispossession, including poverty, segregation, child removal, lack of education, and invisibility in the urban environment. It is a political praxis executed by urban Indigenous women who believe in Indigenous sovereignty and self-determination; engage in a variety of forms of protest, including writing letters to local newspapers, creating organizations to sustain culture and education; and believe that Indigenous peoples have a future within the urban environment. As anthropologist Renya Ramirez contends, while Native people as a whole contribute to the development of the urban Indigenous community, "Native American women are central to sustaining urban Indian community life."[4]

Within the scholarship of Indigenous activism, men continue to dominate, and they dominated the media during the 1960s and 1970s.[5] However, it was Indigenous women who engaged in the everyday forms of labor and who enacted change during this same period.[6] For instance, Hannah Aikens, a longtime Delaware activist in the postwar era, was concerned with correcting the miseducation of the public about Indigenous people, but she was also concerned with the present and convinced that it was Indigenous people who had to do it: “The only people who can speak for the Indians now are the Indians themselves.”[7] While Indigenous activism began to move further into the public sphere, African Americans began to assert their belonging in the city. These two parallel political ideologies within Black and Indigenous America were both about constructing belonging and about challenging their ongoing dispossessions in Detroit in an attempt to claim ownership of the city. However, the claiming of ownership created tension. Native people manufactured their own conception of indigeneity in Detroit by creating cultural and educational spaces in the city. Black people and Indigenous people asserting indigeneity was a direct response to white people dispossessing them in the form of physical displacement, spatial segregation, and cultural erasure. This chapter explores these parallel movements.

In May 1964, an article appeared in the *Detroit Free Press* titled “Indians Becoming Organization of People.” Of course, they had been organized for more than two decades, but the author noticed their more assertive stance in combating stereotypes. “Michigan Indians fear they are losing their proud heritage and their identity,” wrote Don Myers, a member of the press staff. He continued, “They don’t want to live in tepees or wear clothes of animal hides but they just as soon remember how to make them.”[8] The article continues down the path of stereotypes, including discussing the ancient rituals of Indigenous people, but it also included snippets of Indigenous resistance.

Aikens commented on how it was then fashionable for white people to claim an Indigenous heritage. Although in that way it also contributed to Indigenous people becoming stronger in their own heritage. It is important to take a step back and remember the Indigenous activism at the time. In the early 1960s, numerous forms of resistance occurred throughout Indigenous America. The National Indian Youth Council formed in 1961, creating a young, firebrand of Indigenous activists, who would go on to assert their humanity in a variety of ways, including in the fishing-rights movement, which took off in Washington State in 1964.[9] However, urban Indigenous women were at the forefront of resistance to dispossession in urban spaces like Detroit.

One key feature of dispossession is the removal of Indigenous children from Indigenous homes through the foster care system. In the late nineteenth and early part of the twentieth century, the settler colonial state forced

Indigenous children to go to boarding schools; however, during the postwar era, state governments began to take children from Indigenous homes and put them into the foster care system. One way in which urban Indigenous women began to assert their feminism is by creating institutions with the sole job of remaining Indigenous and advocating in front of Congress.

From 1972 through 1974, the Michigan Commission on Indian Affairs (formerly the CIA) traveled around Michigan to get a sense of the needs of Michigan's Indigenous population. By the end of 1974, the commission authored a report, and one of the key concerns of Michigan's Indigenous community was foster care. In a community meeting, one person stated, "An Indian social worker is needed to work with families in all areas of their needs and problems." Another suggested that "more Indian foster care homes are needed for Indian children" and contended that "there is a lack of information about what programs are available and who is eligible."[10] The report concluded that for Michigan's Indigenous community, keeping their children in Indigenous homes was a top priority. The commission argued that their children were being kidnapped like those of a generation before them, and therefore they would miss out on the opportunity to live as Indigenous peoples. In Detroit, the Indigenous community shared similar beliefs; so, too, did Esther Mays.

Figure 2. Esther Shawboose Mays, date unknown. Drawing by Liseth Amaya.

For any community, raising children in their own cultural milieu is important. Esther Mays raised nine children of her own, and, as a child, lived in a variety of homes, albeit Indigenous ones. Her home was known as a place where children could stay. Even as parents struggled with alcoholism, drug abuse, and the instability that being poor, Indigenous, and invisible in Detroit created, Esther would host a variety of youth in her house when they needed a place to stay.[11]

Mays understood the importance of the home as not just an Indigenous woman's place but as a site of contestation to help foster a strong Indigenous identity and to introduce young people to urban Indigenous politics, serving as a role model, and meeting the spiritual needs of many.[12] She made her own children members of organizations and had them participate in meetings. As her daughter remarked, her home was a meeting space, a place where people worked tirelessly on children's rights. She would also always bring in children who needed a place to stay.[13] Coming to terms with the fact that something had to be done to protect children, she decided to create an organization.

In the hub of growing activism across Indian Country and during a moment when federal dollars were pouring into Indigenous communities on reservations and in cities, Native women began to form nonprofit organizations to deal specifically with urban problems.[14] During the era of Indigenous self-determination, Esther Mays founded the Great Lakes Northern Stars in 1974. The Great Lakes Northern Stars was a nonprofit organization dedicated to keeping Native children within Native homes. The organization also sought to work with the entire Detroit and interregional community on a variety of issues, including providing clothing and food for those in need. They would even take in children whose parents had been incarcerated, and would keep them until the parents got out.[15]

It might seem that Mays was engaging in "traditional" women's roles, but it went beyond that. As an urban Indigenous feminist, her activities varied. They included seeking better education and working to make sure that children and those most vulnerable had their basic needs met. She was also a mother and homemaker. Mays and other Indigenous women understood that there would be no Indigenous future in the city without making life better for the next generation. As a part of her protest tactics, she went on to Washington, D.C., in order to testify about the specific problems Native children faced when placed in the foster care system and removed for adoption.

From the late 1960s until the early 1970s, the federal government increasingly decided to undo the decades of bad policy toward Native Americans.

It was known as "Indian Self-Determination." Ushered in by President Richard Nixon during his July 8, 1970 "Special Message to Congress on Indian Affairs," this era of self-determination required that the federal government give Indigenous people control over their affairs and reverse the decades-long policy of government interference and the attempt at assimilating Indigenous people.[16] And by 1974, coupled with Native activism throughout Indian Country, Congress began to take seriously the issue of children being taken out of their homes. They did not do this out of the kindness of their hearts. It was through years of Indigenous women's organizing and activism.[17] As a result, the U.S. House of Representatives and the Senate decided to better understand the government's complicity in the removal of children from Native homes. In April 1974, Esther Mays went to testify before Congress.

On April 8, 1974, at 9:00 A.M., Senator James Abourezk, Democratic, of South Dakota, also the chair of the session, began the 93rd Congress, 2nd session, titled "Problems That American Indian Families Face in Raising Their Children and How These Problems Are Affected by Federal Action or Inaction." Senator Abourezk, who was Lebanese, grew up most of his life in South Dakota near the Rosebud Reservation. He knew almost firsthand the harsh reality facing Indigenous nations.[18] He began: "We have called these hearings today to begin to define the specific problems that American Indian families face in raising their children and how these problems are affected by Federal action or inaction." The bipartisan committee was comprised of eight people. There were also at least thirty-two Indigenous and non-Indigenous attendees who gave testimonies about the difficulties and harms faced by Indigenous communities related to adoption and foster care. They represented a wide range of organizations, including tribal nations, Indigenous community organizations, and psychologists and psychiatrists.

Senator Abourezk acknowledged that agencies, unreasonably, removed Native children from their homes. He argued that nearly 25 percent of Native children were in some form of foster care, at a rate of five to twenty-five times higher than the national average. These policies, unchecked, were abusive and they disregarded Native peoples' demand to have a say in what happened to their children. Over the next two days, the senator hoped that with the testimonies offered they would be "able to propose Federal action and the legal means to protect and develop their families."[19]

The people testifying before Congress used a variety of tactics. Some read written statements and others spoke from the heart. One woman brought her three children and explained that police officers in her hometown, Fallon,

Nevada, pulled her over for drunk driving and brutalized her. The next day, the officers came to her house, kidnapped her children, and helped process them for them for foster care. As a result, she had a difficult time getting her children back. Others testified that Indigenous mothers had hardly any recourse for the kidnapping of their children. And, once taken out of their homes, the children spent extensive time with white families and therefore were not brought up with their Indigenous culture. Toward the end of the day, Esther Mays was supposed to speak; instead, she went first thing the next morning.

The history of Indigenous child removal was based on two assumptions. First, white Americans, backed by the federal government, believed that the best way to deal with the "Indian problem" was to assimilate the children and eradicate their culture. Removing children became a "matter of common sense."[20] It began in the late nineteenth century with the removal of children to boarding schools and using a process of removing their culture. Often, when children returned, they could no longer speak their native language and they looked different from people from their community, which caused great despair. The second assumption was rooted in the larger structure of settler colonialism and its purpose to dispossess Indigenous peoples from their land. It was what anthropologist Patrick Wolfe has called the "logic of elimination."[21]

On April 9, 1974, at 9:00 A.M., Senator Abourezk began the session, stating that the first witness was from Detroit, and her name was Esther Mays. The senator apologized for scheduling her testimony the following day, and stated, "I want to express the committee's gratitude for your staying overnight." Mays, known for her wit, responded, "Since you're handing out compliments, I'd like to compliment you on your timing. It's almost as good as ours." She then began her formal statement.

"My name is Esther Mays and I am from Detroit, Michigan," began Mays. Her identification of Detroit as her hometown, which she was proud of, was not simply a recognition of the place from which she came. It was a representation of her unique identity as an urban Indigenous woman. As Seneca scholar Mishuana Goeman writes, "Embodied geographies thus become pivotal in decolonization projects, and it is here that Native feminisms can play a major role in our thinking about the connection between land, individuals, and constructions of nations."[22] In addition to creating her own organization, she served on the board of directors of the Native American Child Protection Council. Based in Detroit, this organization sought to keep Native children in Native homes and limit the removal of Native children from their homes throughout the state of Michigan. Urban Indigenous feminists worked within their particular geographical spaces as well as in others, demonstrating an awareness of the importance of tribal sovereignty, and knowing that urban Natives are not that far removed from those on the reservation.

In the next part of her testimony, Esther Mays offered four reasons that explained why Indigenous communities struggle to keep their children. These reasons were rooted in larger ideas of Indigenous self-determination. First, non-Indigenous agencies had no respect or regard for the child's cultural and racial heritage. Second, those non-Indigenous homes have no general knowledge about what it is like to be an Indigenous person. Third, children outside of their communities don't learn about their heritage. And when they reach an age when they are able to discover more about themselves, they are caught in limbo, struggling for acceptance in the Native community and deemed unacceptable by the white community. Finally, the adoptive or foster families know nothing about Native culture and histories and therefore cannot relate at all to the child.[23]

Having lived in Detroit since she was sixteen years old and raising children in the city, she understood how difficult it was to raise Indigenous children in a "traditional" cultural way. She believed not so much in tradition but in bringing up youth who could live as urban Indigenous peoples. She mentioned that the Native American Child Protection Council did many holistic things for families, including providing clothing, furniture, transportation, and legal assistance, as well as attending court with parents, simply to make sure they were given the opportunity to keep their children. Mays ended her testimony by offering five recommendations to the committee that would help: She wanted to halt the age restriction that essentially barred elders from taking in children. She recommended a change in the laws that forced Native families to give up their children. She sought better training for social workers who would help families understand Indigenous community needs and the "outside" world and would require training of Native social workers who could do this job. She wanted a full investigation into the practices of agencies that transport children across state and national (Canada) lines. Finally, she requested that she be put on the mailing list in order to keep abreast of the issues.[24] Mays left D.C. that night and returned to the Motor City to continue to do her work as an urban Indigenous feminist. Four years later, on November 8, 1978, President Jimmy Carter signed into law Public Law 95-608, known as the Indian Child Welfare Act of 1978.

Mays continued her work in Detroit and throughout Michigan. She became a well-respected elder in the community. Even the state of Michigan recognized her efforts. On June 26, 1980, Republican governor William Milliken appointed Mays the Detroit representative for the Michigan Commission of Indian Affairs for a two-year term. Her duties varied, including participating on the corrections committee, which helped relatives visit incarcerated family members at correctional institutions throughout Michigan. Shortly after taking the position, she became ill but continued working as hard as she could.

On June 29, 1984, Esther Mays died of congestive heart failure. Her legacy continued through the work of her children, especially in the realm of education. Mays's urban Indigenous feminism centered on Indigenous self-determination, a commitment to justice, and using a variety of tactics to put these ideas into practice.

Black Indigeneity

The discourse and politics of self-determination and community control existed in Detroit at least since the early twentieth century. From the formation of the Nation of Islam and the Universal Negro Improvement Association to Reverend Albert Cleage Jr.'s church, the "Shrine of the Black Madonna," to the Detroit Houseworkers League, Black people were concerned with owning their community and defining themselves in nationalistic ways.[25] From the late 1960s onward, Black radicalism in Detroit was typified with the formation of several organizations. Those included the coalition of Black radicals and theorists, called GOAL (Group on Advanced Leadership), founded in 1961, which included Cleage and Marxist theorists James Boggs and his lifelong partner, the Chinese American, Grace Lee Boggs. Other groups included RAM (Revolutionary Action Movement) and the Republic of New Afrika.[26]

The foundations of Black radicalism in Detroit and throughout the country were based on how African Americans imagined Black indigeneity. Thus, Black indigeneity is the idea that because African Americans were enslaved and exploited for their labor, they deserve the land that they worked. Their exploitation is an essential reason as to why their descendants should be able to claim ownership of land in the United States.[27] Black people in the United States have discursively and historically produced indigeneity and their claims to land because of their labor. The discourse goes something like this: We worked the land, we were promised forty acres and a mule, and our reparations should be land. For example, in March 1968, the Republic of New

Afrika demanded that the U.S. government give them five states in the South. They desired independence and their own land.[28] An important question to ask, though, is where do Indigenous peoples fit in that scenario?

In 1968, a year after the Detroit Rebellion, a Black newspaper titled *East Side Voice of Independent Detroit (ESVID)*, contained a poem about Black history and Black indigeneity. Titled "Black America's Reply to Bigots," the twenty-three-line poem articulated what Black folks could say to racists who argued that they did not belong. The end of the poem captures the core idea of Black indigeneity:

> To those who cry, return to whence you came,
> To those who cry, stay in your place Nigger
> We, the black Americans reply.
> We were here when your pilgrim fathers came
> We gave them corn for their children that first cold cruel winter.
> We came in the ships that followed
> The lawyers, doctors, teachers, and ministers
> We came with the founders of this nation.
> We came in the holes of countless slave ships
> Tortured, stripped of pride and heritage
> We came in chains of steel to free the chains of ignorance from your mind.[29]

Importantly, the members of *ESVID* recognized that Black people had a stake in the United States. Black people had been there as indentured servants and as enslaved Africans. They were the descendants of enslaved Africans who were there at the beginning of the U.S. democratic project. One of the last few lines of the poem demonstrates, perhaps, the most compelling argument for Black belonging and ownership in Detroit (and other parts of the United States): "Our blood, sweat, and tears have purchased our place in this mighty nation."[30] This has been a central theme in Black ideology and political struggle since at least the nineteenth century.[31] During the era of Black Power, for Black activists, land was key.[32] Again, this claim to land causes a problem because it erases the actual history, ongoing presence, and future of Indigenous peoples who have the rightful claim to their space. As literary scholar Shona Jackson writes, "Native displacement and either real or figurative disappearance serves as the necessary or enabling condition of black being . . . and is essential for constitution of that being through the rise of national consciousness and class consolidation."[33] Black people asserted black indigeneity based on their exploited labor and confinement to space.

The basis for Black people's claiming ownership of Detroit and belonging is rooted in their exploited labor. Regarding Creoles in the Caribbean, Jackson contends that "what 'saved' blacks and allowed them to inhabit a native identity connected with the future of the postcolonial state rather than its past is both their greater integration into colonial culture, and through the plantation, their primary identity as workers."[34] With Jackson's observations in mind, I want to offer a few examples of how Blacks have constructed Black indigeneity in Detroit.

Perhaps no two people defined Black radicalism in Detroit more than James "Jimmy" and Grace Lee Boggs. They had worked in radical circles since the 1940s. As historian Stephen Ward observes, "They helped to set the ideological and organizational foundation for the emergence of the Black Power movement."[35] If you considered yourself any type of radical, then you came across James and Grace Boggs in Detroit. It is here that I want to briefly paint a picture of Black radicalism in Detroit, through their political ideology regarding radical social change. It is through their writing that we can see some of the roots of postwar Black radicalism and how they constructed their sense of belonging.

Although only James Boggs's name is on the book, *Racism and Class Struggle: Further Pages from a Black Worker's Notebook* (1970), Grace Lee Boggs contributed significantly to his work through their intellectual partnership. The Boggses believed that radical social transformation should happen at the point of production, and workers should be the ones to usher in this transformation. In the essay titled "The Meaning of the Black Revolt," originally published in 1963, the authors argued that Black Americans learned many of their ideas of anticolonial thinking from decolonization efforts in the Third World.[36] They asserted Black indigeneity through work.

For the Boggses, Black Americans had to accept two facts. First, they "are one of the world's largest minorities, bigger than most of the nations of the world." And, based on the first fact, they "are so organically a part of the way the American system operates that their refusal to play this role can disrupt the system irreparably."[37] The Boggses believed that in order to transform society, Black workers must absolutely move quickly to take over government spaces because the jobs for Black and white workers were becoming more automated.

The Boggses viewed their idea of Black ownership of cities through the lens of the immigrant narrative. Just as white ethnics of a previous generation, who, when they became a majority, took over city politics, Black Americans, who were then becoming the majority in Detroit and cities across the country, were next in line. The Boggses reasoned that "each previous ethnic grouping achieved first-class citizenship chiefly because its leaders became the cities' leaders"; however, "racism is so deeply imbedded in the American psyche from top to bottom, and from left to right, that it cannot even entertain the idea of black political power in cities."[38] While the white power structure would hinder Black Americans from taking over city politics, it would only be temporary and would lead only to the inevitable: Black revolt. This analysis utilized the language of an immigrant narrative, one in line with the white power structure. It followed the settler logic of occupying space, with the silent narrative of Indigenous people only in the background.

The Boggses asserted a strand of radical Black thought that was tied in with the widely circulating idea of internal colonialism.[39] Their goal was to formulate a "revolutionary theory of black urban struggle that would reorganize not just Black communities but American society." The problems of urban Black America dovetailed with those in the developing world. The Boggses believed that "the fundamental problem of the transformation of human activity in advanced America is as deeply rooted as the problem of land reform in countries that have been kept in a state of underdevelopment by colonialism."[40] They also used the history of Indigenous peoples as a warning sign to others: "America has already become a dangerous society. The nation's major cities are becoming police states. There are only two roads open to it. *Either* wholesale extermination of the black population through mass massacres or forced mass migrations onto reservations as with the Indians. . . . *Or* self-government of the major cities by the black majority, mobilized behind leaders and organizations of its own creation and prepared to reorganize the structure of city government and city life from top to bottom."[41] On the surface, this radical idea is a manifesto to Black America to take over their cities by any means necessary, to become a self-determined people. During the 1960s and 1970s, a strand of Black Nationalist thought posited that one way in which Black people could gain control of their lives was by taking over buildings and land in cities, which would be the cultural and political milieu of Black life.[42] Owning land as a socioeconomic possession was a Black political ideology. Although they did not necessarily seek to replace Indigenous peoples, Black Nationalists ignored the agency of urban Indigenous peoples and histories. As a result, they contributed to the historical and present erasure of Indigenous peoples in time and place.[43]

As mentioned above, the Boggses described the Black experience as related to people in the Third World. They connected the underdevelopment of African Americans in U.S. cities to colonized people in underdeveloped countries. They also compared what was happening in Vietnam to the experiences of Black and Indigenous peoples. However, they shifted to a masculine discourse, arguing, "Now the black revolution and the struggle for black power are emerging when all people are clamoring for manhood."[44] In some ways, and with few exceptions, their rhetoric typified that of the Black (male) working-class discourse around social change.

The Black working-class character of Black radical Detroit was also rooted in Black belonging: the relationship between class, nationalism, and race. The meaning of work existed in multiple spheres. Black women had long worked and organized as domestic workers and factory workers prior to and after World War II.[45] From middle-class Black women's groups like the Detroit Housewives Leagues of the 1940s and other Black women's clubs throughout the pre–World War II era, Black women tried to shape conversations about the meaning and importance of women's labor.[46] Black working-class women "constructed their own meanings of citizenship" because they believed that "waged work was absolutely vital to their existence."[47] Indeed, Black women radicals during the Black Power era "protested racism, a discriminatory state, and an economic system that kept them impoverished."[48] They often focused on better working conditions, welfare, and better housing situations. Black women played a major role in the everyday functions of Black Power organizations, including in Detroit.[49]

In the League of Revolutionary Black Workers, Black women were central to the development of the organization. One such person was Marian Kramer. Kramer was born in Baton Rouge, Louisiana, in 1944. As a university student, she became involved in the Congress of Racial Equality (CORE). Her activism would eventually lead her to Detroit. In Detroit, she became involved with numerous organizations, including the West Central Organization (WCO). The WCO tried to combat urban renewal near Wayne State University.

In 1967, General Gordon Baker and Glanton Dowdell, leaders within the League of Revolutionary Black Workers, began to come around the WCO, recruiting members and forming alliances. As a result, Kramer joined and worked on behalf of the League. However, she ended up doing "women's work." Reflecting on that, she commented on the Black male supremacy and rampant sexism within the organization. The women "were the ones doing the typing," she remarked. "They wanted to try and act like our role should be the kitchen, the bedroom, and clerical work. We refused to buckle under that." In addition to their work in the organization, they also resisted in the streets. They fought urban renewal and slumlords, and they helped form tenants' unions and protected people against police brutality.

They also debated about where the League should focus its resistance; they decided it would be at the point of production: in the factories. Women like Kramer disagreed. She reasoned that the factories were important, "but all those men got to come back into the community; they live somewhere. We've got to be organizing in both places."[50] Furthermore, Kramer argued that because women were working in the plants and in the trade unions, they should have been given leadership positions. Black women also had to deal with rampant sexism in the League.

Black men hit on them often. Although Kramer said it was their way of joking, they would call women like her who resisted their advancements "IWW," or "Ignorant Women of the World," rather than "Industrial Workers of the World." In spite of Black male patriarchy, Kramer insisted that Black women were the backbone of the organization. She continued working to organize people outside of the League.

In 1969, she helped organize tenants in the Jeffries and Brewster projects because the city had decided to raise the rent. She, along with members of the League and the Black Panther Party, and the tenants, young and old, met and concluded that they would do a rent strike. Because of the strike, the city of Detroit created some concessions. The city decided not to raise the rent, and it formed tenants' councils.[51]

Kramer left the League in 1971, and would go on to work on welfare rights in Detroit. She began working with the Westside mothers, a welfare-rights organization in the state of Michigan, and, later, cochairing the National Welfare Rights Organization.[52] Women like Kramer sought radical change but understood that transformation should not be at the expense of Black women. It is not clear whether Black women subscribed to the same belief as Black men who engaged in forms of Indigenous erasure. However, other organizations, such as the Third World Women's Alliance, sought to work with other women of color, including Indigenous women.[53] Nevertheless, she did share with women like Esther Mays the ideology that in order to create lasting change, children had to be the center. She remarked, "In order for our children to have a future we've got to eliminate poverty in this country. We've got to participate politically in this fight."[54] The link between poverty and self-determination was not that far removed from urban Indigenous women's ideas of social change.

They understood that in order to help future generations, children must be central, and a focus on children's poverty, education, and discrimination must be at the root of challenging dispossession. Still, Black men's narrow focus on factories did not bode well for their understanding of Indigenous struggles.

In the classic Detroit radicalism study titled *Detroit: I Do Mind Dying* (1975), authors Dan Georgakas and Marvin Surkin studied the activism of Black revolutionaries from 1967 to 1974. I consider this book a primary text of the time period because of its analysis of sources of the time and interviews. A profound contention of the book, from which I draw, is written in the introduction: "More than anywhere else in the United States, the movement led by black workers defined its goals in terms of real power—the power to control the economy, which meant trying to control the shop floor at the point of production."[55] Black workers in Detroit had a very good understanding of racial capitalism—and how race is a central component of class and how Black people often bore a heavier burden of exploitation. A major moment when Detroit's Black radicals articulated Black belonging happened during the construction of the Black Manifesto at the Black Economic Development Conference, held in Detroit, April 26–29, 1969.

Although it was a national conference, with the likes of Michigan congressman John Conyers and Georgia representative Julian Bond there, the League of Revolutionary Black Workers was featured prominently on the steering committee. The committee also included James Boggs. At the meeting, the group demanded $500 million in reparations from white religious organizations. The manifesto stated, "We the black people assembled in Detroit, Michigan for the National Black Economic Development Conference are fully aware that we have been forced to come together because racist white America has exploited our resources, our minds, our bodies, our labor."[56] After outlining how Black people have been exploited, including how exploitation affects the mind and labor, the manifesto outlined the internal colonial discourse prevalent in the mid-twentieth century among Black radicals, "For centuries we have been forced to live as colonized people inside the United States, victimized by the most vicious, racist system in the world." Importantly, this first paragraph ends with "We have helped to build the most industrial country in the world." Black men equated the experience of workers through that which happened to Black men. Because they were exploited and their labor was used to exploit the land, they deserved to own land and assert that this place was their home; they were able to regain their manhood. Though the institutions did not respond positively to these demands, it is significant that they articulated their grievances as to why they deserved certain things, based on their exploited bodies and labor.

Black workers would again assert an idea of their belonging as workers in the city of Detroit two years later. And again, it was at the point of production. The Manifesto of the International Black Workers Congress was delivered at the August 21–22 meeting in Detroit in 1971. The manifesto declared, "We call upon all Third World people to devote their attention to the condition of workers in the United States and other parts of the world," representing the Third World Black internationalism of the time, rooted in the uniqueness of Detroit. The Manifesto's first objective stated, "Workers' control of their places of work—the factories, mines, fields, offices, transportation services and communication facilities—so that the exploitation of labor will cease and no person or corporation will get rich off the labor of another person, but all people will work for the collective benefit of humanity."[57] Taking over all operations of Detroit factories was more than just a minor idea. After all, Detroit was perhaps the most important city in the world when it came to producing cars. If Black workers were to take over the production, they would then also control the social and political component of a new society, one where workers would own it all. In addition, they explicitly articulated that they would eliminate racism and assert self-determination. "An elimination of all forms of racism and self-determination for African people, Chicanos, Puerto Ricans, Asians and Indians who live in the United States and Puerto Rico," read objective number two. The third objective called for the "elimination of all forms of oppression of women in all phases of society, on the job and in the home," perhaps an early iteration of intersectionality.[58] They also believed that cultural expression was essential to social transformation.

Black male Detroiters were not solely trying to take control of city governments and the means of production; they were trying to assert their humanity. It was not simply an attempt to assert some masculine, workers' rights—although that was a part of it—it was fundamentally about asserting the right to live, to be free, and to live without fear and oppression. The struggle for Black self-determination was rooted in radical love and the longing to be treated with basic decency, something that they believed would never happen in white America. Black Detroiters created their idea of belonging, through labor, and believed that they would do it by taking over the means of production. It should not be surprising, however, that they used white Americans—indeed, the veil of whiteness—to construct their belonging and perhaps ignored Indigenous peoples' claim to land and territory.

The discourse of the League of Revolutionary Black Workers was masculine and unfortunately echoed the European idea of land and ownership. Although the League showed some sense of Third World solidarity in their writing, there is no evidence that they actively sought out or worked with Native organizations. Nor is it clear that they imagined a Black and Indigenous future outside of the narrow confines of the Black male laborer. At the same time, they were advocating for radical social change; Black radicals could also contribute to the erasure of Indigenous peoples. Nevertheless, Native Americans formed their own organizations and responded to greater changes in society by asserting their right to sovereignty.

Collaboration and Tensions in Black and Red

While it might seem that Detroit's Black and Indigenous communities collaborated in their struggles for overturning dispossession, this notion is romantic at best and assumes that they were natural allies. To be sure, within national struggles, Black and Indigenous collaborations happened in moments of solidarity. Black and Indigenous peoples participated in the Poor People's Campaign, Stokely Carmichael and Angela Davis actively supported the American Indian Movement, and the Black Panther Party newspaper documented Native struggles for sovereignty.[59] It is not clear, however, if Black and Indigenous peoples' movements intersected in Detroit in systematic ways, and the archives don't reveal that either. There are at least a few reasons, including Indigenous anti-blackness and Black erasure of Indigenous struggles, that perhaps explain why there was not more collaboration in Detroit. However, operating sometimes together and sometimes separately, Black and Indigenous and other movements enacted a national, even global struggle of what historian Jeffrey O. G. Ogbar has called "radical ethnic nationalism."[60]

Collaborations and tension formed the relationship between Black and Indigenous peoples in Detroit and throughout the country. One reason tension existed was because, as the activist Vine Deloria Jr. argued, Black people were fighting for inclusion into the United States while Native people were seeking sovereignty and a respect for their treaties.[61] Little evidence exists that Black and Native peoples who lived in Detroit actually collaborated. However, there was at least one moment when their worlds collided in the effort for solidarity from Detroit outsiders, representing once more that Detroit was a place for non-Detroiters to travel to and meet.

On February 24, 1974, Angela Davis came to Detroit. Davis had been recently acquitted of conspiracy to commit murder when Jonathan Jackson, the younger brother of imprisoned revolutionary George Jackson, who was incarcerated at Soledad Prison, and an acquaintance, shot and killed a judge using guns registered in her name. Davis was joined by Clyde Bellecourt, an Anishinaabe activist and co-founder of the American Indian Movement. Hosted by the Michigan Alliance Against Racist and Political Repression under the National Alliance Against Racist and Political Repression, founded in 1973 as a response to the false imprisonment of Angela Davis, they were there to spread the word about the repression of Black and Indigenous struggles for sovereignty and freedom, and an end to free political prisoners.[62] While this was an important moment, and Black and Indigenous relationships happened in national movements, it is not clear that they happened in Detroit.

While it might appear that Black and Native people were natural allies during the period, that was not always the case. Indeed, Native people expressed real tensions with Black folks who they believed erased them. Black people, at other times, believed that they were often discriminated against. These examples of Black indigeneity in Detroit during the postwar era illustrate some of the challenges that even Black radicals encountered: How can they seek to radically transform society and not think critically about Native people? Whether seeking integration, transformation, or self-determination, African Americans' and Indigenous peoples' movements, in personal and structural ways, were often in tension.

Anti-blackness existed among the Native community. From whence it came, was difficult to tell. However, some observed that Indigenous people simply had adopted prejudice from whites or had heard about "the Blacks" before they even got to Detroit. Furthermore, with the increase in federal funds during President Lyndon Johnson's Great Society legislation in order to combat urban poverty, Detroit's Indigenous community did not want to participate in the poverty programs because Black people held the administrative positions and dominated all of the decision-making, including how money would be allocated. African Americans often ignored Native people.[63] These tensions undergirded Black and Indigenous relationships. Nevertheless, Black people did experience anti-blackness at Native events.

For instance, in a May 1977 issue of the *North American Indian Association Newsletter*, an organ of the North American Indian Association, Sandra Gregory, a Black woman, wrote to the newsletter expressing both her admiration and criticism of the NAIA. Gregory had attended the Indian Princess dance a month before. In her letter, titled "An Open Letter to the Community," Gregory remarked, "First of all, I truly love your newsletter." She continued, "If it wasn't for the newsletter I would probably be lost on information regarding the Native American community of Detroit." She also wanted to know if there were other opportunities to interact with Native people. She ended her praises with a series of questions. "I would like to know why Native Americans aren't as close to the black community as they should be? Are we economically lower than Native Americans? Are we dirt to them (Native Americans)? Remember the Europeans destroyed the equalizing basis toward Native Americans as well as Afro-Americans."[64] Gregory was upset at a particular moment where she believed she experienced invisibility at the dance. "I was appalled to find out how the Native Americans who came thought I was part of the 'brown furniture.' They actually treated me as though I was dirt." Perplexed and angered, she asked, "What have I done to your people?" Finally, she remarked, "The whites treated me with more respect than the Native Americans." Gregory's feeling of invisibility because of her blackness was not uncommon among Native people in the 1970s. Native people surely experienced discrimination in Detroit as far as resources for their community. However, anti-blackness within Native communities existed at least since the nineteenth century, during the era of enslavement.[65] Gregory further stated a common phrase that exists within Black communities: that her family has "Indian in them." She wrote, "In my family because they are originally from the South, were close to the Indians as a matter of fact, there is more Indian in our family than all of the whites claiming their so called ¼ blood that was at the April 23rd Princess Dance." Gregory ended the letter by stating that she would give the Native community one more chance and return to an event in June but hoped that they would "see me and not think I'm an alien from outer space."[66]

Gregory raised a complex question of blackness and indigeneity in a city where Native people, despite gaining more visibility, in general suffered from invisibility. She also held certain assumptions around solidarity. It is not clear that Black and Indigenous people were actively working together on issues in Detroit. She also brought up the issue of whiteness and blood quantum within Indigenous communities. While some argue that Indigenous people are not a racial group and instead nations with distinct cultures, and that is true, it does not mean that they are immune from the issues of racialization, and Gregory tried to hold them accountable. Native people did respond to Gregory's letter.

The first response was from Lincoln Sherwood. He agreed with Gregory. "As a Native American myself, I have noticed how my people are very prejudiced against blacks, even though they should be considered closer to the Indian community than whites." He continued by suggesting that Blacks and Natives should work in solidarity more than whites. "So maybe in the 29th century, maybe even in the 1970s we—Native Americans should realize what the white man has done to us, more than the blacks. We (Native Americans) have 'stereotyped' them (blacks) too much. Let's be considerate to them too, and stop looking at the blacks as though they are brown furniture."[67] Sherwood clearly appreciated Gregory's criticism of anti-blackness in Indigenous communities and wanted them to do better. Others did not agree.

Arlene Shampine, an editor for the *Native Sun Newsletter*, did acknowledge Gregory's pain. However, she only had a little sympathy. "I have had the experience of being 'furniture' also," she remarked. She told a story of a local Black minister who proclaimed to a group of students, "the black people have come a long way in the past few years, not like the American Indian, who was put on reservations and was content to allow the white government to take care of him." She ended her response by stating, "I dislike stereotyping in any form or from any group. Be it white, black, or whatever."[68] Shampine missed an important opportunity not to deflect but to directly engage in a commentary on whiteness and anti-blackness in Native communities. Native youth also had challenges growing up in Detroit.

Sandra Muse grew up on the west side of Detroit, at the intersection of Plymouth and Wyoming, in an all-Black neighborhood. She was one of thirteen children. Her mother and father traveled from Georgia to Detroit in 1949 to work in the factories. After three unsuccessful attempts to land a job, her father finally received one. He became a claims adjustor.

As a white-looking youth, Sandra struggled to fit in with her Black neighbors. She remarked, "When I was a small kid everybody around me was white, for the most part."[69] However, the neighborhood rapidly changed. By the time she attended junior high school, the neighborhood had transformed into a majority Black one. Though MacKenzie High School was the neighborhood high school, she and the other students in the neighborhood were forced to attend Cody High School on the other side of town because of busing legislation to desegregate the schools. By high school, all of her friends were Black and from the neighborhood. Initially, she endured a complicated relationship with the Black folks in her neighborhood.

Reflecting back on her youth, she remarked, "It was weird for me because, here I am, obviously not Black, but definitely not white." While her whiteness was an initial challenge, once they identified her as Indigenous, things changed. The "Black kids in my neighborhood [who] knew me, everything was cool. But if it was a kid from a few blocks away, who didn't know me," she said, "then I could have trouble."[70] However, Black people protected her and her sister from other Black folks, telling them that she was not white. Still, she and her sister would get teased by others who might call them "Pocahontas" in jest. While she felt both protected and invisible, mixed-race Black and Indigenous people did have trouble fitting into a Black and white world.

As mentioned earlier, anti-blackness existed among Detroit's Indigenous community. Some remarked that so-called full bloods would call them "La-hun-jee," which is a derogatory word for Black people. Black people would call the women "Pocahontas" and the men "chiefs." However, Tracy Mays, an Afro-Indigenous person herself, did not take too much offense, stating, "I think it was more ignorance, I don't think it was hatred."[71] A part of the reason they were ignorant was because of the lack of exposure in the Detroit Public Schools. And while they contributed to the erasure of Indigenous identities rooted in stereotypes, Mays understood that in post-Rebellion Detroit, "They were struggling with their own rights."[72] Mays's softening of Indigenous erasure might seem problematic, but she was uniquely positioned to both criticize and understand: She not only grew up around Black people, she was Black and lived with Black people. She understood them and resisted the anti-blackness that might have emerged otherwise.

* * *

What can we take from these brief examples? First, within the context of dispossession, solidarity between oppressed groups is not natural. It takes work. Second, Black and Indigenous peoples responded to their dispossession in different ways that often limited how they viewed their oppression; they often viewed their struggles separately. In addition, with the election of Coleman A. Young as the first African American mayor in Detroit's history in 1974, African Americans controlled politics in Detroit. Though white people left Detroit in large numbers, African Americans did not make room for Native people, thus perpetuating Indigenous invisibility.

CHAPTER 6

Dispossession and the Roots of Culturally Relevant Education

African American and Indigenous peoples created formal and informal independent educational institutions as a response to racism and dispossession. Since the formation of the Nation of Islam schools in the early twentieth century until the creation of Indigenous educational institutions in the 1970s, Black and Native people tried to counter the racist and hegemonic nature of schooling. From the formation of the Nation of Islam schools in the 1930s until right after the Detroit Rebellion in 1967, Black Nationalists were concerned with the creation of education that represented their goals of self-determination, Black representation, and a rejection of white supremacy in the teaching of their children.[1]

Three years before the Detroit Rebellion, the most costly and destructive of the several rebellions that swept across urban America, Hannah Aikens, a Delaware Indian and longtime activist in the city, wrote to Lewis Beeson, secretary of the Michigan Commission of Indian Affairs, citing the importance of language revitalization for Detroit's Native community. Formed in 1952, the Michigan Commission of Indian Affairs served as a do-it-all organization of generally educated Native people in Michigan, who worked with local and state governments on a variety of issues that impacted Michigan's Native communities. Aikens wrote Beeson in response to his request that she speak to an upcoming meeting on "urban Indians," which she had been doing since the 1950s. In the letter, Aikens expressed her regret that she would be unable to make it to L'Anse, Michigan, for a meeting later that month. She had just experienced a terrible car accident in which a young family member had been injured. In addition, she did not have the funds to make the long drive from Detroit to the Upper Peninsula.

Although unable to attend the meeting, she made recommendations for what the group might discuss. For example, she hoped that they would discuss the "preservation of Indian culture," specifically Native languages. Aikens was a fluent speaker of the Delaware language and expressed that being able to speak her language helped her identity as an urban Indigenous person. She suggested that there should be classes taught on the "Chippewa language." She wanted to learn Anishinaabemowin (Chippewa or Ojibwa language) in order to communicate with Anishinaabeg in Detroit. More than that, she wanted Detroit's Indigenous children to learn the language. She advocated for Indigenous peoples' right to their own language, especially given the nature of boarding schools as sites of genocidal practices,[2] which stripped a whole generation of its language of which culture is a central part. "In the past, the use of Indian language was forbidden and students were punished severely if they were caught using it," wrote Aikens. She continued, "I know this condition existed at Mt. Pleasant Indian Boarding School as other such schools throughout the nation."[3]

Both Black and Indigenous peoples challenged dispossession through their focus on education. They understood that building African-centered and Indigenous-centric education would not only help students reject white supremacist education but also help them build their self-esteem. As a result, they would become educated to lead the next generation in what amounted to a form of nation-building, or self-determination.

* * *

Hannah Aikens understood history. She knew, like many women in postwar Detroit, that the connection between culture, language, and sovereignty was profound. In the midst of great social change sweeping across the United States during the mid-1960s, it is not surprising that Detroit's Indigenous population began to assert its right to sovereignty in the postwar period. As historian Dan Cobb argues, Indigenous people transformed the discourse and politics of civil rights into "the language of tribal sovereignty."[4] The role of urban Indigenous women in the assertion of sovereignty in postwar Detroit was crucial for the entire community.

Education was a cornerstone of Indigenous Red Power in the late 1960s, and federal legislation helped. On January 30, 1969, Senator Edward Kennedy, following in the footsteps of his brother, former U.S. attorney general and U.S. senator Robert Kennedy, who was assassinated in 1968, wrote a memorandum to the subcommittee on Indian education, asking for an extension to continue studying the state of Native American children's education. "To a substantial extent, the quality and effectiveness of Indian education is a test of this government's understanding and commitment," he wrote. After nearly two years of investigation on reservation, rural, and urban Indigenous education, Kennedy et al. published *Indian Education: A National Tragedy—A National Challenge* (1969). Among the many findings of the report, one in particular stood out: "Public schools educating Indians rarely include coursework which recognized Indian history, culture or language, and often uses materials and approaches which are derogatory toward Indians." The report concluded, "The primary result of the manner Indians are treated in the history textbooks in use today is a propagation of inaccurate stereotypes."[5] The statistics bore these conclusions out.

On March 5, 1970, the *Detroit News* published an article titled "The Abandonment of the Indian in Detroit's Red Ghetto." In that article, Tom Pawlick wrote the tragic story of the Indigenous Detroit children's educational experience in the Detroit Public Schools. For the story, he interviewed kindergarten teacher, Mrs. Yvonne Walker, and she expressed various sad accounts of the Native children who entered her classroom. "We had an Indian family here a while ago with five children," she said. "The older ones were always getting into fights. People would make remarks, or call them "squaws," she remarked. She continued expressing the deep sorrow that these young children experienced, including the loss of their father to tuberculosis and the mother to cancer. A grandmother took them in; after the grandmother was diagnosed with tuberculosis, the grandchildren were sent to various foster homes.[6]

Mrs. Walker believed that the Native students were "beautiful kids," but they had "a lot of problems." She stated, "One little girl, five years old, has been in the youth home twice. Her parents abandoned her." This story reveals little about the background of these children, except from a deficit perspective, painting them as a problem. Mrs. Walker continued describing the children as students who do "neat work" and who are "very exact" and "eager to learn." However, they are "shy and withdrawn." And, finally, she described one boy who "speaks if you speak first" and replies in a "whisper" and another child who "just sits and cries all morning. He has problems at home, but won't talk about it."[7]

Mrs. Walker seemed like a caring teacher, one deeply invested in bettering the lives of children through education. However, her thoughts on Native children were rooted in centuries-old Native stereotypes. They were silent, stoic, and proud. The painting of these children all appears to reflect poorly on Native people in general, not on the educational system that they were forced into. Indeed, according to a Michigan Commission on Indian Affairs report on Indigenous education in Michigan, high school dropout rates and poor academic achievement could be attributed to numerous factors, including low educational achievement among adults, poverty, inadequate housing, and health problems.[8] In Detroit in particular, Native student achievement and dropout rates could be attributed to a number of factors, including being teased for their Indigenous heritage and the fact that the school curriculum did not reflect their own experiences as urban Native people.[9] Reflecting the political impact of Black Power, Detroit's educational system had begun to change drastically. At a community meeting in 1971, a person observed, "Black Studies programs are being implemented in many schools in Detroit and Indian children are going to be exposed to those. Why can't Indian Studies programs be offered to blacks?"[10]

The Indigenous population in the postwar period erupted, growing from 730 in 1950 to nearly 3,000 by 1970, though a report by the Michigan Commission on Indian Affairs stated that the population was over 6,000. The majority of Native people lived in the Cass Corridor area, on Third Street, near Wayne State University. This was an area of high poverty. It was also the first place where most of Detroit's Native people moved when they arrived in the city. Although they were only 5 percent of the population, they were scattered throughout the city.[11] Most lived in dilapidated housing; many held irregular jobs. Rosemary, an Oneida, who had come from London, Ontario, with her husband, described the condition of Indigenous people in the neighborhood. "I don't trust my kids around this neighborhood," she said, "even in the daytime, it's not safe. I've had my purse snatched and my sister was robbed twice." "My kids have been beaten up on the way to school."[12] She had a right to be fearful. Cass Corridor had the second-highest homicide rate in the city. Russ Wright, a Cherokee employed by the Department of Social Services, similarly explained the harsh reality of Indigenous people, "They come looking for jobs, and sometimes to escape discrimination [in Canada]. But when they get here, all too frequently they end up on Third Street, in the ghetto."[13] In spite of the hardships, Indigenous people pressed on and found power through education.

A 1971 survey conducted in 383 Indigenous households found that, among the children who dropped out of high school, over half had not reached the ninth grade. The report attributed the high dropout rate and general lack of achievement to a combination of factors, including low educational achievement among young adults, poverty, inadequate housing, and health problems.[14] Beyond the statistics, there were social reasons why Indigenous students did not see themselves reflected in the curriculum and believed the curriculum was whitewashed. Furthermore, students felt isolated from their peers because of their Indigenous heritage and some parents believed that school counselors deliberately pushed their children into vocational programs without regard for each student's intellectual interests or curiosities. An Indigenous student who went to high school in Detroit reflected on her experience. Her guidance counselor told her that of the three educational tracks, which included business, general education, and college prep, she should take business courses because it was unlikely that she, as a Native student, would thrive in the college prep track. She was forced to take courses in business.[15]

These narratives further dispossessed Native students from learning in these environments. Nevertheless, Indigenous people found hope. They were inspired by the larger movement for Red Power and the passing of federal legislation such as the Indian Education Act (1972) and the Self-Determination Act of 1975. By the late 1970s, Michigan received a $2.5 million grant from the federal government to educate the state's Indigenous children. Detroit, with nearly 900 Indigenous students enrolled in the district, received the most money in the state, at $117,256.[16] Indigenous women were key in maintaining Indigenous cultures in Detroit, especially during the Red Power movement. This should not be surprising. After all, LaNada Means, a citizen of the Bannock Nation and a founding leader of the occupation of Alcatraz, was in the initial landing party during the occupation of Alcatraz Island, and stayed from beginning to end.[17] They were not interested, however, in maintaining a narrow version of what it meant to be Indigenous. Indeed, these women were motivated by the possibilities of what an Indigenous identity in an urban area could do for Native people, especially for the next generation of Native children. In many ways, fighting for cultural and educational self-determination was the driving force behind Indigenous activism in postwar Detroit.

The idea for an Indigenous school had circulated among Detroit's Indigenous community since 1972, when the North American Indian Association put out a poll to its readership in order to see who might be interested.[18] In 1973, the Detroit school board applied for federal funds under Title 4, which was the 1972 Indian Elementary and Secondary School Assistance Act. Education was sorely needed. Although there are plenty of statistics, Native youth could articulate the challenges they faced in American society. A poem published in the local Indigenous newsletter by an Apache teenager, Debra Jacquez, illustrates the challenges Indigenous youth faced growing up in a Black and white Detroit:

> I am accepted into no-one's society.
> Or either everyone's society.
> To some whites and some blacks,
> I'm either white or a wild savage Indian.
> I want to escape the poverty and disease on a reservation,
> But I don't want to live by the white man's rules.
> I am from a proud people.
> I wish to have knowledge and values accepted as good as the next
> man's.
> I am not white nor am I black, I am an Indian and proud.[19]

This poem reveals the limits of racial literacy in Detroit among the Black and white populations. And Indigenous youth struggled, being stuck in this binary. Therefore, a school that would help them build their cultural knowledge and become educated within their Indigenous heritage, especially during the era of Red Power, was timely and crucial. While there were Native people who worked in the factories, the major source of cultural and educational labor was done by Indigenous women.

The formation of the Detroit Indian Educational and Cultural Center (DIECC) was a significant moment for the Indigenous community for two reasons. First, it asserted their belonging in the city of Detroit and made them a bit more visible to non-Indigenous people. Second, it gave formal recognition to the idea that, in order to build a generation of youth who would live primarily in urban contexts, Indigenous education had to be based on their particular circumstances: urban and a variety of ways of being Indigenous.

The DIECC officially opened in 1974. Its educational purpose had three components. First, the staff wanted to reduce the dropout rate among high school students. Second, they wanted a school environment that could teach both Indigenous and non-Indigenous youth about Indigenous peoples' contribution to Detroit and U.S. history. Finally, they wanted the school to help build the self-esteem of Indigenous youth so that they might carry on Indigenous ways of living in the city going forward. As the brief program description stated: "It is hoped through the knowledge and respect for Native American cultural values and traditions the Native American student will be more effective in his ability to understand himself and better equipped to cope in a public school system that has not geared itself to meet his individual needs."[20]

It also served as a broad cultural, social, and educational center for the community. The first location of the DIECC was at the American Indian Health Service (IHS), which was at Third and Baltimore. Monday through Friday the place was used to help people with their alcohol and drug addictions; on Saturday, the DIECC held school from 9:00 A.M. until 12:00 P.M. In addition to the formal learning and tutoring that students received, the staff also provided emergency services, including optical and dental care, as well as counseling.

The DIECC was a community effort. It was a circle of parents, staff, and children who contributed to its function. Primarily community-member parents, mostly as volunteers, led the staff. Parental involvement was crucial. The staff encouraged parental involvement by institutionalizing it within the educational structure. The vision of this educational model would be to have elders and parents actively participate in the growth and education of their community's children, just like their ancestors had done before them. Therefore, they created the Detroit Indian Parent Advisory Council and the Detroit American Indian Parent Council. Chaired by Esther Mays and Walter Albert, each of these committees guided all decisions. Elders were encouraged to be involved, and they served as counselors to the young people, teaching them about Indigenous histories and cultures and providing general counsel about life.

The educational coordinator was my aunt Judy Mays. Aunt Judy was well qualified. She graduated with a Bachelor of Arts degree in elementary education from Michigan State University.[21] I asked Aunt Judy why she got involved in Indigenous education; she said that it was her mother's influence. She told me that her "mother was involved" and she "knew it meant a lot to her." While she did not plan to do so, she earned her degree in education and so, in many ways, it made sense. She did mention that, though she was concerned with anti-Black prejudice that existed among the Indigenous community, they still trusted her with doing the work that needed to be done.[22] Aunt Judy also saw her mother keep many children in her household so that they would continue living in an Indigenous house. Having learned from her mother the importance of education and sustaining community, Aunt Judy brought this same Indigenous feminist intellectual practice to the educating of Indigenous peoples.

Students listened to pow-wow music, they beaded and did other arts and crafts, and they learned how to make drums. In addition to the craftwork, they also learned about North American Indigenous histories, as well as Detroit's Indigenous history. They had the opportunity to learn Anishinaabemowin. Beyond the nuts and bolts of a culturally relevant and sustaining curriculum, it was important for parents and children to have that space.

The community was ecstatic. "Detroit's Native American children have a place to go now to be together and to learn singing, beadwork, legends, history and all the things it takes to keep Indian heritage alive in the young." There are two significant points about the DIECC. First, it was designed to meet the diverse needs of Indigenous youth in the city of Detroit. With a population made up of a variety of Indigenous ancestries, both mixed-race and multi-tribal, the school needed not only to acknowledge that it was on Anishinaabe territory but also to educate a diverse, urban Indigenous population in a predominantly Black city. Within three years, and picking students up from throughout the city, the DIECC served about one hundred students every Saturday.[23]

Judy Mays wrote a letter to the *Native Sun Newsletter*, encouraging more parents to become involved in the workings of the school. "We now have our school," wrote Mays. In the rhetoric of Red Power, she asked, "Can we let someone else do our work?" Mays understood that in order for the school to work optimally, Indigenous people must be involved; she argued that "Indian parent interest and participation is the only way our school program can proceed as originally planned, for it is you who carry the Indian culture and traditions of your tribe in your hearts."[24] Mays's point about parents holding the traditions within themselves is important, for it reveals that she understood that Indigenous cultures and ways of knowing were not rooted in uncritical musings about how Indigenous people are supposed to live; instead, even in the city of Detroit, those cultures lived and thrived because Indigenous people did. The DIECC did not eliminate anti-Indigenous racism. For instance, during the winter of 1976, Esther Mays and other community leaders went to the Burton Elementary School in order to compel the school to remove the word "squaw" from a songbook, "Music for Young Americans," that was used by third-graders. After the protest, the Wayne County Schools removed it.[25]

By 1980, the program had made significant strides and, by then, had moved downtown to the Adlai Stevenson Building. The school continued to offer Saturday classes, including academic tutoring for some 125 students at Burton Elementary School. It also offered medical and dental care, along with free public transportation. Reporting on the benefits of the school, Judy Mays remarked, "Indian children in public school often are made to feel embarrassed about their heritage." She continued: "Some of my (Saturday) students say history textbooks still show Indians as savages, and that when they go down the hall (in school) non-Indian kids make war whoop noises." In this context, the DIECC was important for building the self-pride of students. "We are trying to instill in them a self-concept and some pride," said Mays, "but the principle goal of the program is to keep Indian kids in school."[26]

The impact on students was significant. Reflecting back on her time at the DIECC, one former student remarked, "It was the first time in our lives that we were able to get together with other Indian kids and learn stuff." [27] Even more, the importance of the DIECC was an exceptional institution because "we learned how to be proud of being Indian—as kids." Of the many things the DIECC staff tried to instill in their students was a respect for nature, a remarkable if not impossible task for urban Indigenous youth. Living in the city, the students saw concrete, abandoned buildings, and urban blight. To show them something different, the staff took the students to Camp Wathana in Holly, Michigan.

Fifty students traveled to Camp Wathana in the summer of 1976. They caught frogs and toads, picked up sticks and leaves for making fires. They went canoeing, rode horses, did archery, and also did beadwork. All did not go as planned, however. They also shared space with the Camp Fire Girls, to whom Charles Eastman spoke at the same camp in 1932.[28] The young white girls who participated in the camp questioned the legitimate identity of these urban Indigenous youth because they did not fit into their fantasies about what Indigenous people were supposed to look like and how they were supposed to act. Following the trip, the newsletter reported, "We had to change the image of the Indian people in many of the girls' minds and straighten out several misconceptions."[29]

The DIECC was also important for cultivating Indigenous identity through cultural teachings and education. It is difficult to measure the social scientific impact of the DIECC. To sum up the success of one year, Judy Mays thanked everyone, from parent volunteers to teachers to student staff for their efforts in working with Indigenous youth. "I also wish to thank the parents and the Indian community for all the support that was received this year to enhance the Program and the education of Native American children in the City of Detroit. . . . Megwech." She continued to implore parents to stay involved, "Get involved we need you! We need each other, the lives of our children are at stake, we must begin to fight for our leaders and educators of the future."[30] However, its meaning as a symbol of Indigenous resistance and resilience should also be celebrated, for to develop an Indigenous educational space with a variety of Indigenous peoples and in a majority Black city was the epitome of Red Power in the postwar era.

Afrocentric Education in Detroit

The Detroit Public Schools have been a central part of the city's cultural and intellectual history.[31] To write about the emergence of an Indigenous school in Detroit, it is imperative to briefly introduce the African-centered educational movement in the city. Indeed, the creation of Medicine Bear American Indian Academy would not have happened without Black American allies and the push for education relevant to the lives and experiences of Black children.

African-centered education, also called Afrocentric education, has long roots going back to the work of scholars Carter G. Woodson, known as the "Father of Black history"; Anna Julia Cooper, often cited as one of the earliest articulators of Black feminism; and W. E. B. Du Bois. The theory of Afrocentric education "approaches knowledge from the perspective of Africa as the origin of human civilization and the descendants of Africans as subjects, rather than objects of history and scientific observation." Furthermore, while the curriculum is centered on the experiences of African-descended peoples, "the pedagogy is multicultural and includes study of all groups in the historical and cultural presence of the United States and the world."[32]

The African-centered education movement began in the early 1960s, although with much earlier roots. The community control of schools was led by Reverend Albert Cleage, activist and leader of the Shrine of the Black Madonna; Chinese American activist Grace Lee Boggs; and Milton and Richard Henry. Together, they formed GOAL in 1962. An ideologically Black Nationalist group, the members conducted some of the first formal protests against the unequal education and vitriolic racism committed against Black children. According to Grace Lee Boggs, the Detroit school system was designed to keep Black children off the streets. They did not receive adequate education, nor did any of the teachers, white or Black, express adequate care for Black students.[33] Thus, members of the Black community began to advocate for Community Control of Schools. They wanted the Black community to have control over the education of their children.[34] By 1967, just four months after the Detroit Rebellion, Reverend Cleage wrote an opinion piece for the *Michigan Chronicle*, Detroit's premiere Black-owned newspaper.

On November 4, 1967, Cleage described the conditions in which Black children existed in Detroit Public Schools and the urgent necessity of Black Nationalism to thwart educational dispossession. He described the "outsiders" to the Black Detroit community as those who drove on the expressway to the inner city but then left to their "'safe' lily-white neighborhoods." He argued that most of the teachers think "of our children as little savages." Using the power of Black discourse, he further contended that "the only kind of black people they feel comfortable around are those who think that everything white is right and everything black should get back." Cleage relied on Black Nationalism to urge parents and community members to understand the importance of children for the development of a nation. "Our children must understand that they are part of a Black Nation," he argued, "which is engaged in a revolution to throw off the shackles of bondage and become a free people." Cleage understood that children were not only objects but also were important subjects for the current and future of the Black revolution. Cleage urged parents to understand that children "are an important part of this Black Revolution and that their ability to learn is therefore important not only to themselves but to their people."[35] If Black children were going to learn, it must be in the spirit of revolution and nation-building.

Cleage also set up the City-Wide Citizens Action Committee (CCAC). The CCAC was a coalition of different organizations across political ideologies. It immediately organized two conferences that focused on Community Control of Schools.[36] The control of Black schools was a national movement.

Educators from around the country participated in national conferences to challenge the treatment of Black youth in schools. On June 8, 1968, administrators, teachers, parents, students, and community activists from all over the country formed the National Association of Afro-American Educators. They viewed education as a "nation-building tool" and as a holistic process that included "anti-colonialism, de-niggerfication, de-programming, self-assertation, self-definition, self-development and survival."[37] In this way, their program sought a complete dismantling of the processes of educational dispossession.

Black advocates for the community control of schools movement worked. In 1972, educators founded the Alexander Crummell School, which became the Aisha Shule Affirmative School for Gifted Children, the first independent

Afrocentric school. And, by 1989, educational activists founded the Nsoroma Institute, the second Afrocentric school.[38] In spite of the efforts of Black Nationalist educators and the formation of independent schools, they could not have anticipated the devastation that would come with the conservative backlash and the election of Ronald Reagan to the White House.

If the 1960s and the early part of the 1970s represented the pinnacle of Black Nationalist activism, the 1980s represented a nadir of sorts for Black people in Detroit. Youth suffered rampant unemployment during the Reagan-era "crack epidemic" and poverty. And murder might have been the worst of the statistics. Black Nationalists could not have predicted the coming wave of poverty and decimation to their communities and schools.

From the late 1970s until the 1990s (and beyond) is what scholars call the era of neoliberalism. At its core, neoliberalism is about the individual's ability to radically transform their own lives, especially through the market, with little government intervention.[39] Neoliberalism is the core tenet that shaped President Ronald Reagan's policies that continued the assault on urban centers across America.[40] Detroit was no exception. The Motor City in the 1980s is remembered for the drugs and violence that impacted the city. A product of Reaganomics, the shift from the war on poverty to a war on the poor and an increase in the criminalization of Black people meant that young people had little chance.[41] Detroit during this time was also known for notorious drug dealers and youth gangs such as YBI (Young Boys Incorporated), the Chambers Brothers, the Curry Brothers, Richard "Maserati Rick" Carter and Demetrius Holloway, and murder-for-hire assassins like the Best Friends. They are now a part of urban lore. The influx of drugs also led to Detroit's having among the highest murder rates in the country in the 1980s. From 1984 through 1985, the murder rate in Detroit was 58 percent, trailing only that in Washington, D.C. (60 percent) and just above that in New Orleans (55 percent). In raw numbers, Detroit had 663 homicides in 1985; in 1994, it decreased to 575. From 1985 to 1994, the homicide rate for Black males ages 18–24 increased while the city's average decreased.[42] In 1985 in Detroit and in other major cities across the country, murder was the leading cause of death among young Black men ages 15 to 34.[43] Thus, during the 1980s young Black men were labeled an "endangered species" as a metaphor to describe the crisis facing them, and there were calls for action.

Many believed education was the way forward. But the education of Black and Indigenous youth was also an example of dispossession. During the neoliberal era, according to anthropologists Michelle Fine and Jessica Ruglis, educational policies implemented by liberal and conservative governments "slowly dispossess[ed] poor students of color from quality education."[44] Furthermore, "dispossession motivated state policy . . . around the contours of race, ethnicity, and class; ironically, in the name of public safety, educational accountability, and personal responsibility."[45] Their chances at success, coupled with the poverty in Detroit, left them with little hope.

The Black community did not sit idly by waiting for the state to continue the dispossession of young Black men. With a coalition of Black mothers from the community and educators from throughout the city, an ad hoc group was formed. The group was led by Joseph Gilbert, who was principal of Detroit's Mackenzie High School, and included Calvin McKinney, principal of Detroit's Brooks Middle School; Geneva Smitherman, of Michigan State University; and Clifford Watson, principal of Detroit's Woodward Elementary School.

They held a conference titled "Improving Self-Concept for At-Risk Black Students, with Emphasis on Saving the Black Male." Nearly 500 people from across the Detroit community attended it. Following the event, an eleven-person committee created a "Male Academy Task Force," which would study the problems facing Black men in Detroit. This resulted in a report on the state of Black males in Detroit.[46] After submitting the report to the Detroit Public Schools Board of Education in November 1990, the board approved a school for Black male youth in the late Spring of 1991. Just a few months prior, in March 1991, the board had elected Dr. Deborah McGriff as the first Black female superintendent of the school district. One of Dr. McGriff's major accomplishments was to empower local schools, thus decentralizing the district from the school board. The initiative was called the "Design for Excellence." It allowed for schools to have more authority over their curriculum and other components of schooling.[47]

In September 1991, the Malcolm X Academy opened on the first floor of Woodward Elementary School with Dr. Clifford Watson serving as the first principal. There was a struggle before the doors opened. The National Organization for Women sued the academy on the basis that the all-Black boys' academy was created to the detriment of Black girls. According to legal scholar Menah Pratt-Clarke, a patriarchal Black Nationalism undergirded the support of the school. According to Pratt-Clarke, those who supported the academy did so under the banner of Black Nationalism for three reasons: "Self-definition to define the needs of the Black race as synonymous with those of Black males, self-determination to determine and decide appropriate laws and policies, and self-reliance depend on the race to implement the policies and procedures."[48] Nevertheless, the school opened, even in the midst of vitriolic racism. Helicopters swirled above the school on opening day in Warrendale, a suburb of Detroit. Dogs were there to sniff for bombs. Both uniformed and plainclothes police were there to make sure students were safe. Someone claimed it reminded them of Little Rock or Boston, when Black people first integrated the school. While Black parents were happy that the first day went without incident, Jeff Testa, a cofounder of People for Equal and Community Education, a group that was adamantly opposed to the Afrocentric academy, expressed his displeasure. "We are opposed to African-centered schools and empowerment all around," he said, "they put the African American into science and history . . . it's all lies."[49]

Testa's words should not be surprising in 1992. They represent an atmosphere of whiteness that did not value Black lives and they demonstrate that some white people would rather forces continue to dispossess Black youth. Other white people agreed with Testa. "The papers talk about how the white people are prejudiced," stated Rosemarie Rembisz, a resident of Detroit, "with its African-centered classes. Once kids are bused, the neighborhood deteriorates." Timothy Slater, a resident of Royal Oak was concerned with the name of Malcolm X. "It appalls me that people would think of naming a school after Malcolm X." In the midst of Spike Lee's film *X*, Slater continued, "It disgusts me to see people, young and old, wearing 'X' hats and shirts. . . . All this for a man who advocated violence and revolution for racial equality." Finally, he declared what many liberal whites do: "If minorities want equal rights and want a figurehead to look for inspiration, why not Dr. Martin Luther King Jr."[50] The main point here is that a large majority of white people from Detroit to its suburbs carried with them ideas of Black inferiority and white superiority from the 1960s and 1970s. The integration, celebration, and foregrounding of Blackness was not tolerable.

The struggle and triumph of Afrocentric education in Detroit is important for a few reasons. First, it was the realization of Black Americans, especially Black women, who wanted a transformative educational experience for Black men, who they believed were suffering the most. Second, it set the stage for Indigenous people to also call on the school board to make education relevant to Indigenous students. It was the perfect opportunity to make Indigenous education a reality. Just like the Black Freedom struggle in the 1960s and 1970s, Indigenous people were able to use a foundation set by Black Americans and remix it, making it their own, for the unique challenges facing Indigenous students. If the Black Nationalist community desired that their children be free from the shackles of white racism, Native people desired that their children be free from the manacles of colonialism.

Indigenous Youth Dispossessed

The context in which Indigenous education formed in Detroit is similar to that of Black youth. A report titled "Empowering Native People, Native American Task Force" offered a sobering reality of the myriad issues facing Native youth. In the 1980s, 49 percent of Native families lived below the poverty line and suffered an unemployment rate averaging 54 percent. By 1990, 64 percent of Detroit's Native children lived in poverty, higher than the 36 percent for white children and 49 percent for Black children. The report described Native communities as resilient but also located the current condition of Native people as a continuation of history. The report also noted a fundamental difference between Native people and others in the United States: the treaty relationship that tribal nations have with the U.S. government. Wayne County consisted of almost 11 percent of the Michigan Indigenous population as a whole. However, because urban Natives did not live on the reservation, they needed local and statewide support. And because they lived in urban areas, "although they form a majority of the Indian population in Michigan, they are very much an invisible and forgotten majority, lost in a vastly larger non-Indian majority."[51]

The educational statistics were just as grim. The Native high school graduation rate was 59.9 percent compared to the statewide rate of 79.6 percent. For those attending college, the graduation rate for Native Americans was 6.2 percent compared to the statewide rate of 14.2 percent. These numbers were crucial because those under 18 years old made up 50 percent of the Native American population in the United States. And they had the highest birth rate of any group in the country. The Native community feared that if something was not done by the "year 2000, devastating consequences for our society will result as the emergence of a dual society with a large and poorly educated underclass (mostly minorities), reduced economic competitiveness of the nation, and higher costs of public services as a result of impoverishment and crime." Still, at the heart of their belief was the necessity to educate Indigenous youth in "traditional" ways within an urban context.

In the fall of 1993, Detroit's Indigenous community presented to the Detroit school board a proposal for a school with an Indigenous curriculum. They hoped that something could be done to educate at least some of the 1,028 Native youth who attended Detroit Public Schools. One of the most important advocates for the school was Kwame Kenyatta. Kenyatta had been on the school board as vice president from November 1992 until October 1997. He would go on to be elected to the Detroit City Council in November 2005, serving there until he resigned in protest at the appointment of an Emergency Financial Manager. He then moved to Mississippi to work with Mayor Chokwe Lumumba, formerly of Detroit, as a compliance officer, ensuring that businesses, government, and nonprofit agencies did not discriminate based on race or gender.[52]

In the early part of 1993, Governor John Engler was trying to get Michigan voters to agree on a ballot that would allow for children to attend independent charter schools. Among voters statewide, 49 percent disapproved. In Wayne County, 51 percent disapproved of the charter schools. At the same time, the Detroit school board debated implementing a public school for Native American students.[53]

Kenyatta said that he would propose to the school board a Native American academy that would benefit Indigenous and non-Indigenous youth who were interested in Indigenous histories and cultures. "The district has the goal of educating all children," Kenyatta said. He reasoned, "You can't educate all children if one group feels left out, if you only call them on one day to dress up." Kenyatta did not stop there. In fact, he articulated the common belief among Indigenous communities throughout the United States: "Thanksgiving represents a day of betrayal and extermination of Native American people." He also noted that this was an opportune time to actualize the Indigenous academy. Kenyatta further stated, "The academy, if approved by the school board, would be similar to existing African-centered academies. It probably would start with primary grades and gradually add grades through high school. Federal money would be sought to pay for setting up the school in a location that hasn't been determined."[54] In some ways, it is not surprising that Kenyatta supported the school; his son attended the Malcolm X Academy. He understood the importance of culturally relevant education and group self-determination.[55] Kenyatta showing solidarity is important for many reasons, perhaps most of all because it was one of the first times in the modern history of Detroit when Black folks not only acknowledged the presence of Indigenous people but also made room for them politically, culturally, and, in this instance, educationally. Reflecting back on her conversations with Kenyatta, Judy Mays recalled, "He liked the idea of having a Native American school in Detroit. And he fought hard for us to be able to get it. So, I credit him as being the one that got Medicine Bear opened as a Detroit public school."

Judy Mays, who by that time had served as the director of the Detroit Indian Educational and Cultural Center for almost two decades, was ecstatic about the move. "There are about 250 Detroit public schools, and not one of them is even named after an American Indian and they're all on Indian land." She assured the public that the curriculum would be multi-tribal, meeting the great diversity that were Indigenous students in Detroit; it would teach Indigenous languages; and it would dispel theories about Christopher Columbus discovering America.[56] The summer before the school opened, Native parents expressed their excitement about it and about what it could mean for the future of Native youth in the nation's Blackest city.

The opening of Medicine Bear Academy was a continuation of the project of Indigenous modernity in the postwar era, a response to educational dispossession and invisibility, and a push for cultural and educational sovereignty. It was a way to define what education might look like for Native people going into the new millennium.

An Ojibwe parent, Thurman Bear, did not accept that Native people and cities were incompatible. He did not believe being in a city culturally deprived him or his children. He was excited about the potential of the school. In an article in the *Detroit Free Press*, Bear argued that the American Indian Academy was "probably going to be a factor in the survival of us as Native American people." Bear also recognized that the school would need to meet the needs of a diverse group of students, with a variety of exposure to their Indigenous cultures. Speaking of his own children, he admitted, "They like *Beavis and Butt-Head*. The children like rap music. We have a Nintendo. We have a VCR. We are 1993 people." Bear's recognition was an admission that in order to teach Detroit's Indigenous youth, they also had to acknowledge that they lived in the present, and weren't tied to some myopic, outdated idea of being Indigenous. He concluded, "I am very pleased that a Native American academy has been proposed," but he insisted that "it's probably something that should have been done 20 or 25 years ago."[57] The academy would also benefit non-Indigenous youth by dispelling stereotypes.

Diane Pierzynowski, a Chippewa, said that her children experienced discrimination in school. Her daughter, Sheila, was asked why she didn't wear "the outfit" or why her family didn't live in a teepee and why they didn't wear moccasins. The academy would, they hoped, dispel some of those stereotypes and simultaneously build the self-esteem of the Indigenous students. On November 23, 1993, the Detroit school board voted to approve the school. And, on June 28, 1994, the board would vote to approve the lease of the school at Historic Fort Wayne, at Livernois Avenue and Fort Street, which was also close to a sacred burial ground.[58] Indeed, this proved ironic.

Historic Fort Wayne, originally built in 1840, is one of the most important historical venues in Detroit that symbolizes U.S. war and dispossession. It also symbolizes the close geographic proximity of the United States to Canada and the history of the British Empire in Detroit. The fort was named after General Mad Anthony Wayne, who defeated the British at the Battle of Fallen Timbers in 1794, which helped the United States gain control of Detroit. The fort was designed to fire cannons capable of hitting sailing vessels and the Canadian shore. Importantly, the fort was designed to ward off not only the British but also their Indigenous allies who never wanted to leave the area in the first place. The fort would become a key place for troops being trained to enter nearly every U.S. conflict, from the Civil War to Vietnam. During these conflicts, the fort held prisoners of war from Italy as well as families having to stay there after the 1967 rebellions.[59]

The Detroit Historical Society, based on the collection of Clarence Burton, owned Historic Fort Wayne. Between 1944 and 1945, archeologist Carl Holmquist of the Michigan Aboriginal Research Club excavated some Indian mounds at Fort Wayne. He recovered twenty-three burial and grave goods that were later donated to the University of Michigan Museum of Anthropology. He left a few mounds untouched. Finally, in 1979, the Detroit Historical Museum opened the Woodland Indian Museum near the burial ground. However, due to lack of funds, the museum was closed in 1991. Ironically, the Detroit Historical Society would not let the people of Medicine Bear use the library. Here, we see the contradictions between how settlers view Indigenous histories and actual Indigenous people. The fort also housed the Tuskegee Airmen Museum. The place was important to Detroit and to Michigan's tribal nations. And the Medicine Bear team was happy to have at least a portion of the eighty-three-acre fort for their use.

The school would begin with grades kindergarten through third grade (a similar tactic used during the opening of the Malcolm X Academy) with plans

Figure 3. Linda Lindsay, left, and Judy Mays, right, August 1994 in front of Historic Fort Wayne, at the opening of Medicine Bear American Indian Academy. Drawing by Liseth Amaya.

to expand to a kindergarten through twelfth-grade model. Although open to all students, 55 percent of all slots were designated for students with Indigenous ancestry and those who lived within a one-mile radius of the school.[60]

Leading up to its opening, the school still had no name. One day, Judy, while planning out the upcoming year with other folks, including Edith Young (Tlingit) and Judy's sister, Linda Lindsay, the group was in search of a name. They threw out some ideas, but they did not stick. Finally, after contemplating for some time, the name "bear" came to mind. Then, it just came to her: Medicine Bear. Judy recalled, "Then, sitting there, I said, 'Medicine Bear.' From the educational experiences that Natives had from the past, I wanted to change that perspective around. And in order to do that we needed healing. And that's why the name Medicine Bear, and for the bear, bear clan [which is the clan she belongs to]. But it was a weird spiritual thing from where the name came from. You know how they say everything goes in a circle, and we were all in a circle and then that name came; it was just like magic."[61] The name of the school was just as important as the curriculum. As Mays recalled earlier, Detroit sits on Anishinaabe land, but there were no schools named after Indigenous people, and Indigenous histories were invisible. School was to be a medicine for students and the community, and attaching "bear" to it was more than a name; it was a responsibility, rooted in Anishinaabe clan responsibilities. As a member of the bear clan, one's role is to be a healer and protector. The school, then, was not only to assert Indigenous sovereignty within the context of Detroit but also to serve as a space for cultural revitalization and healing for students and community, many of whom struggled with their identity as Indigenous people in the city of Detroit because of the systematic erasure of Indigenous people by the city for over a century.

Applications to attend the school, which was open to all Detroit students, were due on June 30, 1994; children and parents, alike, were thrilled. Classes began on August 30. Keith Brant (Mohawk) took his niece to the first day of classes, where she joined 125 other students who would also begin their first day at Medicine Bear. With great optimism, he remarked, "My niece is the first generation to attend public school," he said, "we have never really trusted public schools, but this could be different." Another parent, James Gross, whose son, James Jr. was enrolled in the school, believed that the school would help his son, of Mohawk and Cherokee descent, to "feel good about who he is and help him get in touch with his spiritual side."[62]

The Medicine Bear American Indian Academy's desire was to make sure students were taught from an Indigenous perspective and that they understood the important role their ancestors played in shaping history. Medicine Bear American Indian Academy represents the third public school across America that has a focus on the traditions, customs, and holistic worldview of the North American Indian. Just over twenty years earlier, the urban Indigenous community of the Twin Cities formed the Heart of the Earth Survival School in Minneapolis and the Red School House in St. Paul. As historian Julie L. Davis observes, the schools were designed to "nurture Native youth, strengthen and protect Indian families, and achieve self-determination within urban institutions."[63] Medicine Bear, though in Detroit, was a part of the larger legacy of urban Indigenous communities taking ownership of their children's education for the future. Emphasizing the "first" peoples of

North America, the handbook stated, "We must remember the valuable lessons taught to us by this country's first chemists, doctors, agriculturalists, negotiators, traders, fisherman, orators, veterinarians, spiritual leaders, ecologists, judges, leaders and warriors . . . the Native American Indian." Finally, the fundamental component of centering Indigenous peoples was articulated in the handbook's preface: "A true and accurate study of the history of this country cannot occur without the study and understanding of this country's original inhabitants." This was more than an attempt to engage in the early 1990s multicultural educational models; it was a radical idea to not only teach students from an Indigenous perspective but also to challenge more than a century of history that suggested that Indigenous people no longer existed. The stated vision of Medicine Bear was to educate all students, Indigenous and non-Indigenous. It further stated,

> The Academy will accomplish this mission by meeting the unique and special needs of its students and achieving district, state and national Indian Education goals. Specifically, this academy strives to build a cadre of lifelong learners; educated with a world view and equipped to compete in a global twenty-first century. Through a holistic world view, the students will learn American Indian cultural values, beliefs, oral traditions, languages and life patterns that will equip them with necessary survival skills, and the ability to pass on these skills to future, urban Indian society (and also non-Indian society).
>
> It is also our mission to produce moral, non-racist, goal-oriented, creative productive, emotionally well-adjusted, global citizens with self-esteem being the generator of their academic and life successes.

To be sure, this was a bold mission but a necessary one. After a decades-long struggle to make Indigenous education a reality in a predominantly Black city, Indigenous Detroiters learned from Black tactics but also made it Indigenous. The mission emphasized a key part of being Indigenous in modern Detroit and elsewhere: that the Indigenous community's role in urban areas was to accept the fact that this generation and future ones would be predominantly urban. In this way, making sure that students were able to see that being urban and Indigenous was not, in fact, incompatible, was a revolutionary thought. One of the key struggles of urban Indigenous populations is to have to prove (to non-Indigenous people) that Indigenous people exist and to also illustrate that they are aware of their Indigenous cultures and histories because they have lived in an urban context (something they often had to prove to Indigenous people who grew up on the reservation).

Before coming to school, students also had to sign a pledge that they would "not just get by with a 'C' or 'D'." Instead, they would work hard and earn an "'A' or 'B by giving great quality to any and every task set before me, because I am the winner I am meant to be." Each morning, before classes began, students would make an oath, known as the Indian Pledge of Allegiance. An acrostic poem, which spelled "Indian," read:

I: I will always respect myself and others
N: Never fight or call others names
D: Don't do drugs
I: Improve in School
A: Always respect parents and teachers
N: Never be a drop-out

In addition to this particular pledge, they also had "The Ten Commandments of the Medicine Bear Student," which met the unique situation of students in early 1990s Detroit Public Schools: no drugs, no fighting, and respect for others.[64]

White people did not seem to express the same level of racism in regard to the opening of a school dedicated to Native children as they did for the Malcolm X Academy. There are at least a few possible reasons for this. First, within the white imagination, Native people are people of the past, with no real threat to the white supremacist order. White people believe that they had already conquered Indigenous people and they posed no threat. They consider Native people safe, and that Native people won't ultimately dispossess them by reclaiming land. In contrast, they had fear of a Black planet, where Black children and their families would integrate, lower property values, and mingle with their children. Second, by the 1990s, white people began to claim an unverified Indigenous heritage; it was a cool thing to do. They would listen to rap music, but they never really wanted to be Black. The students in general loved having a Native environment to help them learn about Indigenous histories and to help them develop a greater sense of self.

The Medicine Bear American Indian Academy provided mostly a positive experience for students. And it was essential to include the community, just like the Detroit Indian Educational and Cultural Center (which was still in operation at Pelham Elementary School). Judy recalled that she did not let prejudice of any kind circulate in the school. "Even though there were different races of kids who attended Medicine Bear, we had a lot of whites go there, Blacks, Natives, but we all had that Native spirit family. We considered ourselves a family." The curriculum did not exclude non-Indigenous students, and each person, regardless of age, was treated with respect. Even when conflict arose, the students tried very hard to resolve it in front of everyone. A former staff member recalled, "It was a safe place. We used to have circles where we would get all the teachers and students together in one big circle. We'd talk about what happened to someone if there was a conflict. We'd talk about it until we resolved the issue. The students loved that." The cultural significance of the space was just as important.

SouFy, an Anishinaabe from southwest Detroit, and now a rapper and community activist in the city, recalled how important the aesthetic of Medicine Bear was to his cultural awareness growing up. "When we did our pictures, I had a choker on . . . and I was standing next to a white polar bear in a wicker chair with a Pendleton blanket it on it. In our hallways all you see were animal furs and dream catchers and Native decorations. That helped shape who I was a lot." He recalled that it was a profound experience going to school with other Indigenous youth: "Now that I look back on it, it was great because it was a bunch of Native kids in a poor neighborhood in Detroit, with long hair everywhere, and playing soccer."[65] There were even two totem poles outside of the school. "Now that I look back, it was beautiful, cause there's no school like that now. Everyday when I walked to school I walked past two totem poles. . . . I thank the Creator for that. That did a lot for me when I was younger," remarked SouFy.[66] Other students benefited from the hybrid cultures that existed at Medicine Bear.

Melissa, a Black woman with Cherokee and Creek ancestry, attended Medicine Bear from the beginning. Her parents sent her there because of the small class sizes and because it emphasized her Indigenous heritage. Her experience reveals perhaps Medicine Bear's greatest strength: the ability to meet the cultural needs of mixed-race students and students with multiple Indigenous heritages. "My experience at Medicine Bear was wonderful," recalled Melissa. She continued, "The thing I appreciated most was that it served as a melting pot of students from different cultures." Her comments reflect the challenges facing a school with multiple racial and Indigenous identities. While Detroit was on Anishinaabe land, the school was able to meet the cultural needs of a variety of students.

Melissa thrived in this environment. "It was a school that taught respect from mother earth to relationships with people in general," said Melissa. The school also emphasized the importance of celebrating Black culture, too: "I was proud to attend this school because it also showed appreciation for my culture as well as celebrating Black history month and showing how imperative it was to preserve traditions—Native American and African American." For Melissa, these cultural blendings intersected in the everyday interactions between students and staff, as well as through the use of stories to teach lessons about life and to teach students, no matter their background, to have pride in themselves.

Other students, such as Ashleigh, Black and Anishinaabe, also had fond memories about the importance of learning about Indigenous histories in the school. "I enjoyed learning about the culture and history of Native Americans, of us." Ashleigh was able to connect the history of Indigenous people with her own experience, growing up as Black and Indigenous in Detroit. She recalled that the school was different "because I could learn about how the Indians lived back then, instead of about how they were killed off by white people. That was refreshing and important for me growing up as a Black and Indian child."[67]

The End of An Era

In October 1997, Kwame Kenyatta, the Black Nationalist who had enthusiastically supported Medicine Bear, resigned from the Detroit school board. In listing his accomplishments as a school board member, he cited the creation of a resolution that ultimately approved the Medicine Bear American Indian Academy.[68] By 2000, Judy Mays began to sense that something was not right. And many things began to change during the development of Medicine Bear in the city of Detroit.

In 1994, voters approved a statewide referendum that shifted how education would be financed. It moved from relying on local property taxes to a per-pupil grant that the state of Michigan provided. Detroit at the time continued to lose students. In 1999, Governor John Engler signed into law Public Act 10. This act effectively stripped the power from the Detroit Board of Education, and undemocratically imposed a seven-person reform board; then Mayor Dennis Archer would appoint six members, while the state superintendent of public instruction would serve in the final spot. This effectively ended the elected school board model. Detroit was not without its problems, including high dropout rates; however, when challenged about the constitutionality of the law, the court upheld the takeover.

According to Russ Bellant, a public-school advocate, the takeover of the Detroit Public Schools was unwarranted based on the logic of Governor Engler. "When the 1999 takeover was implemented, DPS had had modestly increasing student enrollment," he wrote. More than this, DPS did not have a deficit; "The District had a $100 million positive fund balance and academic scores in the broad mid-range of districts in the state. There was no performance justification for the takeover."[69] What caused the takeover? Bellant contends, "Conventional wisdom is that the actual reason for the takeover was to take control of $1.2 billion remaining from the $1.5 billion bond approve by voters in 1994. It was a golden egg that tempted too many in Lansing and Detroit."[70] Within the context of the Detroit school takeover in 1999, even though the school district had a deficit, at some point the board was looking to cut monies somewhere. And Medicine Bear became a target. Indeed, the targeting of Medicine Bear, it seems, was a prelude to the school closings that would begin to occur when the district was again taken over by Robert Bobb in 2009.

At the same time as the district-wide takeover, Judy Mays had been asking for another building. In 1996, voters approved a $37 million millage in order to help repair parks and other spots in Detroit, $4.75 million of which would go to the restoration of Historic Fort Wayne. By September 2000, nothing had been done.[71]

On March 29, 2000, Judy Mays received a letter from the Detroit Public Schools' Department of Human Resources. Mays, who had worked in the Detroit Public Schools for twenty-four years, was two years away from retirement. In the letter, Mays was told that her contract as principal of Medicine Bear American Indian Academy would not be renewed because of nepotism. Judy had hired her sister, Tracy Mays, a year earlier, to be the director of the Detroit Indian Educational and Cultural Center, which was in another building (Pelham Elementary School). The irony here is that, since the beginning of the DIECC, a Mays family member had been in a leadership position, including Judy, who had worked for the DIECC for eighteen years. Tracy also reported to a parent council—a mechanism that had been part of the DIECC from the beginning.

There is a crucial difference with nepotism from an Indigenous perspective, according to Cree scholar Shawn Wilson, who writes, "In the dominant system, nepotism generally involves the use of friends and relations in a concerted effort to keep others out."[72] However, "In healthy Indigenous communities," writes Wilson, "the strength of established bonds between people can be used to help uplift others."[73] Arthur Brant said it more succinctly. "What society is calling nepotism," he said, "is how we have survived all these years." He continued, "It is the closeness of our families that brought us this far."[74]

It seems that Judy was targeted because she was a longtime advocate of Indigenous education in Detroit, she was close to retirement, and she consistently asked for better on behalf of her students. "They promised us a new school," she said, and they "looked at property, held meetings about what it would look like." According to Judy, the Detroit Public Schools "even hired an architect." However, nothing happened. On May 26, Judy received a letter that said her contract would not be renewed.

Prior to the school year ending, Judy and the rest of the Indigenous community realized that it was not necessarily about Mays's firing, although that was a part. Her firing would effectively lead to the closing of Medicine Bear. Having long been a part of protest politics in the city of Detroit, the Indigenous community fought, as they had always done. Arthur Brant and Marie Marbly wrote the press release. On June 14, 2000, at 12 noon, on Flag Day, they decided to hold a protest in front of the Detroit Public Schools Center Building, at the corner of Woodward and Putnam.

The press release outlined Judy's credentials. She was a member of the Saginaw Chippewa tribe, she was a native Detroiter, graduating from Mumford High School in 1971, and had earned a Bachelor's degree in elementary education from Michigan State University and a Master's of Education degree in education administration from Wayne State University, as well as a certificate of Indian studies and a Bachelor's of Business Administration. She was the first and former director of the Detroit Indian Educational and Cultural Center. And she served for six years as the principal and founder of Medicine Bear. In 1999, she was awarded the "Booker T. Washington Distinguished Educator Award." The press release also mentioned how the students benefited under her watch as principal: "Under her leadership, the school outscored the Detroit District and State of Michigan MEAP (Michigan Educational Assessment Program) Scores in Reading, Math and Science for the last two years. Three students at the Academy have been designated Great Lakes Scholars. An eighth grader from our first Graduating class received a Full Scholarship at the prestigious Detroit Country Day."[75] Nearly one hundred supporters of Medicine Bear attended the rally. Young children wore their Medicine Bear American

Indian Academy shirts; others wore their Indigenous pow-wow regalia. Students and parents, staff and allies, Indigenous and non-Indigenous held signs that read "Save Our School Medicine Bear" and "Warriors Take Back Fort." The school was important to Detroit's Indigenous community. A mother of two Medicine Bear students remarked, "I was willing to drive way out of my district so that my two daughters could attend Medicine Bear," she said, and, "after they started this school, their grades improved, and one of my daughters is now a Great Lakes Scholar." This parent, like others, was dedicated to the vision that Judy and others created for the school. And, as a result of Judy's firing, the mother remarked, "I will be taking them out of that school, and will have to find a new one."[76] Layla Black Shawl, a grandparent, brought her 5-year-old granddaughter to the protest and remarked, "Judith Mays knows every child, parent and grandparent who comes up to that school. If the child is troubled, she takes him out to a picnic bench to talk with him. The school board should encourage that instead of get rid of it."[77] The most dramatic part of the protest would happen a few moments later.

Judy Mays draped herself in the American flag, which she wore upside down; it is something that her mother always did. "My mother always wore the flag upside down when she battled against wrongdoing," she said, "and I'm just carrying on her tradition."[78] One of the most dramatic moments came when Judy's sister, Tracy, went up to the microphone with her two young daughters, Cree and Seneca. She wrapped her hands around her two long braids, looked at the crowd, pulled the braids together, raised an orange pair of scissors and—just like that—she cut her braids. The crowd gasped; moans and wailings erupted into the warm Detroit sky; people began to cry out. Tracy turned, and handed each of her clipped braids over to her children. She then spoke. "I want (Detroit Public Schools [Superintendent] David Adamany to know why I cut my hair," she said, voice quivering. "I am in mourning for the loss of the city's only Native American principal, because it is like a death, and it is a part of our culture to cut our hair when we are in mourning."[79] While Detroit's Indigenous community fought for Judy and the school, it came to no avail.

On August 1, 2000, Judy's contract was not renewed. Two weeks later, she sued the Detroit Public Schools. She filed paperwork in the Wayne County Circuit Court, charging the Detroit Public Schools for "contract and age, sex, and race discrimination."[80] In addition, the lawsuit stated that Judy was suing the Detroit Public Schools for retaliation because she had complained about an inadequate building, which had two bathrooms—for 20 employees and 130 students; and a playground that had carcinogenic and hazardous materials. In addition, the lawsuit said that she was never questioned about nepotism by the district. Judy did not win her case. And Tracy resigned her position as the director of the Detroit Indian Educational and Cultural Center.

Medicine Bear American Indian Academy, the vision of a mother, the realization of a community, the lifework of a daughter, crumbled. Medicine Bear was officially closed by the school district after the 2001–2 school year. Reflecting on her experience, one student remarked, "I'm not Native, but what [Medicine Bear] meant for me was a really, very diverse and non-discriminatory school with a very tight-knit family feel." I really needed that type of environment as a kid." The closing of Medicine Bear American Indian Academy was different from the closing of Heart of the Earth Survival School and the Red School House. Those schools largely declined because of internal conflicts.[81] Medicine Bear was closed because of larger structural transformations in the city rooted in dispossession. Michigan's takeover of the Detroit Public Schools in 1999 was an example of educational dispossession, and the closing of Medicine Bear was a product of it.[82] The state of Michigan constructed the Detroit Public Schools as "failed" largely for market reasons. The closing of Medicine Bear is a direct result of capitalist interests.[83]

Being fired from Medicine Bear deeply hurt Judy. However, it should not end the great impact she had on Detroit's entire Indigenous community and what she did for children. When asked what the legacy of Medicine Bear was, she remarked:

> We were the third public American Indian school in the country. We were the third one.
>
> It was innovative to have a school like that. And the legacy is that we made it. It was a dream of my mother's—always to have a school for Native American children in Detroit. That was a legacy fulfilled through me by opening and being a part of her dream. To have it opened for kids, that would be the legacy—see someone's' dreams come to fruition. Mom didn't get to see Medicine Bear. That's what drove me—I was driven by that.

Judy is still heartbroken over her firing and the closing of Medicine Bear. However, she does have a sense of the meaning and impact the school had on everyone. "It was a very rewarding experience and I am humbled to have had the opportunity to do some of the things I was able to do," she said. She continued the narrative of working on behalf of her mother Esther's legacy: "Living on for my mom. Taking over for her, that was very gratifying. And I would do it again if I had the chance, in spite of the ending. I would still be at Medicine Bear. But since I left there, my life just went down—depression and all."

Although sad at their school's closing, former students, now adults, currently doing work in Detroit's Indigenous community, have fond memories of Medicine Bear and Judy. However, with the closing of Medicine Bear, the Detroit Indian Educational and Cultural Center soon followed in 2005. Indigenous education in the city of Detroit was no longer the same, and nothing has replaced it.

The history of Medicine Bear American Indian Academy is a history of sovereignty, pain, and struggle. It is also a history of Indigenous triumph. While short-lived, it represents the epitome of Indigenous activism and community will to make Indigenous lives matter, even in a political situation where Black students and perspectives, although tenuous, mattered a bit more. Education happened, and Medicine Bear represents Indigenous sovereignty played out in the postwar terrain of Detroit. The creation of Medicine Bear was the culmination of years of activism against educational dispossession.

The Malcolm X Academy still exists, now as the Paul Robeson Malcolm X Academy (PRMXA). Although the schools had a rocky start, they continue to educate Black children from an Afrocentric perspective. These schools merged in 2010 as a result of financial manager Robert Bobb closing dozens of schools and hardly saving any money as he promised during his tenure. Indeed, during the period from 1999 through 2016 in which the Detroit Public Schools were under emergency financial management, Detroit went into further debt to the tune of $610 million.[84] As PRMXA continues, it demonstrates the long-term possibilities of Black struggle and the short-lived dreams of Native activism to end dispossession in education. It illustrates the benefits and possibilities.

African Americans and Indigenous peoples believed that culturally relevant education would halt dispossession in at least a few ways. First, they reasoned that youth educated in the contemporary ways of local and national politics based in education that affirmed their history and cultures would help them avoid negative portrayal of self. Having a positive image of self would enhance their ability later on to live in a white supremacist world and advocate for their communities but not sell them out. For them, an African-centered and Indigenous-centered education would inform their approach to careers and later inform them in how to deal with local and national politics. Without a quality education, they argued, their respective communities would not be prepared for jobs in the twenty-first century nor would they be able to further the cause of liberation. Second, leaders in education understood that they had an uphill battle. During the 1980s, educational reformers and conservative think tanks placed the national spotlight on Detroit and other urban school districts and began to construct them as failed. This discourse served as a precondition for capitalists to take over the city school district years later.[85] It is within this context, in addition to social issues, that the Black and Indigenous communities had to act in order to avoid the possibility of furthering dispossession because of a lack of educational opportunity.

CONCLUSION

"Where Have All the Indians Gone?": The Afterlife of Dispossession, Detroit

Since the formation of the United States, whenever settlers believe that they are in a moment of crisis, they utilize tropes of Indianness. As historian Philip Deloria contends, the idea of Indianness has changed over time. Though he focused on the American Revolution, urbanization at the turn of the twentieth century, and the postwar era, he argues that whites alter their perception of Indianness during crises in capitalism.[1] In the wake of the 2008 financial crisis that devastated millions of people throughout the United States, in Detroit, it also impacted the General Motors Pontiac brand, and settlers "played Indian" once more to criticize the discontinuation of the Pontiac brand.

Before President George W. Bush and, later, President Barack Obama bailed out General Motors (GM) with a multibillion-dollar plan, GM began cutting costs. The company had $82 billion in assets but $172 billion in liabilities. GM went bankrupt. The bailout did not stop the termination of the Pontiac brand.[2] In January 2010, the last Pontiac automobile emerged from the GM Orion plant in Orion Township, Michigan, which is about thirty miles north of Detroit.[3] In this moment of crisis, elite white men tried to salvage the brand, albeit using the story once again of the actual Odawa war chief.

On August 1, 2009, David Smith, a writer for *WardsAuto* online magazine, used Chief Pontiac to criticize the executives of GM for ending the iconic brand. In the article titled "Chief Pontiac on the Warpath," Smith used age-old savage tropes to comment on the Pontiac closing. "I'll smoke no peace pipes with General Motors Corp," wrote Smith. He continued, "For 83 years GM took advantage of my name by putting it on millions of cars—without sending me a royalty check." Writing as a ventriloquist, he said, "I can forgive many transgressions, but if I were still a young brave, rather than a relic, I'd lead another siege on Detroit and invade GM's headquarters." Smith also channeled Pontiac's voice to criticize GM for sending jobs overseas.

He wrote that General Motors "not only humiliates me by ending the Pontiac brand but also besmirches the name of my Aztec cousins in Mexico by using their name on a Pontiac crossover that has reigned as Chief of the Uglies." Smith engaged in another form of erasure by collapsing Indigenous people in the Americas. After recounting how GM used Pontiac's image, Smith stated, "As chief of the Ottawas, I had two names. One was Pontiac, the other Obwandiyag. I only wish GM had adopted the latter."[4] Smith referred to Pontiac's more accurate phonetic name.

The discontinuation of the Pontiac brand was also the end of one particular brand of Detroit's modernity and, for white men, masculinity. Since the 1920s, Pontiac's image and the brand *were* Detroit. That particular chapter of Detroit would no longer exist. Ironically, white men felt erased, which is a longer part of the history of dispossession in Detroit.

I have tried to demonstrate that an indigenous presence, be it real or imagined, has been central to the development of modern Detroit's cultural and intellectual identity. In fact, if we go back to the Pontiac brand, indigenous presences have been a central part of the city's economic identity as well as its identity as a hardcore, hardworking, innovative place. Detroit is nothing without its Motor City moniker, and, as I have tried to illustrate throughout this book, Detroit is also nothing without its Indigenous cultures, histories, people, and presences. Before there was Detroit, there was Waawayeyaattanong. When Cadillac came and renamed an Indigenous space Fort Pontchartrain, Native people were still there, and he needed them in order to survive. When Detroit's white elite wanted to celebrate the 200-year history of Detroit, they beckoned Indigenous performers to make their celebrated history "authentic." Real and imagined, white settlers' persistent need for Native people and presences demonstrates that they are nothing without Indigenous people and will continue to need them.

The source of Detroit's ingenuity is deeply embedded within elite white male fantasies and the dispossession narratives that they have produced since at least the late nineteenth century. If you saw the city's pitch to be a site for Amazon's headquarters in the fall of 2017, then you see exactly how this narrative went. The video begins with an overview of the Detroit landscape followed immediately by people building things and doing a variety of labor, two familiar images of the story of Detroit. Detroit will remain a settler city, no matter what changes, as long as white and other non-Indigenous people run the city.

Detroit is changing today. More and more white people are moving in. The artists, the hipsters, the bougie coffee drinkers, and the beer snobs—what Richard Florida called the "creative class"—are changing the landscape of Detroit, physically, in name, and in the world's cultural imagination.[5] Of course, Black Americans, the city's largest population, do not have a say in what happens to their city; their rights began to be stripped when the state took over the Detroit Public Schools in 1999 and, more recently, when Governor Rick Snyder stripped power away from the city council and imposed emergency financial manager Kevyn Orr. Still, just as during the height of rapid social change in the 1970s, Indigenous Detroiters are largely invisible. Even Black Detroiters continue to render them invisible.

On Saturday, April 23, 2016, I, along with ten undergraduate and graduate students at Michigan State University, participated in a community day in Detroit. Our goal was to visit four different Black-owned businesses in the city. Of those we visited, my favorite business was that of the biracial (Black-white), German-born Carl Anthony Nielbock, owner of C.A.N. Art Handworks.[6] Nielbock had an amazing story. He came to Detroit in 1984 at the age of twenty-three, after serving for several years as an apprentice to a master craftsman in Germany. He worked on many projects, including the restoration of the infamous Fox Theatre (he got this job in part because the language on the blueprints was in German). He is pretty well known throughout the city. More recently, he has collected discarded art and other artifacts from throughout the Motor City, both because of his craftsmanship and his interest in the collecting of history artifacts. Unbeknownst to most, however, is that he also has become an amateur historian.

During our two-hour-long tour of his place, he told us many stories, but one in particular stood out: his discussion of the Indigenous history of Detroit. He told us of the Battle of Bloody Run, which occurred on July 31, 1763, as a part of the Odawa war chief Pontiac's so-called conspiracy, an Indigenous (many Nations) led assault against British forts in the Midwest, designed to drive the British out of Native homelands once and for all. The British planned a surprise attack on Pontiac and others at Parent's Creek, which is near present-day Elmwood Cemetery. Pontiac and others were not surprised, and they easily defeated their foes. The British would call the blood that flowed in the creek "Bloody Run." Carl stated that one thing he discovered after researching in the Detroit Public Library is that there is *no* presence of "Indians" in Detroit. He wondered aloud, "I wanted to know, what happened to all of the Indians?" In order to rectify this situation, or at least to make the Indigenous people "visible," he created an exhibit in a lot that he owns next to his building. There were red metal stick figures on two sides of a "river" (representing the banks of that creek), with an arrow in their heads and each figure holding a bow and arrow. An elder Black woman proclaimed to Carl, "I'm glad you're doing this." After gently placing her hand on my shoulder, she said to Carl, "We got a First Nations person with us." Carl nodded and smiled. Everyone on the trip realized quickly that I make sure that Indigenous histories of place are acknowledged in Detroit, or in any place they walk. People assumed I would be excited that a Black Detroiter acknowledged Native histories that are often ignored; I was not.

Although I appreciated his resurrection of Native presences in Detroit, it was still predicated on Native invisibility in his actual presence; for instance, more than 8,000 Native people still live in metro Detroit and, if you ask the community, you would probably have to double that number.[7] Second, he also admitted that he was very much a fan of the German author Karl May. May had helped build and sustain the German fascination with Native Americans through his *Winnetou* adventure novels, which have been printed over a hundred million times and translated into dozens of languages.[8] Rhetoric scholar Lisa King observes that some German communities continue to align Native Americanness with German nationalism.[9] Given his affinity for Karl May, it is not surprising that Carl Nielbock also produced those red metal stick figures on his land.

There is much more to be done in order to challenge these stereotypes about Indigenous people. Native people challenge settler narratives when they exist in modernity. If you know any Native person born and raised in Detroit, that person looks, dresses, and acts like fellow Detroiters. Urban Natives are not some special breed of people; they are products of their cultural and social surroundings, just like anyone else.

My encounter with Nielbock represents longer dispossession narratives and Indigenous invisibility in the city. But Indigenous people are trying to change that through forms of creative expression, as I illustrated in Chapter 6. Detroit continues to hold meaning for Detroiters, young and old. Detroit within the cultural imagination of non-Indigenous people represents how settler colonialism works. Detroit represents the epitome of dispossession.

Detroit's dispossession is, according to historian Penelope Edmonds, "a site in which the appropriation of Indigenous land was coupled with aggressive allotment and property speculation, a site in which property relations were constructed quickly through rhetorical celebrations of making a white, civilized space."[10] Detroit is unique because it is now a predominantly Black city. And, currently, venture capitalists and white hipsters have seemingly transplanted the frontier discourse from the nineteenth century, when European settlers moved to the western United States, to the present. There are at least two processes that shape cities of dispossession.

As I have shown throughout this book, narrative dispossessions are a central part of removing and displacing people. Settler capitalists use dispossession narratives not only to erase Indigenous and African American people from the landscape but also to prophesize about their future in Detroit. Take, for instance, Rodney Lockwood. Lockwood is a developer and manager of multifamily and senior housing, mostly in Michigan. He is the chairman/CEO of Lockwood Enterprises. He is also a member of the Mackinac Center for Public Policy (a conservative think tank that creates policies for Michigan and Detroit) and is a past chairman of the Michigan Chamber of Commerce. He lives in Birmingham, Michigan, which is a suburb about twenty miles north of Detroit. He wrote a book titled *Belle Isle: Detroit's Game Changer* (2012), which he self-published. The book can be summed up in this way: a fictional account about how best to change the economy of Detroit through the occupation and complete transformation of Belle Isle, thus, transforming it into a commonwealth. This is completely different from how settlers viewed Detroit in the past. Indeed, in the nineteenth century, the shift from a Native indigeneity to a white indigeneity was about transitioning the city from its Indigenous past and into the hands of white Detroiters, hoping to move away from that Indigenous history. In contemporary Detroit, even within the context of Indigenous erasure, Black indigeneity is the latest version of indigeneity, and white men are attempting to wrest it away from those "indigenous" Black folks by erasing them from even fictional accounts.

Lockwood tells a story that imagines what Belle Isle could be like thirty-five years into the future. The imaginary island is based on three core principles: small government, aesthetic beauty, and respect for all citizens as long as they promote self-reliance. In fact, on January 21, 2013, he pitched the very ideas of this book at an invitation-only meeting for area businesses and civic leaders and politicians at the Detroit Athletic Club.[11] Private investors would purchase the island for $1 billion. The commonwealth would be built for 35,000 people (more on this later). A monorail would connect the commonwealth to Detroit, which would be funded by the payments that citizens make to live on the island. The billions of invested dollars would, without taxpayer money, "launch a construction boom of enormous size and duration, which along with ongoing economic activity, would provide jobs and hope for people of Detroit."[12] The author explicitly states that this idea "is not about creating an island of wealth, even though it does." He continues: "Of course it will attract wealth and wealth is fine, but what will distinguish it from other city-states or small countries is its spirit and optimism. Even the less wealthy will bask in the sunshine of freedom and be lifted by its opportunity. Unfettered from too many rules and regulations, from taxing the wrong things, from inefficient self-serving government, Belle Isle will become the 'Midwest Tiger,' rivaling Singapore and Hong Kong in its economic miracle."[13]

The logic here is "trickle-down economics," which assumes that if wealth is created, it will reach the rest of society. Belle Isle's wealth creation, assumes Lockwood, would benefit all.

The story is based on two main characters: Joseph Sharif and Darin Fraser. Sharif is a Syrian American Muslim. Lockwood writes that he was born in Michigan. He graduated from Michigan State University and attended San Francisco Medical School. He moved up the medical ranks quickly and became director of the Damascus Medical Center in Syria. Fraser (who seems loosely based on Lockwood himself) graduated with a degree in architecture from the University of Michigan and later also got his master's there in urban design. After working for an international urban-design firm in Malaysia and studying under a "great Turkish designer," he was contacted by a group of investors to lead the planning of Belle Isle.

Over several years, Darin urged Joe to come visit the island. It was not until a *Time* magazine article, featuring Darin, did Joe decide to accept Darin's invitation to visit. Joe took a flight from Syria to New York, and then on to Detroit. When he arrived in Detroit, he was taken to Belle Isle by helicopter, which landed on the rooftop of the fifty-seven-story Four Seasons hotel. There, he was met by Darin.[14]

The citizens of Belle Isle will come from everywhere. Joe asks Darin how one becomes a citizen. Darin responds that they must apply to the Citizenship Board. This board consists of three members and, during busier times, more than one board will be operating. The majority of people will come from the United States, but many will also come from France and Great Britain, Central and South America, and Asia. The requirements for citizenship are inherently exclusionary. One cannot be a criminal escaping harsh circumstances elsewhere. "They have to have paid their bills and have good credit." And most potential citizens "have to make a substantial contribution of capital either directly to the Belle Isle Treasury or to a business based in

Belle Isle."[15] "Substantial" means several hundreds of thousands of dollars; for businesses, it would be more. The author does document other ways that the less fortunate can be given citizenship. "We hold 20 percent of our citizenship spots open for exceptions."[16]

The "exceptions" include those who might not have money but can contribute some skill to the betterment of Belle Isle. Darin tells Joe the story of Hector Cabrera, as an example of someone who made it. Darin went to Mexico for a mission trip, and he met Hector. Hector lived in a very simple house, but he had construction skills, spoke a little English, and worked very hard to be successful. Darin told Hector about Belle Isle, and Hector asked if he could come. Darin served as his sponsor. Hector had to write an essay that explained why he wanted to live in a place where "the core values of liberty, freedom, beauty, respect for others, unlimited opportunity and hard work were promoted."[17] Darin flew him up to be interviewed by the board. He was granted approval, pending improvement of his English skills. (Darin advocates English only.) Given Hector's skill set, he would go on to hold two contracts as a landscaper, making the parks on the island look nice, and have a private landscaping business. He has the biggest summer employment business on the island.[18]

The requirements for citizenship and the story of Hector reveal the core principle of this experiment: white indigeneity, rooted in the mythic past of freedom and sovereignty. This narrative, like the U.S. narrative of freedom in general, ignores enslavement and dispossession as the key foundations of this country's past. Belle Isle, too, has a past of dispossession, which the author ignores.

Darin's description—or his lack of mentioning blackness—is not only surprising but also interesting if Detroit's history is important. It reveals the lack of respect for Black people, too, who have their own stake in Detroit's past and present. He only mentions that Detroit will be put into zones with their own police forces and government structures. It is in line with Dan Gilbert's vision for Detroit. Founder of Quicken Loans, Gilbert has helped quickly transform downtown Detroit with the "Detroit 2.0" project. These pioneer logics erase the actual population of Detroit by telling wealthy people and those looking for opportunity that they can occupy land, take over land, and reshape it. They have already done this discursively, which is the simultaneous but under-examined point of settler colonialism: to dispossess first and continuously, through discourse (both images and words). A Detroit 2.0 is not for the citizens already living in Detroit, it is for those who want to venture to the Midwest, just like European settlers and also non-European Americans did more than a century ago.

Lockwood constructs a future of Belle Isle and Detroit, unsurprisingly, without Indigenous people and, for that matter, without Black Americans. The written histories of Belle Isle's past acknowledged the island's Indigenous history, even as they used that history to construct the dichotomy between savagery and civilization. Lockwood's future Belle Isle was a place for new settlers of all kinds, but the majority would be wealthy.

One might wonder, why even write about a fictional project, after all, it is impossible, right? First, it illustrates the continuity between how settlers have viewed and still view land, from the late nineteenth century and in the present. This process is what Palestinian literary scholar Edward Said has called "imaginary geography." He writes, "This universal practice of designating in one's mind a familiar space which is 'ours' and an unfamiliar space beyond 'ours' which is 'theirs' is a way of making geographical distinctions that can be entirely arbitrary."[19] *Belle Isle: Detroit's Game Changer* makes the place very familiar because it is based on Monaco. Lockwood creates a distinction between the residents of Belle Isle (including himself) and the people of Detroit in the text. Indeed, the citizens of Detroit in the book are invisible; just like today, those in power impose policies and projects upon Detroit citizens without their consent (e.g., installing an emergency financial manager). The people are easily manipulated and moved out in order for the futuristic, imaginary geographical construction by the wealthy to succeed. For instance, the author notes that only 45,000 people live within Detroit proper, but it is split into neighborhood zones. Each city has its own government police force and tax rates. The parts of Detroit that did not become part of the new cities were turned into "farms, forest and parks. They're called 'green zones.'" The billion dollars given to the city for the sale of Belle Isle "helped fund the relocation of residents from green zones to the new cities." Second, Lockwood's fictional project dovetails with a common theme experienced by working-class Detroiters today: the wealthy determining what goes on in matters that impact the lives of working-class Detroiters without their input. Finally, it demonstrates the parallels between how colonial imaginings impacted Black and Indigenous people living there today.

Lockwood's Belle Isle dispossession narrative is the evolution of the settler capitalists' indigeneity. It went from a park, locked into nineteenth-century ideas of modernity and nature, to a modern place that is green and efficient but still a place for the wealthy. Elite white men's indigeneity is about erasing the Indigenous history and present, and creating a space in their own imagination. Lockwood's construction of Detroit, as a place built for settler imaginaries, is not new; the concept of progress and modernity through the changing of landscape is as American as cherry pie, or dispossession. Perhaps the least and tragic part of this narrative is that most of us would not be surprised if a billionaire would be able to create their own, neoliberal place of living.

The second process is the physical dispossession of the Indigenous population and displacement of African Americans. An important part of that is also their erasure from the history and cultural imagination. This erasure is deliberate. Finally, to cement the displacement, white men create origin myths, thus altering the history of that place into a place rooted in white men's origins.[20] The dispossession of Detroit is not gentrification. Gentrification cannot fully capture processes of dispossession. Nor can it explain why settlers continue to erase Indigenous people and those, even Black folks, who now, metaphorically represent an "indigenous" population that is being erased from the landscape of Detroit and continue to be displaced by a loss of water and by housing clearance. Dispossession is such a part of the cultural imagination and social and economic policies of Detroit (and of the United States) that the people can now reenact, albeit remixed, versions of displacement from previous centuries, and some people don't even consider it a problem.

Detroit means many things to people. It was and remains a hotbed of radical activism. It is a place to be inspired, both by venture capitalists who see Detroit as a new frontier to expand their business markets and profits and for hipsters to come and make something of themselves. Detroit, still, is a place that was made by and for regular people, especially and including Indigenous people. It is, in fact, Indigenous land. Indigenous people were the first ones here and will continue to remain, despite what venture settlers seek to do. For Indigenous Detroiters, those who remain and who have moved away from the area, it is still home. But for people like Sandra Muse, Detroit, with all of its flaws, is still the place to be:

> I love Detroit. It breaks my heart that Detroit is going through the hard times that it's going through. To me, there was always an Indigenous space within the boundaries of Detroit. There was always a Detroit Indian community. I will always be a Detroit girl. I've been in Ontario twenty-seven years, I think; a long time. I still follow all of the Detroit sports teams: Red Wings, Pistons, Lions. But Detroit is home. It'll always be home. I learned how to survive it, how to deal with my own identity complex as a Native teenager—someone who didn't quite fit in anywhere.

Indigenous people love Detroit. But will the city love Indigenous Detroiters and all Detroiters back?

What Should Detroit Do to Honor Its Indigenous People and Histories?

In concluding this book, I want to make a few recommendations to leaders of Detroit. It is significant that city officials work to honor and respect the Indigenous people and histories of the area. However, we should never forget that Indigenous people still live in Detroit and continue to shape every aspect of the city. As Comanche writer Paul Chaat Smith remarks in *Everything You Know About Indians Is Wrong* (2009), "And for the Americans, who drive Pontiacs and Cherokees and live in places with Indian names . . . we remain a half-remembered presence, both comforting and dangerous, lurking just below the surface."[21] Native people and their presence are resilient and shall remain central to Detroit—regardless of whether others recognize this. Non-Native people who are committed to combating climate change and other issues that threaten our existence should think carefully and strategically about the role that Indigenous people will play in ending all forms of dispossession.

One of the more remarkable things to have happened in Detroit in recent years has been the recognition of Indigenous Peoples' Day. Councilwoman Raquel Castañeda-Lopez, along with Indigenous residents, helped get the resolution passed with Detroit's city council in the fall of 2017. Indigenous Detroiters celebrated this day, like other cities, such as Los Angeles and New York City, at Spirit Plaza. Castañeda-Lopez argued that the city council should consider getting rid of the Christopher Columbus statue in downtown. "It's not about Columbus at all," she remarked. It is about sharing the "stories of people who have been marginalized and forgotten and oppressed for so many generations."[22] Black people also experienced symbolic changes.

In addition to the creation of Indigenous Peoples' Day, African Americans could celebrate the removal of former mayor Albert Cobo's name from the infamous Cobo Center. Symbolically, the name of Cobo is synonymous with Black dispossession given the displacement and removal of Black residents during the 1950s. In August 2019, Chemical Bank purchased the naming rights of Cobo for twenty-two years, for $1.5 million annually. Detroit's Black elite population was excited. As Wendell Anthony, president of the Detroit NAACP noted, "You can't change everything, but you can some things. And I have been wanting and even urging that Cobo Center be renamed. This center being renamed and reclaimed in Black History Month is history." Governor Gretchen Whitmer argued that it was a good move. "We know the name that is coming off this building is synonymous with division," she said. Whitmer also believed that "it's not simply a name change of a building in the great city of Detroit. This is about the next chapter for Michigan, this is about opportunity for all, no matter who you are, and being inclusive in that." Finally, Warren C. Evans, a Wayne County executive, stated bluntly, "They can't take the name off fast enough for me in terms of the history and the city of Detroit." Blaming the problems associated with one man, Evans continued, "We had vibrant African-American neighborhoods in this city until Albert Cobo destroyed them and did it at a time when the rest of the city wasn't receptive to black residents either."[23] The Cobo Center's new name is now the TCF Center because Chemical Bank merged with TCF Bank.

The excitement around the removal of a name like Cobo's should be celebrated. But it also reveals the depths at which dispossession impacts Detroit's Black and working-class citizens. The Cobo name should have been removed. But it does not lead to material changes for Detroit citizens. The name was removed for the purposes of capitalism. Removing a name does not remove the historical effects of racist policies of displacement and removal.

Many things can be done to challenge the long history of dispossession in Detroit. The very first thing the city and the governor of Michigan can do is to acknowledge the wrong that has been and continues to be done to Detroit's Black and Indigenous citizens. In consultation with Black and Indigenous residents, city leaders should consider the following steps:

1. **Formally recognize that Detroit is treaty land**. In settler states, Australia, Canada, and New Zealand, it is not uncommon to hear a government official at least acknowledge that the people are on Indigenous land. I know some might roll their eyes and correctly assert that this is settler "move to innocence"; however, it is important to acknowledge, especially a place that is predominantly Black. For Black people, it would lead to more important conversations, especially within the context of solidarity.
2. **Create a Pontiac statue**. Make a large statue of Pontiac and place it somewhere in downtown Detroit. It could replace the Columbus statue. This statue should be first on the list. This makes sense because one of the city's major historical darlings,

Senator Thomas W. Palmer, wanted to build a grave dedicated to Pontiac. I understand that there are no known pictures of Pontiac, but something must go up. I also think a huge statue, replacing the Columbus one, would be cool.[24] Of course, this has to be done in consultation with Odawa people and created by an Indigenous artist with the help of a historical expert.

3. **Recognize contemporary Indigenous peoples**. While making memorials that acknowledge the history of Indigenous contributions to the city, such as Pontiac, make sure to acknowledge the contributions of Indigenous people today. They continue to show the city that they exist.
4. **Curate Detroit's Indigenous history**. Curate a special history of Indigenous people in the Detroit Historical Museum and at the Detroit Institute of Art. I don't mean the things that only depict Indigenous peoples in the eighteenth and nineteenth centuries; this should include twentieth-century history and beyond. If you need the help of a historian of Native Detroit, you have an expert in myself.
5. **Show Indigenous migrations to Detroit**. Make an exhibit demonstrating the migratory patterns of Indigenous peoples, moving to the Motor City from Canada, Walpole Island, and throughout the United States. Detroit has always been a hub for Indigenous peoples, many who passed through or stayed.
6. **Develop an app**. Create an app in which visitors to and residents of the Motor City can see the history of Indigenous spaces in Detroit.
7. **Celebrate Black-Indigenous History Month**. I understand that Detroit is a predominantly Black city. During Black History Month, there should be a celebration of Black and Indigenous collaborations. Given that many of the city's Indigenous community are mixed race (in this context, Black and Indigenous), this could certainly help expand peoples' understanding of these connections. Did I mention that the "Father of Black History," Carter G. Woodson, wrote one of the first academic articles on the relations between Black and Indigenous peoples? If it makes sense for him, it could make sense for you, too.
8. **Create an Indigenous arts initiative**. To reconcile the unacknowledged and fraught history that Detroit has with Native

people, the city should create an arts initiative for Indigenous youth in Detroit. These youth could work with language instructors, learn how to bead, make drums, learn how to rap, and learn pow-wow dancing and contemporary dancing or even blend the two. The city or a private foundation could provide Indigenous artists a bursary to make their own work, to create new collaborations, or to travel. This would require art material and a studio or, more precisely, space; which leads me to my next point.

9. **Return the land**. Just return the land. It's quite simple. Well, it might not be that simple because the settler nation-state does not want to admit that it was wrong. Frankly, I don't know what this might look like. But the city of Detroit could make space available for Indigenous peoples; I'm sure Belle Isle might be a good place, which is likely unceded territory. In Chicago, Illinois, the Chi-Nations Youth Council, which is a multi-tribal environmental land and social justice organization, leased an abandoned lot in Albany Park in the 35th Ward. The ward is under the jurisdiction of Alderman Carlos Ramirez-Rosa. On this land, the city could build a state-of-the-art youth center that offers counseling and a place to host pow-wows and other cultural events. It would include recreation; a place to hold ceremonies; and a technology and creative-expression space where youth can learn coding, lay down tracks, and be able to communicate with elders when needed. This is not a pipe dream. It's not a return of land in the literal sense, but it's a start. The city could partner with a tribal nation in Michigan to make it happen. Or Dan Gilbert and Mike Illitch could use some of their billionaire pocket change and pay for it. Removing a name of a former mayor and a statue is cool, but what's cooler is giving Indigenous and Black youth a space to be their best selves.
10. **Make new treaties with Black people**. When Europeans kidnapped Africans and brought them to the land of Indigenous nations already living on land that would become the United States, they were taking *Indigenous* peoples in order to exploit their labor. When Europeans permanently settled in what would become the United States, they were dispossessing Indigenous peoples. See the connection? All of the oppressed people were Indigenous. I propose that Indigenous people original to Turtle

> Island form new agreements, treaties, relationships with Black Americans in order to put into practice Indigenous sovereignty. Nations can adopt and incorporate, based on their ceremonial and social practices, the descendants of Indigenous people. It would be one of the most liberating things to happen since the emancipation of the enslaved.

Finally, solidarity between people of African descent and Indigenous peoples in Detroit is essential. We need what Michi Saagiig Nishnaabeg writer and artist Leanne Betasamosake Simpson calls a "radical resurgence." Her understanding of Indigenous futures requires "us to critically and thoroughly look at the roots of the settler colonial present—capitalism, white supremacy, heteropatriarchy, and anti-blackness." Moreover, a radical Indigenous resurgence necessitates us to "name dispossession as the meta-dominating force in our relationship to the [settler state]."[25] Dispossession impacts Black and Indigenous peoples. However, we need a resurgence that helps us build meaningful relationships not just for the now but for our futures. And these relationships must happen across colonial borders and between diasporas.[26]

Black folks can no longer accept the politics of invisibility, even if they might seem insignificant. Indigenous people can no longer engage in a politics of anti-blackness, even out of frustration. If there are white people who want to take a back seat and join that struggle, then they should do so and take direction from Black and Indigenous peoples. All groups should center the relationship between racial capitalism and settler colonialism. We can change things together. However, we need to understand that our histories and current predicaments are rooted in Indigenous genocide and removal and African enslavement and anti-blackness. We can win. We must win! But as we are winning the fight against ongoing dispossession and putting into practice those freedom dreams—we have to simultaneously build our future. We have to remember that solidarity can be fleeting and only when we bond our alliances together can we truly be free.

NOTES

Introduction

1. The recent work of Jodi Byrd and Alyosha Goldstein has been very instructive for me in understanding the shared experiences of colonization and racialization. See Jodi A Byrd, Alyosha Goldstein, Jodi Melamed, and Chandan Reddy, "Predatory Value," *Social Text* 36, no. 2 (June 1, 2018): 1–18; and Jodi Byrd, "Variations Under Domestication: Indigeneity and the Subject of Dispossession," *Social Text* 36, no. 2 (June 1, 2018): 123–41. They use the term "economies of dispossession" to differentiate their use from David Harvey's "accumulation by dispossession." David Harvey, "The 'New' Imperialism: Accumulation by Dispossession," *Socialist Register* 40 (2004): 75-76. What is often missed in describing Harvey's definition of accumulation by dispossession is his understanding of culture, when he writes, "The commodification of cultural forms, histories and intellectual creativity entails wholesale dispossessions" (75). In this way, dispossession, as I argue, is also cultural and ideological in addition to material. Caleb Bush, "Reconsidering Incorporation: Uneven Histories of Capitalist Expansion and Encroachment, Native America," *Studies in Political Economy* 76, no. 1 (2005): 83–109. See also, Robert Nichols, *Theft Is Property: Dispossession and Critical Theory* (Minneapolis: University of Minnesota Press, 2020). He theorizes recursive dispossession "is a form of property generating theft" (9). Nichols's important contribution is combining dispossession with critical theory.

2. Heather Dorries, Robert Henry, David Hugill, Tyler McCreary, and Julie Tomiak, eds, *Settler City Limits: Indigenous Resurgence and Colonial Violence in the Urban Prairie West* (Winnipeg: University of Manitoba Press, 2019). E-book introduction. Accessed August 1, 2020. See also Byrd et al., "Predatory Value," 5, in which they critique racial capitalism for making the assumption that colonialism was one of the original examples of accumulation by dispossession and not an ongoing process. I would challenge their assumption, though. While I agree with their critique of Marx and others who assume that settler colonization is something of the past and not an ongoing phenomenon, I also believe that they miss the point in understanding racial capitalism. What about the colonization of Africa?

3. See Danish Khan and Anirban Karak, "Urban Development by Dispossession: Planetary Urbanization and Primitive Accumulation," *Studies in Political Economy* 99, no. 3 (September 2, 2018): 307–30. Swapna Banerjee-Guha, ed., *Accumulation by Dispossession: Transformative Cities in the New Global Order*, 1st ed. (Los Angeles: SAGE Publications, 2010). See also Naama Blatman-Thomas and Libby Porter, "Placing Property: Theorizing the Urban from Settler Colonial Cities," *International Journal of Urban and Regional Research* 30, no. 1 (2019): 30–45; they argue that property is the fundamental logic through which settler colonial urbanism and dispossession is enacted (42).

4. For a discussion on the relationship between settler colonialism and racial capitalism in urban studies see, Heather Dorries, David Hugill, and Julie Tomiak, "Racial Capitalism and the Production of Settler Colonial Cities," *Geoforum*, August 19, 2019, https://doi.org/10.1016/j.geoforum.2019.07.016. Accessed July 2, 2021. For a discussion of neoliberalism and the restructuring of Black relationship to the U.S. economy, see Michael C. Dawson and Megan Ming Francis, "Black Politics and the Neoliberal Racial Order," *Public Culture* 28, no. 1 (2015): 23–62.

5. Patrick Wolfe, "Settler Colonialism and the Elimination of the Native," *Journal of Genocide Research* 8, no. 4 (December 2006): 388. While scholars often cite Wolfe and Lorenzo Veracini, and for good reason, Palestinian and African scholars have long written about settler colonialism. See Fayez Sayegh, "Zionist Colonialism in Palestine," *Settler Colonial Studies* 2, no. 1 (2012): 206–25; and Bernard Magubane, "The Political Economy of the South African Revolution," *African Journal of Political Economy* 1, no. 1 (1986): 1–28.

6. Tiya Miles, *Ties That Bind: The Story of an Afro-Cherokee Family in Slavery and Freedom* (Berkeley: University of California Press, 2005); Celia E. Naylor, *African Cherokees in Indian Territory: From Chattel to Citizens* (Chapel Hill: University of North Carolina Press, 2009); Arica L. Coleman, *That the Blood Stay Pure: African Americans, Native Americans, and the Predicament of Race and Identity in Virginia* (Bloomington: Indiana University Press, 2013); Tiya Miles, *The House on Diamond Hill: A Cherokee Plantation Story* (Chapel Hill: University of North Carolina Press, 2010); David Chang, *The Color of the Land: Race, Nation, and the Politics of Land Ownership in Oklahoma, 1832–1929* (Minneapolis: University of Minnesota Press, 2010); Kim Cary Warren, *The Quest for Citizenship: African American and Native American Education in Kansas, 1880–1935* (Chapel Hill: University of North Carolina Press, 2010).

7. Patrick Wolfe, *Traces of History: Elementary Structures of Race* (London: Verso, 2016), 2.

8. Robin D. G. Kelley, "The Rest of Us: Rethinking Settler and Native," *American Quarterly* 69, no. 2 (June 2017): 268.

9. Edmund Danziger, *Survival and Regeneration: Detroit's American Indian Community* (Detroit, MI: Wayne State University Press, 1991), 93; Jessi Quizar, "Land of Opportunity: Anti-Black and Settler Logics in the Gentrification of Detroit," *American Indian Culture and Research Journal* 43, no. 2 (May 2019): 113–15. However, Quizar also argues that Black folks today are experiencing similar forms of settler logics as Native people in current discussions of gentrification.

10. Manu Karuka, "Black and Native Visions of Self-Determination," *Journal of the Critical Ethnic Studies Association* 3, no. 2 (2017): 77–98; Justin Leroy, "Black History in Occupied Territory: On the Entanglements of Slavery and Settler Colonialism," *Theory & Event* 19, no. 4 (2016), https://muse.jhu.edu/article/633276; Manu Vimalassery, Juliana Hu Pegues, and Alyosha Goldstein, "Introduction: On Colonial Unknowing," *Theory & Event* 19, no. 4 (October 12, 2016), https://muse.jhu.edu/article/633283.

11. Tiffany Lethabo King, *The Black Shoals: Offshore Formations of Black and Native Studies* (Durham, NC: Duke University Press, 2019), 28.

12. Nick Estes and Roxanne Dunbar-Ortiz, "Examining the Wreckage," *Monthly Review*, July 1, 2020, https://monthlyreview.org/2020/07/01/examining-the-wreckage/. Accessed July 11, 2020. They offer a well-written analysis comparing both Black and Indigenous histories under racial capitalism and settler colonialism. See, again, Dorries, Hugill, and Tomiak, "Racial Capitalism and the Production of Settler Colonial Cities."

13. Jamie Peck and Heather Whiteside, "Financializing Detroit," *Economic Geography* 92, no. 3 (July 2, 2016): 235–68, https://doi.org/10.1080/00130095.2015.1116369; Jason Hackworth, "Defiant Neoliberalism and the Danger of Detroit," *Tijdschrift Voor Economische En*

Sociale Geografie 107, no. 5 (2016): 540–51, https://doi.org/10.1111/tesg.12184; Sarah Phinney, "Detroit's Municipal Bankruptcy and the Case of Austerity Urbanism" (Text, Ottawa, Carleton University, 2016), https://curve.carleton.ca/86ab5ae0-e23b-42dd-97fe-964ebb7ab61c; Terressa A. Benz, "Toxic Cities: Neoliberalism and Environmental Racism in Flint and Detroit Michigan," *Critical Sociology* 45, no. 1 (January 2019): 49–62, https://doi.org/10.1177/0896920517708339; Seth Schindler, "Detroit After Bankruptcy: A Case of *Degrowth Machine Politics*," *Urban Studies* 53, no. 4 (March 2016): 818–36, https://doi.org/10.1177/0042098014563485; David Fasenfest, "Social Sustainability and Urban Inequality: Detroit and the Ravages of Neoliberalism," in *Cities and Inequalities in a Global and Neoliberal World*, ed. Faranak Miraftab, David Wilson, and Ken Salo (London: Routledge, 2015), 15–27. A notable exception is Prentiss A. Dantzler, "The Urban Process under Racial Capitalism: Race, Anti-Blackness, and Capital Accumulation," *Journal of Race, Ethnicity and the City*, June 25, 2021, 1–22.

14. Byrd, "Variations Under Domestication, 130.

15. Aileen Moreton-Robinson, *The White Possessive: Property, Power, and Indigenous Sovereignty* (Minneapolis: University of Minnesota Press, 2016), 4. Rebecca J. Kinney, "'America's Great Comeback Story': The White Possessive in Detroit Tourism," *American Quarterly* 70, no. 4 (2018): 779.

16. N. D. B. Connolly, *A World More Concrete: Real Estate and the Making of Jim Crow South Florida* (Chicago: University of Chicago Press, 2014), 6.

17. "A Monument of Industry: An Unrivaled Cyclopedia of Detroit. Silas Farmer's Wonderful History." *Detroit Free Press*, December 1, 1884. ProQuest Historical Newspapers: Detroit Free Press (1831-1922).

18. George Galster, *Driving Detroit: The Quest for Respect in the Motor City* (Philadelphia: University of Pennsylvania Press, 2012), 6.

19. Thomas Sugrue, *The Origins of the Urban Crisis: Race Inequality in Post-War Detroit* (Princeton, NJ: Princeton University Press, 1996), 126.

20. Ibid.

21. Ibid., 156.

22. Colleen Doody, *Detroit's Cold War: The Origins of Postwar Conservatism* (Urbana: University of Illinois Press, 2013), 48.

23. Ira Katznelson, *When Affirmative Action Was White: An Untold History of Racial Inequality in America* (New York: Norton, 2006), 23.

24. Steve Babson, *Working Detroit: The Making of a Union Town* (Detroit, MI: Wayne State University Press, 1986); Richard Oestreicher, *Working People and Class Consciousness in Detroit, 1875-1900* (Urbana: University of Illinois Press, 1990); John Hartigan Jr., *Racial Situations: Class Predicaments of Whiteness in Detroit* (Princeton, NJ: Princeton University Press, 1999); Rebecca Kinney, *Beautiful Wasteland: The Rise of Detroit as America's Postindustrial Frontier* (Minneapolis: University of Minnesota Press, 2016); Karen R. Miller, *Managing Inequality: Northern Racial Liberalism in Interwar Detroit* (New York: New York University Press, 2015); Heather Thompson, *Whose Detroit? Politics, Labor, and Race in a Modern American City* (Ithaca, NY: Cornell University Press, 2004); Zaragosa Vargas, *Proletarians of the North: A History of Mexican Industrial Workers in Detroit and the Midwest, 1917-1933* (Berkeley: University of California Press, 1993); Sara Safransky, "Rethinking Land Struggle in the Postindustrial City," *Antipode* 49, no. 4 (2016): 1–22; B. J. Widick, *Detroit: City of Race and Class Violence* (Detroit, MI: Wayne State University Press, 1989).

25. Neil Smith, *The New Urban Frontier: Gentrification and the Revanchist City* (London: Routledge, 1996), xiv.

26. Ibid., xv.

27. The following are some of the studies I'm referring to: Jack O. Waddell and O. Michael Watson, eds., *The American Indian in Urban Society* (Boston: Little, Brown, 1971); Jeanne Guillemin, *Urban Renegades: The Cultural Strategy of American Indians* (New York: Columbia University Press, 1975); Sol Tax, "The Impact of Urbanization of American Indians," *Annals of the American Academy of Political Science*, vol. 436, American Indians Today (March 1978), 121–36; Nancy Shoemaker, "Urban Indians and Ethnic Choices: American Indians in Minneapolis, 1920–1950," *Western Historical Quarterly* 9, no. 4 (1988): 431–47; Edward Liebow, "Urban Indian Institutions in Phoenix: Transformation from Headquarters City to Community," *Journal of Ethnic Studies* 18 (Winter 1991): 1–28; Donald Fixico, *The Urban Indian Experience* (Albuquerque: University of New Mexico Press, 2000; David Beck, "Developing a Voice: The Evolution of Native American Self-Determination in an Urban Indian Community," *Wicazo Sa Review* 17, no. 2 (2002): 117–41; Susan Lobo, "Is Urban a Person or Place? Characteristics of Urban Indian Country," in *American Indians and the Urban Experience*, ed. Susan Lobo and Kurt Peters (Walnut Creek, CA: AltaMira Press, 2001).

28. Bonita Lawrence, *"Real" Indians and Others: Mixed-Blood Urban Native Peoples and Indigenous Nationhood* (Lincoln: University of Nebraska Press, 2004); Renya Ramirez, *Native Hubs: Culture, Community, and Belonging in Silicon Valley and Beyond* (Durham, NC: Duke University Press, 2007); Coll Thrush, *Native Seattle: Histories from the Crossing-Over Place* (Seattle: University of Washington Press, 2007); Heather Howard and Craig Proulx, eds., *Aboriginal Peoples in Canadian Cities: Transformations and Continuities* (Waterloo: Wilfrid Laurier University Press, 2011); Nicholas Rosenthal, *Reimagining Indian Country: Native Migration and Identity in Twentieth-Century Los Angeles* (Chapel Hill: University of North Carolina Press, 2012); Evelyn Peters and Chris Andersen, eds., *Indigenous in the City: Contemporary Identities and Cultural Innovation* (Vancouver: University of British Columbia Press, 2013); Chris Andersen, "Urban Landscapes of North America," in *The World of Indigenous North America*, ed. Robert Warrior (New York: Routledge, 2014), 149–70; Coll Thrush, *Indigenous London: Native Travellers at the Heart of Empire* (New Haven, CT: Yale University Press, 2016); Laura Furlan, *Indigenous Cities: Urban Indian Fiction and the Histories of Relocation* (Lincoln: University of Nebraska Press, 2017); Kent Blansett, *A Journey to Freedom: Richard Oakes, Alcatraz, and the Red Power Movement* (New Haven, CT: Yale University Press, 2018); Douglas K. Miller, *Indians on the Move: Native American Mobility and Urbanization in the Twentieth Century* (Chapel Hill: University of North Carolina Press, 2019); Dorries et al., *Settler City Limits*.

29. Although not about Indigenous peoples, Kelly Lytle Hernandez's book *City of Inmates: Conquest, Rebellion, and the Rise of Human Caging in Los Angeles, 1771–1965* (Chapel Hill: University of North Carolina Press, 2017) is important, for she uses settler colonialism as a framework for understanding incarceration in Los Angeles. This is an important step in bridging carceral studies and critical ethnic studies. Lytle Hernandez's work helps us think through how the logics of settler colonialism operate in cities.

30. Frantz Fanon, *The Wretched of the Earth* (New York: Grove Press, 2004), 171.

31. Philip Deloria, *Indians in Unexpected Places* (Lawrence: University Press of Kansas, 2004), 167–68.

32. Stuart Hall, "What Is 'Black' in Black Popular Culture?," in *Black Popular Culture*, ed. Gina Dent (New York: New Press, 1998), 32.

33. See Leanne Betasamosake Simpson, *As We Have Always Done: Indigenous Freedom Through Radical Resistance* (Minneapolis: University of Minnesota Press, 2017), 46–48. She writes

on radical resurgence that challenges settler colonialism. For freedom dreams, see Robin D. G. Kelley, *Freedom Dreams: The Black Radical Imagination* (Boston: Beacon Press, 2002).

34. Mark Rifkin, *Beyond Settler Time: Temporal Sovereignty and Indigenous Self-Determination* (Durham, NC: Duke University Press, 2017), viii.

Chapter 1

1. Frederic Baraga, *A Dictionary of the Otchipwe Language, Explained in English* (Cincinnati: Jos. A. Hermann, 1853). Hathi Trust Digital Library.

2. Clarence Burton, William Stocking, and Gordon Miller, eds., *The City of Detroit Michigan, 1701–1922*, vol. 1 (Detroit: S. J. Clarke Publishing Co., 1922), 40. According to Burton, the Huron called Detroit "karontaen," which meant "the coast of the straits."

3. Helen Hornbeck Tanner, "The Location of Indian Tribes in Southeastern Michigan and Northern Ohio," in *Indians of Northern Ohio and Southeastern Michigan* (New York: Garland Publishing, 1974), 326–27.

4. Richard White, *The Middle Ground: Indians, Empires, and Republics in the Great Lakes Region, 1650–1815* (New York: Cambridge University Press, 2011), 1–2. Chapter 1 tells the story of these encounters and conflicts between Algonquian and Haudenosaunee peoples.

5. Tanner, "The Location of Indian Tribes," 329.

6. For a summary of the uses and misuses of the Middle Ground thesis, see Andrew Lipman, "Reviews in American History," *Reviews in American History* 44, no. 1 (March 2016): 24–30.

For examples of how others have demonstrated the limits of the Middle Ground, see Robert Michael Morrissey, *Empire by Collaboration: Indians, Colonists, and Governments in Colonial Illinois Country* (Philadelphia: University of Pennsylvania Press, 2015); Brett Rushforth, *Bonds of Alliance: Indigenous and Atlantic Slavery in the New World* (Chapel Hill: University of North Carolina Press, 2012); and Kathleen DuVal, *The Native Ground: Indians and Colonists in the Heart of the Continent* (Philadelphia: University of Pennsylvania Press, 2007).

7. Richard White, *The Middle Ground: Indians, Empires, and Republics in the Great Lakes Region, 1650–1815* (New York: Cambridge University Press, 2011), xxvi–xxvii

8. Ibid., xxvi.

9. My only focus is on Detroit. However, the Treaty of Greenville (1795) really opened up Michigan and Ohio for further dispossession.

10. Peter Cozzens, *Tecumseh and the Prophet: The Shawnee Brothers Who Defied a Nation* (New York: Knopf, 2020).

11. See Jeremy Scahill, "Scholar Robin D. G. Kelley on How Today's Abolitionist Movement Can Fundamentally Change the Country," *The Intercept*, June 27, 2020, https://theintercept.com/2020/06/27/robin-dg-kelley-intercepted/. Accessed June 29, 2020.

12. Martin Case, *The Relentless Business of Treaties: How Indigenous Land Became U.S. Property* (St. Paul: Minnesota Historical Society Press, 2018), chap. 1, "Speculators: Territory: 1783–1800." Ebook.

13. Tiya Miles, *The Dawn of Detroit: A Chronicle of Slavery and Freedom in the City of the Straits*New York: New Press, 2017), 6. It is important to note that enslavement had been going on in the Great Lakes area and among Native people prior to European forms of enslavement. See Rushforth, *Bonds of Alliance*. There were qualitative differences, though. Native people took captives to replace those lost from families, whereas Europeans used chattel slavery for profit. However, this would change, especially in the southeast.

14. Miles, *Dawn of Detroit*, 2. See Rushforth, *Bonds of Alliance*, 276.

15. Rushforth, *Bonds of Alliance*, 276.

16. Edward Littlejohn, "Black Before the Bar: A History of Slavery, Race Laws, and Cases in Detroit and Michigan," *Journal of Law in Society* 18, no. 1 (Spring 2018): 41.

17. Karolyn Smardz Frost, "African American and African Canadian Transnationalism Along the Detroit River Borderland: The Example of Madison J. Lightfoot," *Journal of American Ethnic History* 32, no. 2 (2013): 80–81.

18. Karolyn Smardz Frost, *I've Got a Home in Glory Land: A Lost Tale of the Underground Railroad*, 1st ed. (New York: Farrar, Straus and Giroux, 2008), 189. See also Littlejohn, "Before the Bar," 41.

19. Constitution of Michigan of 1835, www.legislature.mi.gov/documents/historical /miconstitution1835.htm. Accessed October 30, 2020.

20. John N. Low, *Imprints: The Pokagon Band of Potawatomi Indians and the City of Chicago* (East Lansing: Michigan State University Press, 2016), 24–25.

21. Herb Boyd, *Black Detroit: A People's History of Self-Determination* (New York: Harper-Collins, 2017), 40–41.

22. Richard Thomas, *Life for Us Is What We Make It: Building Black Community in Detroit, 1915–1945* (Bloomington: Indiana University Press, 1992), 5.

23. "Indians," *Detroit Daily Free Press*, April 29, 1853.

24. Jean O'Brien, *Firsting and Lasting: Writing Indians Out of Existence in New England* (Minneapolis: University of Minnesota Press, 2010), xiii.

25. Friend Palmer, *Early Days in Detroit: Papers Written by General Friend Palmer of Detroit; Being His Personal Reminiscences of Important Events and Descriptions of the City for Over Eighty Years*, ed. H. P. Hunt and C. M. June (Detroit, MI: Hunt & June, 1906), 383.

26. Ibid., 17.

27. Ibid., 772.

28. Colleen Boyd and Coll Thrush, eds., *Phantom Past, Indigenous Presence: Native Ghosts in North American Culture and History* (Lincoln: University of Nebraska Press, 2011), ix.

29. Palmer, *Early Days in Detroit*, 772.

30. "Byron Farwell, "Black Hawk," in *The Encyclopedia of Nineteenth-Century Land Warfare: An Illustrated World View* (New York: Norton, 2001), 108.

31. Kerry Trask, *Black Hawk: The Battle for the Heart of America* (New York: Henry Holt, 2006).

32. Ibid., 219.

33. Sauk chief Black Hawk, *Autobiography of Ma-Ka-Tai-Me-She-Kia-Kiak, or Black Hawk* (Good Press, 2019), 82.

34. Trask, *Black Hawk*, 301.

35. Ibid., 302.

36. For an extensive history of Buffalo Bill's Wild West show and the experiences of Indigenous performers, see, L. G. Moses, *Wild West Shows and the Images of American Indians, 1883–1933*, 1st ed. (Albuquerque: University of New Mexico, 1996).

37. Philip Deloria, *Playing Indian* (New Haven: Yale University Press, 1998), 98.

38. Robert M. Utley, *Sitting Bull: The Life and Times of an American Patriot* (New York: Henry Holt, 2008), 265.

39. See, for example, James Joseph Buss, *Winning the West with Words: Language and Conquest in the Lower Great Lakes* (Norman: University of Oklahoma Press, 2011).

40. "The Indian General, Buffalo Bill's Company and Sitting Bull Reach Detroit: Sitting Bull Receives Mayor Grummond and Other Dignitaries," *Detroit Free Press* (Detroit, MI, September 5, 1885), 4.

41. Linda Scarangella McNenly, *Native Performers in Wild West Shows: From Buffalo Bill to Euro Disney* (Norman: University of Oklahoma Press, 2012). McNenly argues, "Wild West shows were also nation-building projects in that they shaped the construction of American identity and attempted to define, situate, and justify the place of Native peoples in America" (71).

42. "The Indian General," *Detroit Free Press*, September 5, 1885.

43. See C. Joseph Genetin-Pilawa, *Crooked Paths to Allotment: The Fight over Federal Indian Policy After the Civil War* (Chapel Hill: University of North Carolina Press, 2012), 28, and Frederick Hoxie, *This Indian Country: American Indian Political Activism and the Place They Made* (New York: Penguin, 2012).

44. "The Indian General," *Detroit Free Press*, September 5, 1885, 4

45. Ibid.

46. Ibid.

47. McNenly, *Native Performers in Wild West Shows.*

48. "Old Relics: Some Valuable Remembrances of the Indian Chief 'Pontiac,'" *Detroit Free Press*, February 4, 1872.

49. "The City of Pontiac: No Other Michigan Community Has Brighter Prospects," *Detroit Free Press*, April 9, 1899, sec. C.

50. Henry J. Richmond, "Apple Island: Home of Pontiac Conspirator: Legends Concerning the Death and Burial of the Great Chief Who Once Territorialized All Michigan; The Sacred Place of the Red Men; Is the Big Mound a Tomb?" *Detroit News-Tribune*, August 3, 1913.

51. Karen Marrero, "Founding Families: Power and Authority of Mixed French and Native Lineages in Eighteenth-Century Detroit" (Ph.D. diss., Yale University, 2011), 52. Marrero's book *Detroit's Hidden Channels: The Power of French-Indigenous Families in the Eighteenth Century* (East Lansing: Michigan State University Press, 2020) is more focused on the families and less on people like Burton.

52. Clarence Burton, *Journal of Pontiac's Conspiracy*, ed. M. Agnes Burton (Detroit: Speaker-Hines Print Co., 1912).

53. "Who Was Silas Farmer?" Night Train to Detroit, nighttraintodetroit.com/2010/01/20/who-was-silas-farmer.

54. Silas Farmer, *The History of Detroit and Michigan: Or, The Metropolis Illustrated; a Chronological Cyclopedia of the Past and Present, Including a Full Record of Territorial Days in Michigan, and the Annals of Wayne County* (Detroit: Silas Farmer & Co., 1884); Silas Farmer, *All About Detroit: An Illustrated Guide, Map, and Historical Souvenir, with Local Stories* (Detroit: Silas Farmer & Co., 1899). See also Silas Farmer, *Detroit Past and Present, or 1870 vs. 1890* (Detroit: Preston National Bank, 1890).

55. Silas Farmer, C. L. Arnold, Mary Catharine Crowley, Clarence Burton, and A. H. Griffith., eds., *The Bi-Centenary of the Founding of Detroit, 1701–1901: Being the Official Celebration of July 24, 25, 26, 1901*. Issued Under Direction of the Common Council of the City of Detroit (Detroit: Chas. M. Rousseau & Sons, 1902).

56. I used historical search engines of the *Detroit Free Press* and the *Detroit News*, as well as one on historical newspapers. While constrained by the time period of the digital repository, it does present an important case for exploring how indigeneity functioned at the key point of city development.

57. "The Box," *Detroit Free Press,* October 6, 1900.

58. Historiographer, "Historical Notes—No. XVIII: That Old Pontiac Tree," *Detroit Free Press,* March 6, 1881.

59. U.S. Census.

60. "Historical Event: Unveiling of Tablet on Site of Old Fort," *Detroit Free Press,* November30, 1899.

61. "Pontiac's Conspiracy: Tablet Commemorative of Its Defeat Unveiled Some of the American Revolution," *Parsons Weekly Blade* (Kansas), December 1, 1899.

62. Farmer et al., *The Bi-Centenary,* 12, 14.

63. Sidney Olson, *Young Henry Ford: A Picture History of the First Forty Years* (Detroit, MI: Wayne State University Press, 1963), 115.

64. Coll Thrush, "Monument, Mobility, and Modernity; or, The Sachem of Southwark and Other Surprising Commemorations," *Ethnohistory* 61, no. 4 (Fall 2014): 609.

65. Ibid.

66. Scott Morgensen, "Cutting to the Roots of Colonial Masculinity," in *Indigenous Men and Masculinities: Legacies, Identities, Regeneration,* ed. Robert Alexander Innes and Kim Anderson (Winnipeg: University of Manitoba Press, 2015), 38–61.

67. Kristin Hoganson, *Fighting for American Manhood: How Gender Politics Provoked the Spanish-American and Philippine Wars* (New Haven, CT: Yale University Press, 1998).

68. David Katzman, *Before the Ghetto: Black Detroit in the Nineteenth Century* (Urbana: University of Illinois Press, 1973).

69. For a discussion of the history of the noble savage, see Robert Berkhofer Jr., *The White Man's Indian: Images of the American Indian from Columbus to the Present* (New York: Vintage, 1979), 73–80.

70. Fred Carlisle, *Wayne County Chronography of Notable Events in the History of the Northwest Territory and Wayne County: Period Embraced, 1531–1890; Together with Biographical Sketches of the Early Explorers and Pioneers.* (Detroit: O. S. Gulley, Borman & Co. Printers, 1890).

71. William Curtis, "Pontiac's Grave: Wm. E. Curtis Tells of Senator Palmer's Mound," *Detroit Free Press,* August 8, 1901.

72. Ibid.

73. "Ex-Senator Palmer at Home: How Detroit's Distinguished Citizen Passes His Resting Days After Busy Public Life," *Detroit Free Press,* December 4, 1904.

74. "Indians Wednesday A.M.," *Detroit Free Press,* July 23, 1901.

75. Deloria, *Playing Indian,* 5.

76. William R. Nester, *"Haughty Conquerors": Amherst and the Great Indian Uprising of 1763* (Westport, CT: Praeger, 2000), 283.

77. For an example of this longstanding perspective, see Anthony F. C. Wallace, *Jefferson and the Indians: The Tragic Fate of the First Americans* (Cambridge, MA: Belknap Press, 1999).

78. Edward Said, *Orientalism* (New York: Vintage, 1979), 55.

79. Henry J. Richmond, "Apple Island: Home of Pontiac Conspirator: Legends Concerning the Death and Burial of the Great Chief Who Once Territorialized All Michigan; The Sacred Place of the Red Men; Is the Big Mound a Tomb?," *Detroit News Tribune,* August 3, 1913.

80. Ibid.

81. Ibid.

82. Coll Thrush, "Hauntings as Histories: Indigenous Ghosts and the Urban Past in Seattle," in *Phantom Past, Indigenous Presence: Native Ghosts in North American Culture and History,* ed. Colleen Boyd and Coll Thrush (Lincoln: University of Nebraska Press, 2011), 76.

83. "Indians Will Assail Detroit: Attack by Pontiac and His Redskins Will Be Feature of Cadillaqua Celebration," *Detroit Free Press*, April 23, 1912.

84. Ibid.

85. "Historical Floats—Cadillaqua: Detroit in Its Infancy Looking Back into the Silent Past," *Detroit Free Press*, July 21, 1912.

86. Charles Ward, "If Pontiac Should Come to Detroit in 1918," *Detroit Free Press*, December 9, 1917.

87. Ibid.

88. Ibid.

89. Ibid.

90. Ibid.

91. Ibid.

92. Beatrice Bigony, "A Brief History of Native Americans in Detroit," *Michigan History* 67, no. 2 (Summer 1977): 161.

93. Bruce Braun, *The Intemperate Rainforest: Nature, Culture and Power on Canada's West Coast* (Minneapolis: University of Minnesota Press, 2002), 8.

94. "Excursion on the Morning Star: Walpole Island and Its Inhabitants," *Detroit Free Press*, June 20, 1867.

95. Mishuana Goeman, "Land as Life: Unsettling the Logics of Containment," in *Native Studies Keywords*, ed. Stephanie Nohelani Teves, Andrea Smith, and Michelle Raheja (Tucson: University of Arizona Press, 2015), 73.

96. Ibid.

97. "Another Double Sheet Next Sunday," *Detroit Free Press*, September 13, 1874, ProQuest Historical Newspapers: Detroit Free Press (1831–22).

98. "Sayings and Doings," *Detroit Free Press*, December 9, 1874, ProQuest Historical Newspapers: Detroit Free Press (1831–22).

99. "20 Lo's from Canada visit Detroit," *Detroit Free Press*, June 2, 1875.

100. "Indian Chief Waylays Palefaces' Street Cars," *Detroit Free Press*, November 6, 1913.

101. "Claim Island: Walpole Chippewas Declare That Detroit's Famous Playground Belongs to Them," *Detroit Free Press*, April 8, 1906.

102. Ibid.

103. Ibid.

104. Claudio Saunt, "Telling Stories: The Political Uses of Myth and History in the Cherokee and Creek Nations," *Journal of American History* 93, no. 3 (December 2006): 676.

105. Miles, *The Dawn of Detroit*.

106. Ibid., 17. Miles notes that there were three categories of enslaved people: "those possessed by the French and their Indian allies, those owned by British officers and businessmen, and those held during the period of American occupation and settlement prior to Michigan statehood" (17–18).

107. "Alcoholism Kills Josephine Kidroe: Negro-Indian Woman Who Held Long Police Record Is Dead," *Detroit Free Press*, October 31, 1906.

108. Forrester B. Washington, "The Detroit Newcomers' Greeting," in *The Survey: Social, Charitable, Civic: A Journal of Constructive Philanthropy* (Charity Organization Society of the City of New York, 1917), 334.

109. Richard Thomas, *Life for Us Is What We Make It: Building Black Community in Detroit, 1915–1945* (Bloomington: Indiana University Press, 1992).

110. "Walpole Island Injun Is Eager to See Real War: Comes to Detroit to See Redskins Battle Cowboys in Moving Picture Show," *Detroit Free Press*, December 20, 1912.

111. Khalil Gibran Muhammad, *The Condemnation of Blackness: Race, Crime, and the Making of Modern Urban America* (Cambridge, MA: Harvard University Press, 2010), 4-5.

112. Miles, *The Dawn of Detroit.*

113. Sarah Haley, *No Mercy Here: Gender, Punishment, and the Making of Jim Crow Modernity* (Chapel Hill: University of North Carolina Press, 2016), 35.

114. Kali N. Gross, *Colored Amazons: Crime, Violence, and Black Women in the City of Brotherly Love, 1880-1910*, (Durham, NC: Duke University Press, 2006), 4.

115. Ibid., 4.

116. Haley, *No Mercy Here*, 10.

117. Cathy Cohen, "Punks, Bulldaggers, and Welfare Queens: The Radical Potential of Queer Politics," *GLQ: A Journal of Lesbian and Gay Studies* 3 (1997): 437–65. A classic essay, I think one of the important arguments that Cohen offers for Josephine Kidroe is that her being Black and Indigenous in Detroit is a marginalized, nonnormative identity, and one in which she had to deal with multiple oppressions. Though documentation is scant, I believe that Kidroe suffered marginalization and political discrimination for the simple fact of being of these two heritages, and she was ostracized by both Black people and Indigenous people.

118. Melissa Harris-Perry, *Sister Citizen: Shame, Stereotypes, and Black Women in America* (New Haven, CT: Yale University Press, 2011), 55.

119. Ibid.

120. Victoria Wolcott, "The Culture of the Informal Economy: Numbers Runners in Inter-War Black Detroit," *Radical History Review*, Fall 1997, 46–75.

121. Katherine McKittrick, *Demonic Grounds: Black Women and the Cartographies of Struggle* (Minneapolis: University of Minnesota Press, 2006), xiii.

Chapter 2

1. George Cortelyou, "Detroit's Biggest Parade," *Detroit Free Press*, July 13, 1901.

2. See S. M. Barrett, *Geronimo's Story of His Life* (1906). Digital Reprint.

3. David Roediger, *The Wages of Whiteness: Race and the Making of the American Working Class* (New York: Verso, 1991), 124. Cheryl Harris, "Whiteness as Property," *Harvard Law Review* 106, no. 8 (1993): 1714-16.

4. Jean O'Brien, *Firsting and Lasting: Writing Indians Out of Existence in New England* (Minneapolis: University of Minnesota Press, 2010), xv.

5. Kevin Bruyneel, "Codename Geronimo: Settler Memory and the Production of American Statism," *Settler Colonial Studies* 6, no. 4 (October 2016): 351.

6. There is a host of literature on world's fairs and how they promoted empire and U.S. cultural imperialism. Robert W. Rydell, *All the World's a Fair: Visions of Empire at American International Expositions, 1876-1916* (Chicago: University of Chicago Press, 1987); Adria L. Imada, *Aloha America: Hula Circuits Through the U.S. Empire* (Durham, NC: Duke University Press, 2012); John E. Findling, *Chicago's Great World's Fairs* (New York: St. Martin's, 1994); John E. Findling and Kimberly D. Pelle, eds., *Encyclopedia of World's Fairs and Expositions* (Jefferson, NC: McFarland & Co., 2008); TJ Boisseau and Abigail M. Markwyn, eds., *Gendering the Fair: Histories of Women and Gender at World's Fairs* (Urbana: University of Illinois Press, 2010); Jim Zwick, *Inuit Entertainers in the United States: From the Chicago World's Fair Through the Birth of Hollywood.* (West Conshohocken, PA: Infinity Publishing Co., 2006); Mabel Wilson, *Negro Building: Black Americans in the*

World of Fairs and Museums (Berkeley: University of California Press, 2012). Settlers celebrating their past were also an important part in other settler places such as South Africa. See Ciraj Rassool and Leslie Witz, "The 1952 Jan Van Riebeeck Tercentenary Festival: Constructing and Contesting Public National History in South Africa," *Journal of African History* 34, no. 3 (Nov. 1993): 447–68.

7. Jane Jacobs, *Edge of Empire: Postcolonialism and the City* (London: Routledge, 1996), 159.

8. G. Wayne Miller, *Car Crazy: The Battle for Supremacy Between Ford and Olds and the Dawn of the Automobile Age* (New York: PublicAffairs, 2015), 14.

9. Silas Farmer, C. L. Arnold, Mary Catharine Crowley, Clarence Burton, A. H. Griffith, eds., *The Bi-Centenary of the Founding of Detroit, 1701–1901: Being the Official Celebration of July 24, 25, 26, 1901. Issued Under Direction of the Common Council of the City of Detroit* (Detroit, MI: Chas. M. Rousseau & Sons, 1902), 12.

10. Ibid., 14.

11. Ibid.

12. Ibid., 17.

13. Ibid.

14. "50 Indians for Bicentenary," *Detroit Free Press*, June 6, 1901.

15. To be clear, this makes sense on many levels, with massive amounts of immigration from Europe over the past twenty to thirty or more years. However, Detroit's manufacturing boom was just on the horizon, and European immigrants wanted a chance to make it big. Contrary to a pervasive belief, English has never been the official language of the United States.

16. Khalil Gibran Muhammad, *The Condemnation of Blackness: Race, Crime, and the Making of Modern Urban America* (Cambridge, MA: Harvard University Press, 2010), 4.

17. A. J. Stovall, *The Growth of Black Elected Officials in the City of Detroit, 1870–1973* (Lewiston, NY: Mellen University Press, 1996), 29.

18. "150,000 People Saw Yesterday's Parade," *Evening News Detroit*, July 26, 1901.

19. Stovall, *The Growth of Black Elected Officials*, 3.

20. Richard Thomas, *Life for Us Is What We Make It: Building Black Community in Detroit, 1915–1945* (Bloomington: Indiana University Press, 1992). Veta Smith Tucker, "Uncertain Freedom in Frontier Detroit," in *A Fluid Frontier: Slavery, Resistance, and the Underground Railroad in the Detroit River Borderland*, ed. Veta Smith Tucker and Karolyn Smardz (Detroit, MI: Wayne State University Press, 2016).

21. "Colored Men Suggest Tablets: Mark the House in Which Harper's Ferry Raid Was Planned," *Detroit Free Press*, May 26, 1901.

22. Wilma Wood Hendrickson, ed., *Detroit Perspectives: Crossroads and Turning Points* (Detroit, MI: Wayne State University Press, 1991), 255. This excerpt is from Forrester Washington, "History," in *The Negro in Detroit: A Survey in the Conditions of a Negro Group in a Northern Industrial Center During the War Prosperity Period* (Detroit, MI: Associated Charities, 1920).

23. Thomas, *Life for Us Is What We Make It*, 10–12.

24. Ibid., 17.

25. Hendrickson, *Detroit Perspectives*, 255.

26. "Colored Men Protesting: Will Not Take Part as Such in the Bicentennial; Union Men Withdraw from Committee; Allege That the Color Line Has Been Drawn," *Detroit Free Press*, May 23, 1901.

27. "Courteous to State Officials: Bicentenary Committee Will Not Return; Colored People Not Slighted," *Detroit Free Press*, May 24, 1901.

28. Ibid.

29. Ibid.

30. Ibid.

31. Ibid.

32. "Colored Men Protesting," *Detroit Free Press*, May 23, 1901.

33. "Colored Men Suggest Tablets," *Detroit Free Press*, May 26, 1901.

34. Ibid.

35. "Indians Wednesday A.M.," *Detroit Free Press*, July 23, 1901. This person's name was B. Baptiste and was said to have worked for the U.S. railroad.

36. "The Landing of Cadillac," *Detroit News-Tribune*, July 24, 1901.

37. Ibid.

38. Ibid.

39. Ibid.

40. Ibid.

41. Helen Hornbeck Tanner, "The Location of Indian Tribes in Southeastern Michigan and Northern Ohio," in *Indians of Northern Ohio and Southeastern Michigan* (New York: Garland, 1974), 327.

42. "Nations Passed in Review," *Detroit Free Press*, July 26, 1901.

43. "Cadillac Receives Keys to the City: Mayor Maybury Bids Him Again to Resume His Rule Over the City He Founded," *Detroit Free Press*, July 25, 1901.

44. Ibid.

45. Ibid.

46. Ibid.

47. Ibid.

48. Ibid.

49. Anne McClintock, *Imperial Leather: Race, Gender and Sexuality in the Colonial Contest* (New York and London: Routledge, 1995), 29.

50. Aldo Rossi, *The Architecture of the City* (Cambridge, MA: MIT Press, 1999), 24.

51. Farmer, *The Bi-Centenary*, 292.

52. Ibid.

53. Ibid., 294.

54. Karen Marrero, *Detroit's Hidden Channels: The Power of French-Indigenous Families in the Eighteenth Century* (Winnipeg: University of Manitoba Press, 7–8.

55. McClintock, *Imperial Leather*, 26.

56. John Hartigan Jr., *Racial Situations: Class Predicaments of Whiteness in Detroit* (Princeton, NJ: Princeton University Press, 1999).

57. "Cadillac Chair Will Be Removed," *Detroit Free Press*, February 22, 1905, p. 12.

58. "Sleuth Discovers Cadillac's Chair," *Detroit Free Press*, September 11, 1921 p. 44.

59. "Cadillac's Chair Going to Oblivion," *Detroit Free Press*, October 22, 1941, p. 15. For more information, see Dan Austin, *Forgotten Landmarks of Detroit* (Charleston, SC: History Press, 2012), 146.

60. "Detroit's Bicentenary Celebration Programme," *Detroit Free Press*, July 20, 1901.

61. Susan Davis, *Parades and Power: Street Theatre in Nineteenth-Century Philadelphia* (Philadelphia: Temple University Press, 1986), 5.

62. Farmer, *The Bi-Centenary*, 17–19.

63. William Maybury, *Fifth Annual Message of William C. Maybury Mayor of Detroit to the Common Council* (Detroit: Thos. Smith Press, 1902).

64. In 2001, Detroit celebrated the 300th-year founding of the city. Legendary singer and songwriter Stevie Wonder headlined the event with a concert. Elliott Wells-Reid, "Tricentennial Celebration," *The Michigan Daily*, July 22, 2001, http://www.michigandaily.com/uncategorized/tricentennial-celebration/. Accessed July 3, 2021.

65. Farmer, *The Bi-Centenary*, 9–10.

66. "Money Left Over: Probable Financial Result of the Bicentenary," *Detroit Free Press*, July 28, 1901.

67. *Detroit Bicentenary*, 11.

Chapter 3

1. Antonio Gramsci, "Americanism and Fordism," in *The Gramsci Reader*, ed. David Forgacs (New York: New York University Press, 2000), 278–80.

2. Ibid.

3. Beth Bates, *The Making of Black Detroit in the Age of Henry Ford* (Chapel Hill: University of North Carolina Press, 2012), 26–27.

4. Kevin Whalen, *Native Students at Work: American Indian Labor and Sherman Institute's Outing Program, 1900–1945* (Seattle: University of Washington Press, 2016). Whalen demonstrates that students did, however, manipulate the meaning of the work and used it to travel, to make money, and to provide a general sense of freedom.

5. Bates, *The Making of Black Detroit*, 16–21. Coleman A. Young, Detroit's first Black mayor, was a member of one of the families who came to Detroit in 1923. His family, like others, moved to Detroit for better opportunities.

6. Ulysses W. Boykin, *A Hand Book on the Detroit Negro* (Detroit, MI: The Minority Study Associates, 1943), https://catalog.hathitrust.org/Record/001874776, 15. Accessed Jul 4, 2021.

7. Sarah Haley, *No Mercy Here: Gender, Punishment, and the Making of Jim Crow Modernity* (Chapel Hill: University of North Carolina Press, 2016).

8. Darlene Clark Hine, *Hine Sight: Black Women and the Re-Construction of American History* Bloomington: Indiana University Press, 1997), 89, 90. For a history of young Black girls' experience during the great migration, see, Marcia Chatelain, *South Side Girls: Growing Up in the Great Migration* (Durham, NC: Duke University Press, 2015).

9. Katherine J. Curtis White, "Women in the Migration: Economic Activity of Black and White Southern-Born Female Migrants in 1920, 1940, and 1970," *Social Science History* 29, no. 3 (September 2005): 418.

10. Boykin, *A Hand Book on the Detroit Negro*, 53–54.

11. Ibid., 96.

12. Victoria Wolcott, "The Culture of the Informal Economy: Numbers Runners in Inter-War Black Detroit," *Radical History Review*, Fall 1997, 64.

13. Darlene Clark Hine, "African American Women and Their Communities in the Twentieth Century: The Foundation and Future of Black Women's Studies," *Black Women Gender + Families* 1, no. 1 (Spring 2007): 131.

14. William A. Sundstrom, "Last Hired, First Fired? Unemployment and Urban Black Workers During the Great Depression," *Journal of Economic History* 52, no. 2 (June 1992): 415–29, https://doi.org/10.1017/S0022050700010834.

15. Frederick Hoxie, *A Final Promise: The Campaign to Assimilate the Indians* (Lincoln: University of Nebraska Press, 2001).

16. Richard H. Pratt, "The Advantages of Mingling Indians with Whites," in *Writings by the "Friends of the Indian,"* ed. Francis Paul Prucha (Cambridge, MA: Harvard University Press, 1973), 261.

17. Ziibiwing Center Project Team, "American Indian Boarding Schools" (Mt. Pleasant, MI: Ziibiwing Center of Anishinabe Culture and Lifeways, 2011), 10.

18. Ibid., 11.

19. Brenda Childs, *Boarding School Seasons: American Indian Families, 1900–1940* (Lincoln: University of Nebraska Press, 2000), see introduction.

20. For a brief discussion of the differences between the SAI and African American uplift organizations, see Lucy Maddox, *Citizen Indians: Native American Intellectuals, Race, and Reform* (Ithaca, NY: Cornell University Press, 2006), chap. 2, "General Principles and Universal Interests: The Politics of Reform," 74–78. Here, Maddox argues that because the United States treated Blacks and Native people as so different from each other, their collaboration was unlikely.

21. Hazel Hertzberg, *The Search for an American Indian Identity: Modern Pan-Indian Movements* (Syracuse, NY: Syracuse University Press, 1971).

22. Philip Deloria, "Four Thousand Invitations," *American Indian Quarterly* 37, no. 3 (Summer 2013): 27.

23. Fayette McKenzie to W. E. B. Du Bois, January 9, 1904, in Aptheker.

24. Kevin Gaines, *Uplifting the Race: Black Leadership, Politics and Culture in the Twentieth Century* (Chapel Hill, NC: University of North Carolina Press, 1996), xiv.

25. Frederick E. Hoxie, *This Indian Country: American Indian Political Activism and the Place They Made* (New York: Penguin, 2012), 226.

26. Cristina Stanciu, "Americanization on Native Terms: The Society of American Indians, Citizenship Debates, and Tropes of 'Racial Difference,'" *Native American and Indigenous Studies Journal* 6, no. 1 (May 2019): 112.

27. Ibid.

28. Society of American Indians, *Constitution and By-Laws: The Society of American Indians* (Washington DC, 1916), 4. Lawrence Revision.

29. Kyle T. Mays, "Transnational Progressivism: African Americans, Native Americans, and the Universal Races Congress of 1911," *American Indian Quarterly* 37, no. 3 (Summer 2013).

30. Deloria, "Four Thousand Invitations," 35.

31. Karen R. Miller, *Managing Inequality: Northern Racial Liberalism in Interwar Detroit* (New York: New York University Press, 2015), 4.

32. Stanciu, "Americanization on Native Terms," 125. For a history of the peyote movement, see Thomas C. Maroukis, *The Peyote Road: Religious Freedom and the Native American Church* (Norman: University of Oklahoma Press, 2010).

33. Deloria, "Four Thousand Invitations," 30.

34. "Famous Folks," *Detroit News*, October 24, 1921, p. 16.

35. Zitkala Ša, "Zitkala Ša on the Paris Peace Conference, 1919," in *Talking Back to Civilization*, ed. Frederick Hoxie (Boston: Bedford St./Martin's, 2001), 129–30.

36. "Indians Open Big Pow-Wow: International Convention to Ask U.S. to Educate Reds with Whites," *Detroit News*, October 25, 1921.

37. "American Indians, Convening in Detroit, Object to the Way They Are Characterized in the Movies and Say They Are Not Wild," *Detroit News*, October 28, 1921.

38. "Indians Open Big Pow-Wow, *Detroit News*, October 25, 1921.

39. Ibid.

40. Ibid.

41. Ibid.

42. Ibid.

43. "On Assimilation Lo," *Detroit News*, October 30, 1921.

44. Ibid.

45. Ibid.

46. Philip Deloria, *Playing Indian* (New Haven, CT: Yale University Press, 1998), 4.

47. "Doctor Declares Modern Training Is Bad for White Men and Worse for Indians." *Detroit News*, October 28, 1921.

48. Ibid.

49. Hoxie, *This Indian Country*, 273.

50. K. Tsianina Lomawaima, "The Society of American Indians," American History, Oxford Research Encyclopedias. http://americanhistory.oxfordre.com/view/10.1093/acrefore/9780199329175.001.0001/acrefore-9780199329175-e-31. Accessed August 17, 2016.

51. Fayette McKenzie to Arthur C. Parker, October 31, 1911. Papers of the Society of American Indians, The Newberry Library, Chicago, Illinois.

52. David Martinez, *Dakota Philosopher: Charles Eastman and American Indian Thought* (Minneapolis: Minnesota Historical Society Press, 2009), xi.

53. Mark Rifkin, *When Did Indians Become Straight? Kinship, the History of Sexuality, and Native Sovereignty*, 1st ed. (New York: Oxford University Press, 2011), 8.

54. "Manhood," *Detroit Free Press*, May 21, 1899, ProQuest Historical Newspapers: Detroit Free Press (1831–1922).

55. Brendan Hokowhitu, "Producing Elite Indigenous Masculinities," *Settler Colonial Studies* 2, no. 2 (2012): 29.

56. Mays, "Transnational Progressivism, 243–61.

57. Charles Eastman, *From Deep Woods to Civilization* (Boston: Little, Brown, and Rowfield, 1916), 187.

58. Charles Eastman, "Opening Address," *American Indian*, October 2, 1921, 145.

59. Ibid., 147.

60. Ibid.

61. Gail Bederman, *Manliness and Civilization: A Cultural History of Gender and Race in the United States, 1880–1917* (Chicago: University of Chicago Press, 1995), 27.

62. Charles Eastman, *The Soul of the Indian* (New York: Johnson Reprint Corporation, 1971), 105–6.

63. Ibid.

64. Ibid., 114–15.

65. Eastman, "Opening Address," 149.

66. Hokowhitu, "Elite Indigenous Masculinities," 33.

67. Ibid., 146.

68. Raymond Wilson, *Ohiyesa: Charles Eastman, Santee Sioux* (Urbana: University of Illinois Press, 1983), 176.

69. Theodore D. Sargent, *The Life of Elaine Goodale Eastman* (Lincoln: University of Nebraska Press, 2005), 106.

70. Charles Eastman, "Indians as Citizens," Comment and Opinion on Topics of Today, *Detroit Free Press*, April 8, 1906.

71. Ibid., 130.

72. Wilson, *Ohiyesa*, 190.

73. Nina Mjagkij, *Light in the Darkness: African Americans and the YMCA, 1852–1946* (Lexington: University Press of Kentucky, 1994), 17.

74. Ibid., 50.

75. Ibid., 36–39.

76. Ibid., 126–27.

77. A. G. Struder, *One Hundred Years with Youth: The Story of the Detroit YMCA, 1852–1952.*

78. Ibid., 1.

79. See Karen Marrero, *Detroit's Hidden Channels: The Power of French-Indigenous Families in the Eighteenth Century* (Winnipeg: University of Manitoba Press), 1–20. In this book, Marrero skillfully illustrates how gender and Indigenous French families were central to the creation of Detroit.

80. Ibid., 37–38.

81. Ibid.

82. Ibid., 7.

83. Ibid., 159.

84. Paula Lupkin, *Manhood Factories: YMCA Architecture and the Making of Modern Urban Culture* (Minneapolis, MN: University of Minnesota Press, 2003), xvi.

85. Ibid.

86. Struder, *One Hundred Years with Youth,* 94.

87. Ibid.

88. Ibid.

89. Wilson, Ohiyesa, 88.

90. Lupkin, *Manhood Factories*, 182.

91. "Y Friendly Indians to Indulge in Pow-Wow," *Detroit Free Press*, May 17, 1931.

92. "Father-Son-Week Plans Accepted: 'Boy Problem' to Be Given Close Study Feb. 6–26," *Detroit Free Press*, January 24, 1930.

93. "Y to Celebrate 66th Anniversary: National President to Appear on Program Thursday Night," *Detroit Free Press*, February 2, 1930, p. 12.

94. "68th Annual Report of the Detroit Young Men's Christian Association," January-December, 1932, Box 1. Detroit YMCA Administrative Annual Reports, 1930–1935, Bentley Historical Library, University of Michigan.

95. Kiara M. Vigil, "Charles Eastman's 'School of the Woods': Re-Creation Related to Childhood, Race, Gender, and Nation at Camp Oahe," *American Quarterly* 70, no. 1 (2018): 27.

96. Deloria, *Playing Indian*, 101.

97. Ibid.

98. Gore, "Sitting Bull's Follower," *Detroit Free Press*, July 17, 1932.

99. Charles A. Eastman, *Indian Scout Craft and Lore* (formerly titled *Indian Scout Talks*), (New York: Dover Publications, 1974), 1–2.

100. "Spirit of Indian Days Seen in Fine Pageant Enacted by Kiddies for Red Cross," *Detroit Free Press*, August 25, 1918, ProQuest Historical Newspapers: Detroit Free Press (1831–1922).

101. "Chief Will Attend 'Y' Camp Opening: Ohiyesa Arrives June 22 in Full Indian Dress," *Detroit News*, June 13, 1936, p. 5.

102. "YMCA Show to Depict Past: Benefits of Joining to Be Stressed," *Detroit News*, February 17, 1935. p. 13.

103. "Michigan Indians Before the coming of French Settlers," *Detroit News*, May 14, 1938.

104. Jackson D. Haag, "Chief Ohiyesa Visits Detroit: Sioux Leader a Doctor, His Son a Detroiter, Indian Race Changing," *Detroit News*, December 31, 1939.

105. Ibid.

106. "Indian Chief Is Dead at 80: Dr. Eastman (Ohiyesa) Was Writer, Lecturer," *Detroit News*, January 9, 1939; Wilson, *Ohiyesa*, 188.

107. Martinez, *Dakota Philosopher*, 6.

108. Philip Deloria, *Indians in Unexpected Places* (Lawrence, KS: University Press of Kansas, 2004), 238.

Chapter 4

1. Michael C. Dawson, *Black Visions: The Roots of Contemporary African-American Political Ideologies* (Chicago: University of Chicago Press, 2003), 21, 85–86. See also Tony N. Brown, Ebony M. Duncan, and Heather Hensman Kettrey, "Black Nationalist Tendencies and Their Association with Perceived Inefficacy of the Civil Rights Movement and of Black Elected Officials," *Sociology of Race and Ethnicity* 3, no. 2 (April 1, 2017): 188–201.

2. Keisha N. Blain, "'For the Rights of Dark People in Every Part of the World': Pearl Sherrod, Black Internationalist Feminism, and Afro-Asian Politics During the 1930s," *Souls: A Critical Journal of Black Politics, Culture, and Society* 17, nos. 1–2 (June 2015): 90–112. See also Daryl Michael Scott, "How Black Nationalism Became Sui Generis," *Fire!!!* 1, no. 2 (Summer 2012): 6–63; and J. Herman Blake, "Black Nationalism," *Annals of the American Academy of Political and Social Science* 382 (March 1969): 15–25.

3. Alex Zamalin, *Black Utopia: The History of an Idea from Black Nationalism to Afrofuturism* (New York: Columbia University Press, 2019), 5–7.

4. Judith Weisenfeld, *New World A-Coming: Black Religion and Racial Identity During the Great Migration* (New York: NYU Press, 2017), 67–69.

5. Ibid., 46–53.

6. Ibid., 24–25.

7. Beth Bates, "'Double V for Victory' Mobilizes Black Detroit, 1941–1946," in *Freedom North: Black Freedom Struggles Outside the South, 1940–1980*, ed. Jeanne Theoharis and Komozi Woodard, (New York: Palgrave Macmillan, 2003), 133.

8. Renya Ramirez, *Native Hubs: Culture, Community, and Belonging in Silicon Valley and Beyond* (Durham, NC: Duke University Press, 2007), 3.

9. Megan Shockley, "Working for Democracy: Working-Class African-American Women, Citizenship, and Civil Rights in Detroit, 1940–1954," *Michigan Historical Review* 29, no. 2 (Fall 2003): 128.

10. Bates, "'Double V for Victory,'" 21.

11. See Keisha N. Blain, *Set the World on Fire: Black Nationalist Women and the Global Struggle for Freedom* (Philadelphia: University of Pennsylvania Press, 2018), 12–13. Blain does an exceptional job explaining the unique and ongoing labor of Black women in the UNIA, as well as in other Black Nationalist and diasporic groups during the early part of the twentieth century. Erik McDuffie, "'A New Day Has Dawned for the UNIA': Garveyism, the Diasporic Midwest, and West Africa, 1920–80," *Journal of West African History* 2, no. 1 (2016): 104, https://doi.org/10.14321/jwestafrihist.2.1.0073. For a full discussion of the life of William Sherrill, who was a prominent activist, and his role in developing the UNIA, see Kenneth S. Jolly, *By Our Own Strength: William Sherrill, the UNIA, and the Fight for African American Self-Determination in Detroit*, 1st ed. (New York: Peter Lang, 2013). See also Blain, *Set the World on Fire*.

12. "Economic Citizenship Called Need of the Day: A. Phillip Randolph Heard by 200 at Urban League Dinner," *Pittsburgh Courier*, March 23, 1940, ProQuest Historical Newspapers: Pittsburgh Courier.

13. Arthur Huff Fauset, "I Write as I See," *Pittsburgh Courier*, February 7, 1942, ProQuest Historical Newspapers: Pittsburgh Courier.

14. "Victory at Home, Victory Abroad Sweeps Nation," *Pittsburgh Courier*, March 21, 1942, ProQuest Historical Newspapers: Pittsburgh Courier.

15. Paul C. Rosier, *Serving Their Country: American Indian Politics and Patriotism in the Twentieth Century* (Cambridge, MA: Harvard University Press, 2009).

16. Joel Stone, "Detroit: The 'Arsenal of Democracy,'" 1. https://detroithistorical.org/sites/default/files/pdfs/AoD%20Paperv2.pdf. Accessed Jul 4, 2021.

17. James M. Gregory, *The Southern Diaspora: How the Great Migrations of Black and White Southerners Transformed America* (Chapel Hill: University of North Carolina Press, 2005).

18. Colleen Doody, *Detroit's Cold War: The Origins of Postwar Conservatism* (Urbana: University of Illinois Press, 2013), 49.

19. David M. P. Freund, *Colored Property: State Policy and White Racial Politics in Suburban America* (Chicago: University of Chicago Press, 2010), 6.

20. Ibid.

21. While whites may not have targeted them systematically, Native people likely only had the opportunity to live in the poorest areas. See, for example, Detroit Historiographer, *Annual Report of the Historiographer of the City of Detroit* (Northern Micrographics, 1883), 69. On June 12, 1908, the author wrote, "Jacob's Village, the worst of all Detroit's tenement districts, located at Orleans and Macomb Streets, was ordered destroyed by the Board of Health. The population was composed of Negroes, Whites, Indians and Italians."

22. Kent Blansett, *A Journey to Freedom: Richard Oakes, Alcatraz, and the Red Power Movement* (New Haven, CT: Yale University Press, 2018), 77.

23. Public Law 68-175, STAT 253, June 2, 1924; Enrolled Act and Resolutions of Congress, 1789–1996; General Records of the U.S. Government; Record Group 11; National Archives. www.archives.gov/historical-docs/todays-doc/?dod-date=602. Accessed July 3, 2020.

24. "Indians in Floor Show," *Detroit News*, January 14, 1937. See also Gordon Douglas Northrup, "Pan-Indianism in the Metropolis: A Case Study of an Emergent Ethno-Syncretic Revitalization Movement" (Ph.D. diss., Michigan State University, 1970), 114.

25. Edmund Danziger, *Survival and Regeneration: Detroit's American Indian Community.* (Detroit, MI: Wayne State University Press, 1991), 36–37.

26. Tanner Howard, "Native American Routes: The Ancient Trails Hidden in Chicago's Grid System," *Guardian*, January 17, 2019, sec. Cities, www.theguardian.com/cities/2019/jan/17/native-american-routes-the-ancient-trails-hidden-in-chicagos-grid-system. Accessed August 14, 2020.

27. For a detailed view of more local trails now turned into streets and modern highways, see "Detroit Urbanism: Uncovering the History of Our Roads, Borders, and Built Environment," http://detroiturbanism.blogspot.com/2016/01/retracing-detroits-native-american.html. Accessed October 3, 2019.

28. George S. Bush, "Indians in City Hold Old-Style Pow-Wow," *Detroit Free Press*, April 5, 1948. p. 12.

29. Ibid.

30. Ralph West, "The Adjustment of the American Indian in Detroit: A Descriptive Study," master's thesis, Wayne State University, 1950), 56.

31. Ibid., 58–59.

32. "YWCA Official inducted into Indian Club," *Detroit Free Press*, April 17, 1944.

33. "Service Parade," *Detroit Free Press*, September 2, 1943, p. 5.

34. William Bright, "The Sociolinguistics of the 'S–Word': Squaw in American Placenames," *Names* 48, no. 3–4 (December 2000): 211–14; Rayna Green, "The Pocahontas Perplex: The Image of Indian Women in American Culture," *Massachusetts Review* 16, no. 4 (1975): 703–5.

35. "Fightin' Word: Indians Raise Squawk over Term 'Squaw,'" *Detroit Free Press*, January 6, 1947.

36. Arthur Kornhauser, *Attitudes of Detroit People Toward Detroit: Summary of a Detailed Report* (Detroit: Wayne State University Press, 1952), 1, 2.

37. Donald Fixico, *Termination and Relocation: Federal Indian Policy, 1945–1960*. Albuquerque: University of New Mexico Press, 1986, 191. While I single out Fixico, even other scholarship that discusses urban Indigenous history largely frames Native people as incompatible with cities, highlighting their struggles instead of understanding the broad range of experiences, including those that "made a way out of no way." For alternative views that consider Native peoples' agency in traveling to cities, see Douglas K. Miller, *Indians on the Move: Native American Mobility and Urbanization in the Twentieth Century* (Chapel Hill: University of North Carolina Press, 2019).

38. Douglas K. Miller, *Indians on the Move: Native American Mobility and Urbanization in the Twentieth Century* (Chapel Hill: University of North Carolina Press, 2019), 4.

39. "Indians Seek Point-4 Plan," *Detroit Free Press*, June 10, 1957, p. 19.

40. "Sioux to Appear in Palms Lobby," *Detroit Free Press*, February 7, 1951, p. 23.

41. Interview with Helen Kelley, conducted by Blackside, Inc., on June 6, 1989, for *Eyes on the Prize II: America at the Racial Crossroads 1965 to 1985*. Washington University Libraries, Film and Media Archive, Henry Hampton Collection.

42. Interview on WNDTV, New York City, May 28, 1963. Taken from "Urban Renewal Under Fire" by William B. Dickinson Jr., http://library.cqpress.com/cqresearcher/cqresrre1963082100. Accessed September 11, 2019.

43. Josephine Gomon, "First Annual Report of the Detroit Housing Commission" (Detroit, MI: Bulletin Control and Printing Bureau, 1934), 20.

44. Ibid., 18.

45. Ibid., 20.

46. Ibid., 21.

47. Joe T. Darden, Richard Hill, June Thomas, and Richard Thomas, *Detroit: Race and Uneven Development*, Comparative American Cities (Philadelphia: Temple University Press, 1987), 155.

48. A. J. Stovall, *The Growth of Black Elected Officials in the City of Detroit, 1870–1973* (Lewiston, NY: Mellen Press, 1996), 6.

49. *Profile of Critical Social Welfare and Economic Problems Facing Negro People in the Detroit Community* (Detroit, 1959), http://hdl.handle.net/2027/mdp.39015071308368, 15.

50. Kenneth Clark, *Dark Ghetto: Dilemmas of Social Power* (New York: Harper & Row, 1965), 11. Although a part of an era that used the term "internal colonies," it is an apt usage. Though they might forget the First Nations in the United States, assuming they believed the majority of them lived on reservations, both the ghetto and reservation were designed to confine people in certain spaces, control their mobility, and determine the economic and political capabilities of the people. For other examples of "internal colonialism" see, Robert Blauner, "Internal

Colonialism and Ghetto Revolt," *Social Problems* 16, no. 4 (Spring 1969): 393–408; and Robert Staples, "Race and Colonialism: The Domestic Case in Theory and Practice," *Black Scholar* 7, no. 9 (June 1976): 37–48.

51. Ibid., 158.

52. Patrick Wolfe, "Settler Colonialism and the Elimination of the Native," *Journal of Genocide Research* 8, no. 4 (December 2006): 387.

53. June Manning Thomas, "Redevelopment in Detroit," in *Mapping Detroit: Land, Community, and Shaping a City* (Detroit, MI: Wayne State University Press, 2015), 51.

54. Evelyn Seely Steward, "Racial Bars Complicate Slum Crisis: Blight-Area Tenants Find Moving Difficult." *Detroit Free Press*, May 4, 1956, p. 3.

55. For a detailed look at the housing crisis in the 1940s and 1950s, see Chapter 2, "Detroit's Time Bomb: Race and Housing in the 1940s," in Thomas Sugrue's *The Origins of the Urban Crisis: Race and Inequality in Postwar Detroit* (Princeton, NJ: Princeton University Press, 1996).

56. Keeanga-Yamahtta Taylor, *Race for Profit: How Banks and the Real Estate Industry Undermined Black Homeownership* (Chapel Hill: University of North Carolina Press, 2019), 2.

57. Detroit Urban League, *Profile of Critical Social Welfare and Economic Problems Facing Negro People in the Detroit Community* (Detroit, MI, 1959), http://hdl.handle.net/2027/mdp.39015071308368, 16.

58. Rebecca Kinney, "The Mechanics of Race: The Discursive Production of Detroit's Landscape of Difference" (PhD. diss., University of California San Diego, 2011).

59. Albert E. Cobo, "Mayor Candidates Trade Accusations," *Detroit Free Press*, November 5, 1969, Newspapers.com.

60. "Candidates Discuss Strikes and Street," *Detroit Free Press*, November 2, 1949, Newspapers.com.

61. Doody, *Detroit's Cold War*, 62–63.

62. James Ransom, "Cobo Clashes with Inglis, Favoring Slum Razing for Housing," *Detroit Free Press*, December 15, 1949, Newspapers.com.

63. Carl Almbald Papers, Walter Reuther Library, folder 12 (1953 booklet).

64. Harold Norris, Law Professor and Civil Rights Advocate, www.michjewishhistory.org/gallery/2018/05/harold-norris.html. Accessed June 5, 2020.

65. Harold Norris, "Dislocation Without Relocation, Excerpts from Talk Opposing Mayor Cobo's Urban Renewal Policy," in *Some Reflections on Law, Lawyers, and the Bill of Rights: A Collection of Writings* (Detroit: Michigan Law Book Society, 1983), 813–15.

66. Carl Almbald Papers. Carl W. Almbald Collection, Box 3, folder 26, Wayne State University Walter Reuther Library Archives.

67. Sugrue, *The Origins of the Urban Crisis*, 207.

68. See ibid., chap. 8, "Homeowner's Rights: White Resistance and the Rise of Antiliberalism," 209–11.

69. Richard Rothstein, *The Color of Law: A Forgotten History of How Our Government Segregated America*, Repr. ed. (New York: Liveright, 2018), 78.

70. Darden et al., *Detroit*, 174.

71. Cheryl Harris, "Whiteness as Property," *Harvard Law Review* 106, no. 8 (1993): 1714–16.

72. Aileen Moreton-Robinson, *The White Possessive: Property, Power, and Indigenous Sovereignty* (Minneapolis: University of Minnesota Press, 2016), 4.

73. Taylor, *Race for Profit*, 17.

74. *A Profile of the Detroit Negro, 1955–1964* (Detroit, 1965), 5. https://books.google.com/books?id=lc3iAAAAMAAJ&focus=searchwithinvolume&q=rent. Accessed July 4, 2021.

Chapter 5

1. Lewis Cook, "Detroit's Forgotten People—American Indians," *North American Indian Association Newsletter*, 6, no. 6 (June 1976): 4

2. American Indian Chicago Conference, University of Chicago, June 13–20, 1961, pp. 5–6. https://files.eric.ed.gov/fulltext/ED030518.pdf. Accessed January 31, 2021.

3. Shona Jackson, *Creole Indigeneity: Between Myth and Nation in the Caribbean* (Minneapolis: University of Minnesota Press, 2012), 42.

4. Renya Ramirez, *Native Hubs: Culture, Community, and Belonging in Silicon Valley and Beyond* (Durham: Duke University Press, 2007), 3–4.

5. The scholarship during the Red Power movement is broad, but there continues to be a lack of scholarship on the contributions of women. Nevertheless, there are important works on Red Power, including Kent Blansett, *A Journey to Freedom: Richard Oakes, Alcatraz, and the Red Power Movement* (New Haven, CT: Yale University Press, 2018); Paul R. McKenzie-Jones, *Clyde Warrior: Tradition, Community, and Red Power*, 1st ed. (Norman: University of Oklahoma Press, 2015); and Paul Chaat Smith and Robert Warrior, *Like a Hurricane: The American Indian Movement from Alcatraz to Wounded Knee* (Boston: South End Press, 1995).

6. Susan Applegate Krouse and Heather Howard, eds., *Keeping the Campfires Going: Native Women's Activism in Urban Communities* (Lincoln: University of Nebraska Press, 2009).

7. Don Myers, "Indians Becoming Organization People," *Detroit Free Press*, May 19, 1964, p. 8D.

8. Ibid.

9. Bradley Shreve, *Red Power Rising: The National Indian Youth Council and the Origins of Native Activism* (Norman: University of Oklahoma Press, 2011). For a detailed look at the origins of the National Indian Youth Council, see chap. 4 (pp. 94–118); for a look at the fish-ins, see chap. 5, (pp. 119–38).

10. James R. Hillman, ed., *The Minutes of the Michigan Commission on Indian Affairs, 1956–1977*, vol 1. (Canal, OH: Hillman Publishing Co., 1990). The Commission was created to be a collection of leaders who represented different parts of the entire state of Michigan's Indigenous population.

11. Sandra Muse interview with the author, August 2, 2014.

12. Susan Lobo, "Urban Clan Mothers: Key Households in Cities," in *Keeping the Campfires Going: Native Women's Activism in Urban Communities*, ed. Susan Applegate Krouse (Lincoln: University of Nebraska Press, 2009), 18.

13. Judy Mays interview with the author, June 25, 2014.

14. See Dean J. Kotlowski, "Alcatraz, Wounded Knee, and Beyond: The Nixon and Ford Administrations Respond to Native American Protest," *Pacific Historical Review* 72, no. 2 (2003): 201–27, 204, https://doi.org/10.1525/phr.2003.72.2.201.

15. Judy Mays interview with June 25, 2014.

16. Richard Nixon, "Special Message to the Congress on Indian Affairs," July 8, 1970. Online by Gerhard Peters and John T. Woolley, The American Presidency Project. https://www.presidency.ucsb.edu/documents/special-message-the-congress-indian-affairs. Accessed July 5, 2021.

17. Margaret D. Jacobs, *White Mother to a Dark Race: Settler Colonialism, Maternalism, and the Removal of Indigenous Children in the American West and Australia, 1880–1940*, ill. ed. (Lincoln: University of Nebraska Press, 2011), 429.

18. James G. Abourezk and Fred Harris, *Advise and Dissent: Memoirs of an Ex-Senator*, repr. ed. (Lincoln, NE: Bison Books, 2013).

19. "Indian Child Welfare Program: Problems That American Indian Families Face in Raising Their Children and How These Problems Are Affected by Federal Action or Inaction," Subcommittee on Indian Affairs of the Committee on Interior and Insular Affairs (Washington DC: Government Printing Office, 1974), 2.

20. Margaret D. Jacobs, "The Habit of Elimination: Indigenous Child Removal in Settler Colonial Nations in the Twentieth Century," in *Colonial Genocide in North America*, ed. Andrew Woolford, Jeff Benvenuto, and Alexander Laban Hinton (Durham, NC: Duke University Press, 2014), 193. See also Margaret D. Jacobs, *A Generation Removed: The Fostering and Adoption of Indigenous Children in the Postwar World* (Lincoln: University of Nebraska Press, 2014).

21. Patrick Wolfe, "Settler Colonialism and the Elimination of the Native," *Journal of Genocide Research* 8, no. 4 (December 2006): 387–89.

22. Mishuana Goeman, *Mark My Words: Native Women Mapping Our Nations* (Minneapolis: University of Minnesota Press, 2013), 12.

23. "Indian Child Welfare Program," 160–61.

24. Ibid.

25. For an overview of Black religious nationalism in Detroit, see Angela Dillard, *Faith in the City: Preaching Radical Social Change in Detroit* (Ann Arbor: University of Michigan Press, 2007).

26. Peniel Joseph, *Waiting 'Til the Midnight Hour: A Narrative History of Black Power in America* (New York: Henry Holt, 2006), 55–63. Joseph offers an overview of early components of Black radicalism in Detroit from the late 1950s until the mid-1960s.

27. In contemporary times, this discourse is tied to reparations. See William A. Darity and A. Kirsten Mullen, *From Here to Equality: Reparations for Black Americans in the Twenty-First Century* (Chapel Hill: University of North Carolina Press, 2020).

28. For a history of the Republic of New Afrika and Black self-determination in Detroit, see Edward Onaci, *Free the Land: The Republic of New Afrika and the Pursuit of a Black Nation-State* (Chapel Hill: University of North Carolina Press, 2020), 42.

29. "Black America's Reply to Bigots," *The Ghetto Speaks: East Side Voice of Independent Detroit*, vol. 1, no. 8 (1968). Bentley Library, University of Michigan.

30. Ibid.

31. For the Black Power era, see Komozi Woodard *A Nation Within a Nation: Amiri Baraka (LeRoi Jones) and Black Power Politics* (Chapel Hill: University of North Carolina Press, 1999); and William L. Van Deburg, *A New Day in Babylon: The Black Power Movement and American Culture, 1965–1975* (Chicago: University of Chicago Press, 1992).

32. Russell Rickford, "'We Can't Grow Food on All This Concrete': The Land Question, Agrarianism, and Black Nationalist Thought in the Late 1960s and 1970s," *Journal of American History* 103, no. 4 (March 2017): 956–59.

33. Jackson, *Creole Indigeneity*, 2012), 29.

34. Ibid., 87.

35. Stephen M. Ward, *In Love and Struggle: The Revolutionary Lives of James and Grace Lee Boggs* (Chapel Hill: University of North Carolina Press, 2020), 6.

36. James Boggs, *Racism and the Class Struggle: Further Pages from a Black Worker's Notebook* (New York: Monthly Review Press, 1970), 16.

37. Ibid.

38. Ibid., 162.

39. Robert Blauner, "Internal Colonialism and Ghetto Revolt," *Social Problems* 16, no. 4 (Spring 1969): 393–408; Robert Staples, "Race and Colonialism: The Domestic Case in Theory and Practice," *Black Scholar* 7, no. 9 (June 1976): 37–48.

40. Boggs, *Racism and the Class Struggle*, 165.

41. James Boggs and Grace Lee Boggs, "The City Is the Black Man's Land," in *Racism and the Class Struggle: Further Pages from a Worker's Notebook* (New York: Monthly Review Press, 1970), 40.

42. Rickford, "'We Can't Grow Food on All This Concrete,'" 957-64.

43. Jackson, *Creole Indigeneity*, 3.

44. Boggs, *Racism and the Class Struggle*, 50.

45. Megan Shockley, "Working for Democracy: Working-Class African-American Women, Citizenship, and Civil Rights in Detroit, 1940-1954," *Michigan Historical Review* 29, no. 2 (Fall 2003): 133.

46. Premilla Nadasen, *Welfare Warriors: The Welfare Rights Movement in the United States*, 1st ed. (New York: Routledge, 2004), 107.

47. Megan Taylor Shockley, *We, Too, Are Americans: African American Women in Detroit and Richmond, 1940–54* (Urbana: University of Illinois Press, 2003), 7.

48. Rhonda Y. Williams, "Black Women, Urban Politics, and Engendering Black Power," in *The Black Power Movement*, ed. Peniel E. Joseph, 1st ed. (New York: Routledge, 2006), 81.

49. For histories of Black women in the struggle for civil rights and Black Power, see Bettye Collier-Thomas and V. P. Franklin, eds., *Sisters in the Struggle: African-American Women in the Civil Rights–Black Power Movement* (New York: NYU Press, 2001); Annelise Orleck, *Storming Caesars Palace: How Black Mothers Fought Their Own War on Poverty*, annotated ed. (New York: Beacon Press, 2006); and Nadasen, *Welfare Warriors*. For a discussion of Detroit, see Dara R. Walker, "Black Power, Education, and Youth Politics in Detroit, 1966-1973," Ph.D. diss., Rutgers University, 2018).

50. Walker, "Black Power, Education, and Youth Politics," 104.

51. Marian Kramer, Oral History, August 6, 2007, University of Michigan-Dearborn. https://sites.google.com/a/umich.edu/motor-city-voices/work-showcase/kramer. Accessed February 1, 2021.

52. Ibid.

53. Stephen Ward, "The Third World Women's Alliance: Black Feminist Radicalism and Black Power Politics," in *The Black Power Movement: Rethinking the Civil Rights–Black Power Era* (New York: Routledge, 2006), 119–44. Ward argues that they were founded in direct response to patriarchy.

54. Robert Mast, ed., "Struggles of Women," in *Detroit Lives* (Philadelphia, PA: Temple University Press, 1994), 106.

55. Dan Georgakas and Marvin Surkin, *Detroit: I Do Mind Dying: A Study in Urban Revolution* (New York: St. Martin's Press, 1975), 5.

56. "Jim Forman Delivers Black Manifesto at Riverside Church." https://snccdigital.org/events/jim-forman-delivers-black-manifesto-at-riverside-church/. Accessed January 10, 2019.

57. "Draft Proposal: Manifest of the International Black Workers Congress," www.marxists.org/history/erol/ncm-1/bwc-manifesto.htm. Accessed January 10, 2019.

58. Combahee River Collective, “The Combahee River Collective Statement,” in *How We Get Free: Black Feminism and the Combahee River Collective*, ed. Keeanga-Yamahtta Taylor (Chicago: Haymarket Books, 2017), 15–27.

59. See Kyle T. Mays, *An Afro-Indigenous History of the United States* (Boston: Beacon Press, 2021), chap. 6, “Black Power, Red Power, and the Struggle for Freedom and Sovereignty.”

60. Jeffrey O. G. Ogbar, *Black Power: Radical Politics and African American Identity* (Baltimore: Johns Hopkins University Press, 2004), 188.

61. Vine Deloria Jr., *Custer Died for Your Sins: An Indian Manifesto* (New York: Macmillan, 1969), 168-72.

62. Jack Burdock, “Angela Davis Hails Young Election, STRESS Abolition,” *Detroit Free Press*, February 24, 1974, Newspapers.com.

63. Beatrice A. Bigony, “Native Americans in Detroit,” in *Immigrants and Migrants: The Detroit Ethnic Experience*, Ethnic Studies Reader (Detroit, MI: Wayne State University Press, 1974), 354, 364.

64. “Indian Princess Dance,” *Native Sun Newsletter*, vol. 7, May 1977

65. Tiya Miles, *Ties That Bind: The Story of an Afro-Cherokee Family in Slavery and Freedom* (Berkeley: University of California Press, 2005), 5.

66. “Indian Princess Dance,” *Native Sun Newsletter*, May 1977.

67. Ibid., 7 no. 7, July 1977.

68. Ibid.

69. Sandra Muse interview with the author, August 2, 2014.

70. Ibid.

71. Tracy Mays interview with the author, June 25, 2014.

72. Ibid.

Chapter 6

1. Kefentse K. Chike, “From Black Power to the New Milinium [*sic*]: The Evolution of African Centered Education in Detroit, Michigan, 1970-2000” (Ph.D. diss., Michigan State University, 2011), 23-25.

2. Andrew Woolford, *This Benevolent Experiment: Indigenous Boarding Schools, Genocide, and Redress in Canada and the United States* (Winnipeg: University of Manitoba Press, 2015).

3. Hannah Aikens “Aikens to Lewis Beeson,” August 19, 1964. Record Group 66, Box 1, Folder 1, Library of Michigan, Lansing, MI.

4. Daniel Cobb, *Native Activism in Cold War America: The Struggle for Sovereignty* (Norman: University of Oklahoma Press, 2008), 4.

5. Edward Kennedy, et al. “Indian Education: A National Tragedy—A National Challenge (Washington, DC: U.S. Government Printing Office, November 3, 1969), 22. His brother served as chair of the subcommittee on Indian Education in 1967.

6. Tom Pawlick, “The Abandonment of the Indian in Detroit’s Red Ghetto,” *Detroit News*, March 5, 1970.

7. Ibid.

8. Michigan Commission on Indian Affairs, *A Study of the Socioeconomic Status of Michigan Indians* (Lansing, MI: Commission on Indian Affairs, 1971), 44.

9. Beatrice A. Bigony, “Native Americans in Detroit,” in *Immigrants and Migrants: The Detroit Ethnic Experience*, Ethnic Studies Reader (Detroit, MI: Wayne State University Press, 1974), 354.

10. Ibid.

11. Edmund Danziger, *Survival and Regeneration: Detroit's American Indian Community.* (Detroit, MI: Wayne State University Press, 1991), 57.

12. Pawlick, "The Abandonment of the Indian," *Detroit News*, March 5, 1970.

13. Ibid.

14. Michigan Commission on Indian Affairs, *Socioeconomic Status of Michigan Indians*, 29.

15. Interview with the author, August 2, 2014.

16. *Michigan Department of Education News*, June 28, 1977.

17. Donna Langston, "American Indian Women's Activism in the 1960s and 1970s," *Hypatia* 18, no. 2 (Spring 2003): 120.

18. *North American Indian Association Newsletter*, 2, no. 11 (November 1972). It had a readership of about 750 people. It is likely that the majority were Indigenous, but surely some were non-Indigenous.

19. *North American Indian Association Newsletter*, 3, no. 3 (March 1973). Library of Michigan.

20. Detroit Indian Educational and Cultural Center pamphlet written by Judith Mays.

21. Danziger, *Survival and Regeneration*, 147–48.

22. Judy Mays interview with the author June 25, 2014.

23. *Native Sun Newsletter*, 6, no. 5 (1976).

24. Ibid.

25. *Native Sun Newsletter*, 6, no. 1 (January 1976).

26. Pow Wow Links Indian Pupils to Past." *Detroit Free Press*, June 3, 1980, p. 23.

27. Sandra Muse interview with the author, August 2, 2014.

28. Russell Gore, "Sitting Bull's Follower Who Won Paleface Wisdom: Raised to Hate White, Now Is a Doctor Here," *Detroit News*, July 17, 1932.

29. *North American Indian Association Newsletter*, 5, no. 6 (June 1975).

30. Ibid.

31. Jeffrey Mirel, *The Rise and Fall of an Urban School System: Detroit, 1907–1981* (Ann Arbor: University of Michigan Press, 1999).

32. Clifford Watson and Geneva Smitherman, *Educating African American Males: Detroit's Malcolm X Academy Solution* (Chicago: Third World Press, 1996), 55.

33. Grace Boggs, *Living for Change*, Repr. ed. (Minneapolis: University of Minnesota Press, 2016), 120–21.

34. Chike, "From Black Power to the New Milinium [*sic*]," 26–29.

35. Reverend Albert Cleage Jr., "What Do We Owe Our Children?" *Michigan Chronicle*, November 4, 1967. https://riseupdetroit.org/wp-content/uploads/2019/01/Inner-City-Parents-Council-Flyer-1967.pdf. Accessed July 5, 2021.

36. Ibid., 140–41.

37. Preston Wilcox, "The Meaning of Community Control," reprinted from *Foresight* magazine, 1969, i. Walter P. Reuther Library, Archives of Labor and Urban Affairs, Wayne State University. https://riseupdetroit.org/wp-content/uploads/2019/03/The-Meaning-of-Community-Control.pdf?iframe=true&width=100%&height=100%. Accessed July 5, 2021.

38. Ibid., 55–58.

39. David Harvey, *A Brief History of Neoliberalism* (Cambridge: Oxford University Press, 2007). Harvey notes, "Neoliberalism is in the first instance a theory of political economic practices that proposes that human well-being can best be advanced by liberating individual entrepreneurial freedoms and skills within an institutional framework characterized by strong private

property rights, free markets, and free trade. The role of the state is to create and preserve an institutional framework appropriate to such practices. The state has to guarantee, for example, the quality and integrity of money. It must also set up those military, defence, police, and legal structures and functions required to secure private property rights and to guarantee, by force if need be, the proper functioning of markets" (2).

40. See Manuel B. Aalbers, "Debate on Neoliberalism in and After the Neoliberal Crisis," *International Journal of Urban and Regional Research* 37, no. 3 (May 2013): 1053–57. Aalbers notes that there are many versions of neoliberalism.

41. For an analysis of this shift, see Elizabeth Hinton, *From the War on Poverty to the War on Crime: The Making of Mass Incarceration in America* (Cambridge, MA: Harvard University Press, 2016). See also Michelle Alexander's *The New Jim Crow: Mass Incarceration in the Age of Colorblindness* (New York: New Press, 2011).

42. Pamela K. Lattimore, James Trudeau, K. Jack Riley, Jordan Leiter, and Steven Edwards, "Homicide in Eight U.S. Cities: Trends, Context, and Policy Implications" (Washington, DC: U.S. Department of Justice, December 1997), 15, 32.

43. "Murders: The Solution Isn't Just a Matter Just for the Police," *Detroit Free Press* May 16, 1986, p. 8A

44. Michelle Fine and Jessica Ruglis, "Circuits and Consequences of Dispossession: The Racialized Realignment of the Public Sphere for U.S. Youth," *Transforming Anthropology* 17, no. 1 (2009): 21, https://doi.org/10.1111/j.1548-7466.2009.01037.x.

45. Ibid., 2.

46. Ibid., 37.

47. Jeffery Robinson, "The Detroit Public School System, 1980–2000," in "The African Centered School Movement and the Detroit Public School System" (Ph.D. diss., Michigan State University, 2008), 64–91.

48. Menah Pratt-Clarke, *Critical Race, Feminism, and Education: A Social Justice Model*, 2010 ed. (New York: Palgrave Macmillan, 2011), 120.

49. Debra Adams and Margaret Trimer-Hartley, "Academy Opens Without Incident; Detroiters Cheerfully Cope with Chaos," *Detroit Free Press*, September 30, 1992, Newspapers.com.

50. "Does the Academy Belong in Warrendale?" *Detroit Free Press*, August 15, 1992. Newspapers.com.

51. "Empowering Native People, Native American Task Force," Michigan Documents Collection, Michigan State University (Harris, MI: Hannahville Printing, 1990).

52. Steve Neavling, "Kwame Kenyatta, Hits Road for Watchdog Job in Mississippi." August 27, 2013. http://motorcitymuckraker.com/2013/08/27/ex-councilman-kenyatta-hits-road-for-gig-in-in-mississippi/.

53. Chris Christoff, "Engler School Plan Has Spotty Approval," *Detroit Free Press*, October 27, 1993, p. 6.

54. Debra Adams, "Detroit Considers Indian Academy," *Detroit Free Press*, October 27, 1993, p. 6.

55. Adams and Trimer-Hartley, "Academy Opens Without Incident."

56. Ibid.

57. Martin F. Kohn, "Native Values," *Detroit Free Press*, November 14, 1993, p. 81.

58. Cecil Angel, "Academy to Focus on Indian Culture," *Detroit Free Press*, July 16, 1994, p. 3A.

59. "Detroit's American Start Fort with a Mission." www.historicfortwaynecoalition.com/historical_insights.html. Accessed July 5, 2021.

60. "Medicine Bear American Indian Academy Handbook," 1994. From the personal collection of Tracy Mays.

61. Judy Mays interview with the author, June 25, 2014.

62. Margaret Trimer-Hartley and Joan Richardson "First Day Is a Learning Experience," *Detroit Free Press*, August 31, 1994.

63. Julie L. Davis, *Survival Schools: The American Indian Movement and Community Education in the Twin Cities* (Minneapolis: University of Minnesota Press, 2013), 6.

64. "Medicine Bear American Indian Academy Handbook."

65. SouFy interview with the author, September 11, 2016

66. Ibid.

67. Ashleigh interview with the author, August 20, 2014.

68. Jennifer Juarez, "Kenyatta Quits Detroit School Board," *Detroit Free Press*, November 1, 1997, p. 11.

69. Russ Bellant, "Robert Bobb and the Failure of Public Act 72: A Case Study." https://detroitdebtmoratorium.org/robert-bobb-and-the-failure-of-public-act-72-a-case-study/, 2. March 8, 2011. Accessed July 5, 2021.

70. Ibid.

71. Mark Puls, "Despite $4 Million Repair Tax, Fort Wayne In," *Detroit News*, September 25, 2000, p. 1A.

72. Shawn Wilson, *Research as Ceremony: Indigenous Research Methods* (Halifax & Winnipeg, Manitoba, Canada: Fernwood Publishing, 2008), 81.

73. Ibid.

74. Shawn D. Lewis, "Parents Support Fired Principal," *Detroit News*, June 13, 2000, p. 8D.

75. Press Release, "Trail of Tears 2000: Broken Promises, Broken Treaties."

76. Lewis, "Parents Support Fired Principal," *Detroit News*, June 13, 2000.

77. Shawn Lewis, "Principal Protest Turns Personal: Leader of Native-American Academy Cuts Hair to Mourn Firing by Detroit Schools," *Detroit News*, June 15, 2000, p. 1C.

78. Ibid., p. 6C.

79. Shawn Lewis, "Principal Protest Turns Personal- Leader of Native-American Academy Cuts Hair to 'mourn' Firing by Detroit Schools," *Detroit News*, June 15, 2000, sec. C.

80. Shawn Lewis, "Fired Academy Principal Sues," *Detroit News*, August 15, 2000, section D.

81. Davis, *Survival Schools*, 173–75.

82. AJ Rice, "Manufacturing Failure: Revitalization, Black Dispossession, and the Takeover of Detroit Public Schools" (Ph.D. diss., Michigan State University, 2021).

83. AJ Rice, "Encountering Reform: Race, Power, and the Unmaking of Detroit Public Schools" (Ph.D. diss., Michigan State University, 2020), especially chap. 1, "The Production of 'Educational Failure': The Case of Detroit Public Schools," 32–41.

84. George K. Pitchford, Esq., "Review of Detroit Public Schools During State Management," *Allen Law Group*, November 8, 2019, 2.

85. Rice, "Encountering Reform."

Conclusion

1. Philip Deloria, *Playing Indian* (New Haven and London: Yale University Press, 1998), 98–99.

2. Chris Isidore, "GM Bankruptcy: End of an Era," *CNN Money*, June 2, 2009, https://money.cnn.com/2009/06/01/news/companies/gm_bankruptcy/. Accessed October 30, 2019.

3. Paul A. Einstein, "Pontiac Hits End of the Road After 82 Years," *NBC News*, December 2, 2009, sec. Business, www.nbcnews.com/id/34224218/ns/business-the_driver_seat/t/pontiac-hits-end-road-after-years/#.XbmHkyUpA0o. Accessed October 30, 2019.

4. David C. Smith, "Chief Pontiac on the Warpath: 'GM Uses My Name, Gratis, for 83 Years, and Now This?'" *WardsAuto*, 8th ed., August 1, 2009, 43, https://www.wardsauto.com/news-analysis/chief-pontiac-warpath. Accessed October 30, 2019.

5. Richard Florida, *The Rise of the Creative Class: And How It's Transforming Work, Leisure, Community and Everyday Life* (New York: BasicCivitas Books, 2002). To be fair—even if that is hard to accept, Florida does seem to have at least reconsidered his idea of the creative class in his latest book. See Richard Florida, *The New Urban Crisis: How Our Cities Are Increasing Inequality, Deepening Segregation, and Failing the Middle Class—and What We Can Do About It* (New York: Basic Books, 2017). However, it took him fifteen years to recognize the pitfalls of this argument.

6. About C. A. N. Art Handworks, https://canarts.portfoliobox.io/ourcompany. Accessed July 2, 2021.

7. For instance, according to community reports in the 1980s, the census was inaccurate in counting Native people in Detroit. The 1980 census counted about 6,000 plus; a joint study between the University of Michigan and the Detroit American Indian Center said the number was likely upward of 18,000.

8. Lisa Michelle King, "Revisiting Winnetou: The Karl May Museum, Cultural Appropriation, and Indigenous Self-Representation," *Studies in American Indian Literatures* 28, no. 2 (2016): 30

9. Ibid.

10. Penelope Edmonds, *Urbanizing Frontiers: Indigenous Peoples and Settlers in the 19th Century Pacific Rim Cities* (Vancouver: University of British Columbia Press, 2010), 12.

11. Tom Henderson, "Belle Isle: Motown's Monaco: Developer Envisions Independent Commonwealth," www.mackinac.org/archives/2013/011213CDB-belle.pdf. Accessed August 16, 2020.

12. Rodney Lockwood, *Belle Isle: Detroit's Game Changer*. Bingham Farms, MI: Self-Published, 2012.

13. Ibid., 6.

14. Ibid., 13–15.

15. Ibid., 54.

16. Ibid., 55.

17. Ibid., 31–32.

18. Ibid., 54.

19. Edward Said, *Orientalism* (New York: Vintage, 1979), 54.

20. Jean O'Brien, *Firsting and Lasting: Writing Indians Out of Existence in New England* (Minneapolis, MN: University of Minnesota Press, 2010), xiii.

21. Paul Chaat Smith, *Everything You Know About Indians Is Wrong* (Minneapolis: University of Minnesota Press, 2009), 6.

22. Christine Ferretti, "Detroit Celebrates First Indigenous Peoples' Day in Place of Columbus Day," *Detroit News*, October 8, 2018, www.detroitnews.com/story/news/local/detroit-city/2018/10/08/detroit-celebrating-indigenous-peoples-day-not-columbus-day/1564458002/.

23. Branden Hunter, "Bye Bye, Cobo: Former Racist Mayor's Name to Be Taken off Convention Center," *Michigan Chronicle*, February 27, 2019.

24. "Replace Chris Columbus Statue in Downtown Detroit with a Real Hero," The Raiz Up Collective, Change.org, 2017, www.change.org/p/detroit-city-council-replace-chris-columbus-statue-in-downtown-detroit-with-a-real-hero. The Raiz Up collective advocated for this in 2017.

25. Leanne Betasamosake Simpson, *As We Have Always Done: Indigenous Freedom Through Radical Resistance* (Minneapolis: University of Minnesota Press, 2017), 48.

26. Keisha-Khan Y. Perry, *Black Women Against the Land Grab: The Fight for Racial Justice in Brazil* (Minneapolis: University of Minnesota Press, 2013), xx.

INDEX

Aalbers, Manuel B., 204n40
Abourezk, James, 119, 120
Afrocentric education: Black Nationalism and, 144; community control of schools movement and, 122, 144–46; Detroit Public Schools financing and, 163; educational dispossession and, 144–49; gender and, 146–47, 147–48; impact on Indigenous education, 148–49, 150–51; Medicine Bear American Indian Academy and, 144, 155–56; opposition to, 148. *See also* culturally relevant education; Malcolm X Academy
Afro-Indigenous peoples, ix, 3–4, 41–42, 134. *See also* Kidroe, Josephine; also under Mays
Afro-Indigenous studies, 3
Aikens, Hannah, 105, 116, 135–36
Aisha Shule Affirmative School for Gifted Children, 145–46
Albert, Walter, 141
Alexander, Michelle, 204n41
Alexander Crummell School, 145
Algonquian peoples, 11–12, 37, 183n4
Ali, Noble Drew, 95
Amaya, Liseth, 60, 117, 153
Amazon.com, Inc., 166
American Indian Health Service (IHS), 141
Anishinabee people: Anishinabeg names for Detroit, 11; Miami band, 12; migration oral histories, 11; Mississauga band, 12; Odawa band, 12–14, 18, 37; Potawatomi band, 12, 13, 37; Saulter bands, 12; Three Fires Confederacy, 37–38
"An Open Letter to the Community" (Gregory), 131–32
Anthony, Wendell, 174–75
anti-blackness, 42–46, 131–34, 141, 178
Archer, Dennis, 158–59
Arnold, C. L., 48–49
Asleigh (student), 158
assimilation: automobile industry and, 64; boarding schools, 64, 67–70, 98, 117, 120, 136; resistance *vs.*, 78; savage warrior stereotype and, 76; Society of American Indians and, 68–78; termination of Native tribal land rights and, 104–6
authenticity, 24–25, 36–37, 55, 71–72, 89–90, 100, 166
automobile industry: Fordism and, 64–65; manufacturing boom and, 189n15; wartime, 5–6, 97

Baker, Gordon, 126
Baldwin. James, 106
Battle of Bloody Run, 167–68
Battle of Little Big Horn, 23
Bear, Thurman, 151
Beaver, Austin, 39–40
Bederman, Gail, 82
Beeson, Lewis, 135
Bellant, Russ, 159
Bellecourt, Clyde, 131
Belle Isle, 9, 40–41, 55–56, 169–73, 177
Belle Isle (Lockwood), 169–73
belonging: Black belonging, 3, 47, 51, 52–55, 66–67, 128; Black indigeneity and, 115, 122–30, 131, 169, 171; Indigenous belonging, 7–8, 81–83; ownership of the city and, 116
Beracini, Lorenzo, 180n5
bicentennial celebration (1901): allegorical parade pageantry, 61–62; Black participation, 50–55; citizenship and, 46; Detroit modernity and, 46–47; Indigenous erasure and, 59–60; Indigenous participation, 46, 49, 51, 55–58; pageantry and, 47–48, 61–62; Parade of Nations, 49, 51, 53–54, 54–55; performance of Cadillac, 46–47, 55–58

Bkejwanong (Walpole Island), 37–38. *See also* Walpole Island First Nations people
"Black America's Reply to Bigots" (1968), 123
Blackburn, Thornton and Ruth, 15
Blackburn Riots, 15
Black dispossession: challenging dispossession, 175–78; housing and, 106–12; symbolic changes and, 174–75; urban renewal and, 110–12
Black Economic Development Conference (1969), 128–29
Black Hawk, 19, 31
Black indigeneity, 115, 122–30, 131, 169, 171
Black-Indigenous History Month, 176
Black Manifesto (1969), 128–29
Black Nationalism: Black indigeneity *vs.*, 115; community control of schools movement and, 122, 144–46; culturally relevant education and, 122, 135, 144–46; gender and, 147–48; Nation of Islam and, 94–95, 122, 135; religious nationalism and, 94–95, 200n25
Black Power movement, 6, 114, 123–24, 126, 138, 200n31, 201n49
Black radicalism, 122–30, 127–28, 147–48, 200n26
Black Shawl, Layla, 161
Black women, 65, 66–67, 128, 201n49
Blain, Keisha N., 195n11
Blansett, Kent, 98
boarding schools, 64, 67–70, 98, 117, 120, 136
Bobb, Robert, 159, 163
Boggs, Grace Lee, 122, 124, 144
Boggs, James, 122, 124, 128
Booker T. Washington Trade Association, 67
Bowen, Anthony, 85
Boyd, Colleen, 18
Boykin, Ulysses S., 65–66
Brant, Arthur, 160
Brant, Keith, 154
Brown, John, 16
Bruyneel, Kevin, 47–48, 61–62
Buffalo Bill's Wild West show, 21, 24–25, 184n36, 185n41
Bunche, Ralph, 103
Bureau of Indian Affairs, 70, 72, 75, 104
Burton, Clarence, 27, 29, 34, 41, 152, 183n2. *See also* Detroit Historical Society
Burton Elementary School, 142
Bush, George S., 100
Bush, George W., 165
Byrd, Jodi A., 179n1
Cadillac, Antoine de la Mothe: bicentennial performance of, 47, 55–58, 58–61; narrative dispossession and, 34, 46–47; origin narratives and, 103–4; settler memories of French occupation, 11, 12, 30, 34, 86–87, 103, 112, 166
Camp Fire Girls, 90
Camp Oahe, 89
Camp Ohiyesa, 88–90
Camp Wathana, 143
C.A.N. Art Handworks, 167–68, 206n6
carceral politics, 43–44, 204n41
Carmichael, Stokely, 130
Chrysler, 5–6
citizenship: Black belonging and, 4, 11, 15, 41, 52–55, 96–99; economic citizenship, 96–97; freedom narratives and, 171; Indigenous citizenship, 73, 75–76, 76–77, 98; labor exploitation and, 9, 111, 122–30; land dispossession and, 14; second-class citizenship, 2, 4, 15, 41, 96–99, 111
Citizenship Act (1924), 78
City-Wide Citizens Action Committee (CCAC), 145
Clark Hine, Darlene, 65, 67
Cleage, Albert, Jr., 122, 144–45
Cobb, Dan, 136
Cobo, Albert, 109–10, 112, 174
Cobo Center (TCF Center), 174–75
Cody, William F., 25. *See also* Buffalo Bill's Wild West show
Cohen, Cathy, 188n117
Colored Vigilant Committee, 16
Community Control of Schools movement, 144–46
Cook, Louis, 114
Coolidge, Sherman, 70
Cooper, Anna Julia, 144
Cooper, James Fenimore, 16–17
Cornell, George, viii
Cortelyou, George, 46
Couzens, James "Jim," 74–75
culturally relevant education: Black Nationalism and, 122, 135, 144–46; boarding schools and, 67–68, 70, 120, 136; cultural revitalization and, 154; Detroit Public Schools takeover and, 1–2, 158–59, 162; educational dispossession and, 163–64; Indigenous-centric education, 143–44, 149–58; language revitalization, 135–36; Nation of Islam schools, 135; opposition to, 156; Red Power movement and,

136–44; self-determination and, 136–44, 144–49, 150–51, 154. *See also* Afrocentric education; Indigenous education

Danziger, Edmund, ix
Darden, Joe, 107–8
Davis, Angela, 130–31
Davis, Julie L., 154
Dawes Act (1887), 69–70, 77
Dawn of Detroit (Miles), 14, 187n106
Dawson, Michael, 94
DeBaptiste, George, 16
"Declaration of Indian Purpose," 114–15
Deloria, Phillip, 32, 68–69, 72, 76, 89–90, 165
Deloria, Vine, Jr., 130
Detroit: overview of, 5–8, 11; Cass Corridor area, 98, 138; challenging dispossession, 175–78; creative class and, 166–69, 206n5; DPS takeover, 1–2, 159, 162; education financing, 158–59; emergency takeover and bankruptcy, 1–2; imaginary geographies of, 169–72; Indigenous migration to Great lakes area, 11, 176; Indigenous names for, 11, 183n2; Motor City moniker, 48, 64; tricentennial, 191n64; as violent, 12–13, 17, 50, 146
Detroit 2.0 project, 6–7, 171
Detroit American Indian Parent Council, 141
Detroit Anti-Slavery Society, 15
Detroit City Planning Commission, 107
Detroit Historical Museum, 152, 176
Detroit Historical Society, 152–53, 159
Detroit Houseworkers League, 122
Detroit Housing Commission (DHC), 106–7, 110
Detroit: I Do Mind Dying (Georgakas and Surkin), 128
Detroit Indian Educational and Cultural Center (DIECC), 140–43, 151, 156–57, 159–63
Detroit Indian Parent Advisory Council, 141
Detroit Institute of Art, 31, 61, 176
Detroit Pistons, vii
Detroit Public Housing Tenants Council, 110
Detroit Public Schools: community control of schools movement, 122, 144–46; drop out rates, 138, 139–40, 159; federal legislation and, 139–40; takeover of, 1–2, 158–59, 162
Detroit Rebellion (1967), 6, 9, 134, 135, 145, 152
Detroit's Hidden Channels (Marrero), 27, 185n51, 194n79
Detroit Urban League, 96, 108
disappearance narratives: Indigenous erasure, 16–17, 18–19, 21, 38–39, 55, 92, 123–24; as site of dispossession, 3–4; space reclamation and, 36–41. *See also* Indigenous erasure
displacement: Black displacement, 173, 174; foster care system and, 116–22; Indigenous displacement, 123–24, 173; slum clearance and, 4, 106–12, 127
dispossession: use of term, 1–5, 48, 179n1; challenging dispossession, 175–78
Douglass, Frederick, 52
Dowdell, Glanton, 126
Du Bois, W. E. B., 69, 71, 80, 144
Dunbar-Ortiz, Roxanne, 180n12

Earhart, Harry B., 88
Eastman, Charles Alexander: biographical overview, 81–83; Camp Ohiyesa and, 85, 88–91; Camp Wathana and, 143; challenges to white masculinity and, 78–84; death of, 91–93; Detroit YMCA and, 85–91; impact on settler imaginaries, 80–84, 89–92; SAI and, 68, 70
Eastman, Charles "Ohi," Jr., 85
Eastman, Elaine Goodale, 84
Eastman, Jacob. *See* Eastman, Charles Alexander
East Side Voice of Independent Detroit (ESVID), 123
economic security: Black women and, 65; migration and, 65; racial capitalism and, 2, 111–12; as site of dispossession, 2; urban renewal and, 111; welfare rights organizing, 127
Edmonds, Penelope, 168–69
educational dispossession: assimilation projects as, 64; boarding schools, 64, 67–70, 98, 117, 120, 136; culturally relevant education and, 163–64; DPS takeover and, 158–59, 162; dispossession of Indigenous youth and, 148–52; poverty and, 146–47, 149–50. *See also* culturally relevant education
Edwards, George, 109
employment security: 64–67, 97–98. *See also* poverty
"Empowering Native People, Native American Task Force," 149
Engler, John, 150, 158–59

enslavement: African enslavement, 3, 13, 14, 16; categories of, 183n13, 187n106; Detroit Underground Railroad and, 16, 52, 86; of Indigenous people, 13–14, 183n13
Estes, Nick, 180n12
Evans, Warren C., 175
Everything You Know About Indians (Smith), 174
expressive culture, 4. *See also* performance of dispossession, memorialization

Fanon, Frantz, 8
Fard, W. D., 94–95
Farmer, Silas, 5, 27–28, 59, 62, 87
Fauset, Arthur Huff, 96–97
Federal Housing Act (1949), 107–8
Ferguson, William, 50
Fine, Michelle, 147
Finney, Seymour, 50, 53
First Nations people, 36–38, 73, 100
fishing rights movement, 116, 199n9
Five Tribes, 3–4
Fixico, Donald, 104, 197n37
Florida, Richard, 166, 167, 206n5
Ford, Henry, 5, 28–29, 48, 64
Fordism, 64
Fox Nation, 19
Fraser, Darin, 170–71
freedom dreams: challenging dispossession and, 175–78; citizenship and, 171; Detroit Underground Railroad and, 16, 52, 86; diasporic Black freedom, 52; freedom/unfreedom relationship, 41–42; Indigenous belonging and, 7–8, 81–83
French, Caroline, 15
Freund, David, 97–98

Gaines, Kevin, 69, 71, 80, 144
gender: Afrocentric education and, 146–47, 147–48; anti-blackness and, 43–45; Black male patriarchy, 127, 146–48, 201n53; Camp Fire Girls performance, 90; Housewives' League of Detroit, 66–67, 128; indigeneity and, 43–45; Indigenous dispossession and, 78–79; League of Revolutionary Black Workers and, 126–27, 128–30; savage warrior stereotype and, 83, 89–90; settler memory and, 27, 86, 185n51, 194n79; settler patriarchy gaze, 44, 178; urban Indigenous feminism and, 115–16. *See also* masculinity; patriarchy
General Motors (GM), 5–6, 165–66
Genetin-Pilawa, C. Joseph, 23–24
Georgakas, Dan, 128
Geronimo, 25, 46
Gilbert, Dan, 6–7, 171, 177
Gilbert, Joseph, 147
Gitchi-Manadoo (the Great Spirit), viii, 11
GOAL (Group on Advanced Leadership), 122, 144
Goeman, Mishuana, 37–38, 120
Goldstein, Alyosha, 179n1
Gramsci, Antonio, 64
Gratiot Redevelopment Project, 109–10
Greater Detroit Homeowners' Association Council, 110–11
Great Lake Northern Stars, 118
Gregory, Sandra, 131–32
Gross, James, 154

Haag, Jackson D., 91
Haley, Sarah, 43, 44, 65
Harris, Cheryl, 111–12
Harris-Perry, Melissa, 44
Harvey, David, 64, 179n1, 203n39
Haudenosaunee people, 11–12, 37, 183n4
Heart of the Earth Survival School (Minneapolis), 154, 162
Henry, Milton, 144
Henry, Richard, 144
heteropatriarchy, 83, 178
Hill, A. W., 53–54
Hinton, Elizabeth, 204n41
Historic Fort Wayne, 152–53, 159–63
Hokowhitu, Brendan, 79, 83
Holmquist, Carl, 152
House Concurrent Resolution 108, 114–15
Housewives' League of Detroit, 66–67, 128
housing: Black dispossession and, 106–12; internal colonialism and, 107, 125, 197n50; migration and, 64–65, 65–66, 95; mixed race people and, 111; poverty and, 4, 106–12, 127; tenant organizing, 127; urban renewal, 106–12, 196n21. *See also* reservation systems
Housing Corporation of America, 109–10
Hoxie, Frederick, 70, 77
Hudson, Joseph L., 87
Hull, William, 13
Hunton, William, 88–89
Huron people, 12, 183

Illitch, Mike, 177
Indian Child Welfare Act (1978), 121

Indian Citizenship Act (1924), 76, 98
Indian Claims Commission (1946), 78
Indian Education (Kennedy, et al.), 137
Indian Education Act (1972), 139
Indian Elementary and Secondary School Assistance Act (1972), 139
Indian Fireside Council of Detroit, 99
Indian Pledge of Allegiance, 156
Indian Relocation Act (1956), 104
Indian Scout Talks (Eastman), 90
indigeneity: African indigeneity, 3; Black Indigeneity, 115, 122–30, 131, 169, 171; Black Nationalism *vs.*, 115; construction of modern Detroit and, 46–49, 62–63; postwar shifts and, 102–3; white indigeneity, 116, 169–73
Indigenous dispossession: challenging dispossession, 175–78; naturalization of, 3–4; poverty and, 77, 131, 138–40, 149; symbolic changes and, 174–75; urban renewal and, 111–12
Indigenous education: boarding schools and, 67–68, 70, 120, 136; DPS financing and, 163; impact of Afrocentric education on, 148–49, 150–51. *See also* culturally relevant education; Medicine Bear American Indian Academy
Indigenous erasure: authenticity and, 24–25, 36–37, 55, 71–72, 89–90, 100, 166; believed disappearance of Indigenous people, 16–17; bicentennial celebration and, 59–60; Black indigeneity and, 115, 122–30, 131, 169, 171; Black participation in, 52–53, 54–55; boarding schools, 64, 67–70, 98, 117, 120, 136; child removal and, 116–22; disappearance narrative, 16–17, 18–19, 21, 38–39, 55, 92, 123–24; narratives of the past and, 45; postwar indigeneity shifts, 102–3; race consciousness and, 71–72; savage warrior stereotype and, 17, 17, 18–19, 20, 71–72; tensions between Black and Indigenous peoples and, 130–34; vanishing Indian trope, 7, 16–17, 55, 57, 100
Indigenous futures, 178
Indigenous Nationalism, 96–97
Indigenous People's Day, 174
Indigenous women, 67–68, 90, 136–37, 139, 140
Indigenous youth, 140, 149–52
Inglis, James, 109
internal colonial discourse, 107, 125, 128, 197n50
invisibility, politics of: Black people and, 178; imaginary geographies of settler colonialism and, 169–72; Indigenous people and, 167–68, 178; Princess Dance letter and, 131–33

Jackson, Andrew, 18, 19
Jackson, Shona, 123–24
Jacobs, Jane, 47
Jacquez, Debra, 140
Jefferson, Thomas, 13
Jim Crow racism, 42–43, 50, 52, 55, 71
Johnson, Lyndon, 131
Joseph, Peniel, 200n26

Kanter, Joseph, 110
Kelley, Helen, 106
Kelley, Robin D. G., 3
Kellogg, Laura Cornelius, 70
Kennedy, Edward, 136–37
Kennedy, Robert, 136–37, 202n5
Kenyatta, Kwame, 150–51, 158
Kidroe, Josephine, 41–45, 188n117
King, Charles Brady, 48
King, Lisa, 168
Kornhauser, Arthur, 102
Kramer, Marian, 126–27

labor: Black belonging and, 9, 111, 122–30; boarding schools and, 67–68; Ford Motors and, 5, 64–65; gender and, 43, 65; Indigenous labor, 115–16; treatment of Black people *vs.* Indigenous people and, 3, 14, 110–12, 177–78. *See also* enslavement
LaFerte, Daniel, 55
Lambert, William, 16
land dispossession: Black settlement and, 14–15; challenging land dispossession, 40–41, 175–78; Dawes Act (1887), 69–70, 77; disappearance and, 16–17, 18–19, 21, 38–39, 55, 92, 123–24; European occupation of Detroit, 11–17; enslavement and, 13, 14; Indigenous masculinity *vs.* settler masculinity and, 29–30; Indigenous reclamation of space and, 37–41; land claim discourse and, 37–38; land speculation and, 13–14; nationalist racial rhetoric and, 71; reparations and, 122, 200n27; termination of land rights and, 104–6; treaties with Black people and, 177–78. *See also* displacement; removal; settler colonialism; urban renewal

Landmarks of Wayne County and Detroit (Farmer), 5
League of Revolutionary Black Workers, 126–27, 128–30
Lee, Spike, 148
Lightfoot, Tabitha, 15
Lindsay, Linda, 153
Lockwood, Rodney, 169–73
Loft, Frederick Ogilvie, 73
Lomawaima, K. Tsianina, 78
Lumumba, Chokwe, 150–51, 158
Lupkin, Paula, 88, 89
Lytle Hernandez, Kelly, 182n29

Maddox, Lucy, 191n5
Malcolm X Academy, 147–48, 150, 152–53, 156, 163
"Male Academy Task Force," 147
"Manhood" (poem), 78–79
Manifesto of the International Black Workers Congress (1971), 129
Marbly, Marie, 160
Marrero, Karen, 27, 185n51, 194n79
Martinez, David, 78, 92
masculinity: Indigenous challenges to white masculinity, 78–84; Indigenous masculinity, 29–30, 78–84; memorialization and, 58–59, 78–79; modernity and, 29–30, 32–33, 166; origin narratives and, 58–61; savage warrior stereotype and, 82–83, 89–90; settler colonialism and, 21, 24, 32–33, 58, 59–60, 83; settler masculinity, 29–30, 87–89; settler memories and, 47, 55–58; urban development and, 29–30; violence narratives and, 29–30; warfare and, 82–83
May, Karl, 168
Maybury, William C., 28–30, 48–49, 54, 55, 57–58, 62
Mays, Esther Shawboose, vii, viii, 98, 117–22, 127, 141, 142, 162–63
Mays, Judy, vii, ix; contract cancellation and firing, 159–63; DIECC and, 141; discrimination lawsuit, 161–62; naming of Medicine Bear, 153–54; parent involvement, 143–44
Mays, Robert Isiah, 98
Mays, Tracy, 134, 159, 161–62
McClintock, Anne, 58, 59
McGriff, Deborah, 147
McKenzie, Fayette, 69, 78, 85
McKinney, Calvin, 147
McNenley, Linda Scarangella, 185n41
Means, LaNada, 139
Medicine Bear American Indian Academy: African-centered education and, 144, 155–58; closing of, 158–63; diversity of, 156–58; legacy of, 162–63; Judy Mays and, 162–63; mission of, 153–56; opposition to, 156. *See also* culturally relevant education
Melissa (student), 157–58
memorialization: of Black achievements, 54; racial ideologies and, 46–48; masculinity and, 58–59, 78–79; settler memorialization and, 46–48; as site of dispossession, 2. *See also* bicentennial celebration (1901)
Miami people, 12
Michigan Alliance Against Racist and Political Repression, 131
Michigan Commission on Indian Affairs (formerly CIA), 117, 122, 136, 138, 199n10
Michilimackinac band, 12, 13
migration: Black migrations, 51–52, 64–67, 95, 97, 106–7, 191n8; challenging Indigenous dispossession, 176; cultural formation and, 98–106; employment security, 64–67; housing and, 65–66, 95; Indigenous migrations, 11, 98–106, 176; wartime manufacturing and, 97
Miles, Tiya, 14, 42, 187n106
Miller, Douglas K., 104
Miller, Karen R., 72
Mission Field Indians of California, 73
Mississaugi people, 12
mobility: reservation systems and, 14, 67, 76, 98, 101–2, 197n50; Walpole First Nations people, 36–41. *See also* migration
modernity: assimilation ideology and, 104; automobile industry and, 5, 48; bicentennial celebration and, 46–47; construction of modern Detroit and, 46–49, 62–63; indigeneity and, 46–49, 62–63; land claim discourse and, 37–38; masculinity and, 29–30, 32–33, 166; origin narratives and, 103–4; savage warrior stereotype and, 17–18, 29–32, 38–40, 56, 60, 61, 76, 172; settler colonialism and, 2–3, 44, 178; urban Indigenous communities and, 151; Walpole First Nations and, 37–41; YMCA and, 88
Monroe, William, 16
Montezuma, Carlos, 70, 73, 74, 75
Moorish Science Temple (MST), 94, 95
Moreton-Robinson, Aileen, 112
Morgensen, Scott, 30

Mount Pleasant Indian Industrial School, 67–68
Muhammad, Elijah, 95
Muhammad, Khalil G., 50
Muse, Sandra, 133, 173
Myers, Don, 116

narrative dispossession: use of term, 1–5, 8–9, 17, 169; Belle Isle narrative and, 169–73; blackness and, 6–8, 54; creative class and, 166–69; Indigenous resistance to, 40–41; modernity and, 31–36, 54; Pontiac and, 8, 26, 27–36; recommended challenges to, 175–78; settler capitalism and, 169–73; settler narratives, 17–21; use of legends as, 33–34
narrative of progress, 17–18, 29–32, 38, 71–72, 90
narratives of the past: authenticity and, 24–25, 36–37, 55, 71–72, 89–90, 100, 166; Indigenous erasure and, 45; memorialization as site of dispossession, 2; settler memories of French occupation, 11, 12, 30, 34, 86–87, 103, 112, 166. *See also* memorialization
National Association for the Advancement of Colored People (NAACP), 71, 96, 174–75
National Association of Afro-American Educators, 145
National Indian Youth Council, 116, 199n9
National Organization for Women, 147
National Welfare Rights Organization, 127
Nation of Islam, 94–95, 122, 135
Native American Child Protection Council, 120–21
Native American Church, 72, 192n32
neoliberalism, 3, 146, 203n39, 204n40
Nester, William R., 32
Nielbock, Carl Anthony, 167–68
Nixon, Richard, 119
Norris, Harold, 109–10
North American Indian Association (NAIA), 95, 100, 102, 114, 131–32, 139, 203n18. *See also* North American Indian Club
North American Indian Association Newsletter, 114, 131–32, 203n18
North American Indian Club, 99, 100, 101, 105. *See also* North American Indian Association (NAIA)
Northwest Ordinance of 1787, 14
Nsoroma Institute, 146

Obama, Barack, 165
O'Brien, Jean, 17, 46–47
Odawa people, 12–14, 18, 37. *See also* Pontiac (Chief)
Ogbar, Jeffrey O. G., 130
Ohiyesa, Chief, 79, 84–85, 88–89, 91–92. *See also* Eastman, Charles
Olds, Ransom E., 48
Oldsmobile, 48
One Hundred Years with Youth (Struder), 86–87, 88–89
origin narratives: masculinity and, 58–61; modernity and, 103–4; settler memories of landing in Detroit, 11, 12, 30, 34, 86–87, 103, 112, 166; whiteness and, 173
Orr, Kevyn, 167

pageantry, 2, 47, 50–51, 89. *See also* memorialization; performance of dispossession
Palmer, Robert E., 103
Palmer, Thomas W., 17, 22, 31–32, 48, 175–76
Pan-American Exposition (1901), 49
Parker, Arthur, 70, 73, 74, 75
patriarchy: Black male patriarchy, 127, 146–48, 201n53; heteropatriarchy, 83, 178; settler patriarchal gaze, 44, 178
patriotism, 82–83, 97
Paul Robeson Malcolm X Academy (PRMXA), 163. *See also* Malcolm X Academy
Pawlick, Tom, 137
People for Equal and Community Education, 148
performance of dispossession: construction of modern Detroit and, 46–49, 62–63; Indigenous participation in challenges to, 23–25, 105–6; modernity and, 46–48; performance of colonization and, 48; racial ideologies and, 46–48; settler performances of, 17, 46–48. *See also* bicentennial celebration (1901)
Peyote movement, 72, 192n32
physical dispossession. *See* land dispossession; displacement; removal; urban renewal
Pierzynowski, Diane, 152
Poindexter, Thomas, 110–11
Pontiac (Chief): Battle of Bloody Run and, 167–68; burial and gravesite, 31–34; memorialization of, 28–30, 31–36, 175–76; narrative dispossession and, 8, 26, 27–36; Pontiac's conspiracy, 13, 26, 27–29, 131, 167

Pontiac (General Motors brand), vii, 5, 8, 26, 165–66, 174, 178, 182n33
Potawatomi people, 12, 13, 37
poverty: Black communities and, 106–12, 146–47; education and, 146–17, 149–50; housing and, 4, 106–12, 127; Indigenous communities and, 77, 131, 138–40, 149; Poor People's Campaign, 130; self-determination and, 127–28; urban Indigenous communities and, 77, 131, 138–41, 149, 196n21; welfare rights organizing, 127. *See also* reservation systems
Pratt-Clarke, Menah, 147–48
Princess Dance letter, 131–33
progress narratives, 34–35

queerness, 44
Quizar, Jessi, 180n9

"Racial Bars Complicate Slum Crisis" (Detroit Free Press), 108
racial capitalism: critiques of, 124–30; economic security and, 2, 111–12, 128; enslavement and, 13–14; narrative dispossession and, 169–73; removal and, 13–14; settler colonialism and, 2–3, 13, 179n2, 179n4, 180n12; urban renewal and, 2–3, 107, 111–12, 179n4. *See also* settler capitalism
racial uplift discourse: Black middle class and, 52–55, 69, 71, 80, 96, 144; nationalist racial rhetoric and, 71; savage warrior stereotype and, 75, 76; SAI and, 68–78; sovereignty and, 68
racism: Detroit as majority-Black city and, 6; human rights discourse and, 97; Indigenous challenges to, 100–104; Jim Crow racism, 42–43, 50, 52, 55, 71
Racism and Class Struggle (Boggs), 124
RAM (Revolutionary Action Movement), 122
Ramirez, Reyna, 115
Ramirez-Rosa, Carlos, 177
Randolph, A. Phillip, 96
reclamation of land: Belle Isle and, 40–41; land claim discourse and, 37–38, 40–41; Walpole Island First Nations people, 9, 36–41, 42–43. *See also* land dispossession
recommendations for challenging dispossession, 174–78
Red Cloud, 25
Red Power movement, 136–44, 199n5
Red School House (St. Paul), 154, 162
Rembisz, Rosemarie, 148
removal: enslavement and, 13–14; foster care system and, 116–22; racial capitalism and, 13–14; relocation and, 104, 197n37; reservation systems and, 14, 67, 76, 98, 101–2, 197n50; slum clearance and, 4, 106–12, 127; termination of land rights and, 104–6; urban renewal and, 4, 106–12. *See also* disappearance narratives
reparations, 122, 200n27
Republic of New Afrika, 122, 200n28
reservation systems, 14, 67, 76, 98, 101–2, 197n50
resistance to dispossession: artmaking and, 4, 142, 176–77; assimilation *vs.*, 78; Black and Indigenous peoples and, 130–34; Black Indigeneity, 115, 122–30; Black radicalism and, 122–30; creative expression and, 168; expressive culture as, 4; radical activism and, 113; radical ethnic nationalism and, 130; sites of resistance and, 4–5; solidarity as, 130, 132–33, 150–51, 175, 178; urban Indigenous feminism and, 115–22
respectability politics, 50–55
Reuther, Walter, 103
Richmond, Henry, 33–34
Roosevelt, Franklin Delano, 5
Rosemary (Oneida), 138
Ruglis, Jessica, 147

Sa, Zitkala, 70, 73
Said, Edward, 32, 172
Sands, Thomas, 40
Sauk Nation, 19, 31
savage warrior stereotype: use of term, 186n69; assimilation and, 76; gender and, 83, 89–90; Indigenous erasure and, 17, 18–19, 20, 71–72; masculinity and, 82–83, 89–90; modernity and, 17–18, 29–32, 38–40, 56, 60, 61, 76, 172; narrative of progress and, 17–18, 29–32, 38, 71–72, 90; noble savage trope and, 27–28, 186n69; racial uplift discourse and, 75, 76
self-determination: Black indigeneity and, 115, 122–30, 131, 169, 171; Black self-determination, 4, 66–67, 94–95, 96–98, 122, 127–30, 147–48, 150–51, 200n28; cultural formation and, 95–96, 99; economic self-determination, 66–67, 94, 127–30; Indigenous self-determination, 95–96, 99, 105, 119–21, 136–44, 154;

land rights and, 104–6; urban Indigenous feminism and, 115, 119–21
Self-Determination Act (1975), 139
Set the World on Fire (Blain), 195n11
settler capitalism, 2–3, 107, 111–12, 169–73, 179n4. *See also* racial capitalism
settler colonialism: use of term, 2–3; African & Palestinian scholarship on, 180n5; Black people and, 51; cultural imagination of non-Indigenous people and, 168–69; freedom dreams and, 8, 178, 182n33; frontier discourse, 6–7, 169; imaginary geographies of, 169–72; internal colonialism, 107, 197n50; Middle Ground thesis and, 12–13, 183n6; racial capitalism and, 2–3, 13, 179n2, 179n4, 180n12; settler capitalism and, 2, 4–5, 13, 169, 172–73; settler masculinity and, 21, 24, 32–33, 58, 59–60; settler memory and, 11, 12, 30, 34, 86–87, 103, 112, 166; urban renewal and, 107–8, 110–12, 182n29. *See also* land dispossession
settler imaginaries, 41, 80–84, 85, 89–92
settler memory: use of term, 47–48, 61–62; of Black Detroiters, 51, 52–55; of Cadillac, 55–58; Cass/Pontiac story, 18; Detroit identity and, 47; of French occupation, 11, 12, 27, 30, 34, 86–87, 103, 112, 166, 185n51, 194n79; gender and, 27, 86, 185n51, 194n79; Indigenous erasure and, 47; masculinity and, 47, 55–58; pageantry and, 47–48, 61–62; settler colonialism and, 11, 12, 30, 34, 86–87, 103, 112, 166; settler masculine origins, 58–61; whiteness and, 47
settler narratives: disappearing Indigenous narrative, 18–19; dispossession and, 110; Indigenous past discourse, 18–19; Friend Palmer and, 17–21; Thomas W. Palmer and, 17, 22, 31–32, 48, 175–76; violence and, 12–13, 17, 29–30
sexualities: Black dispossession and, 65–66; Indigenous dispossession and, 44, 78–79, 102
Seymour, A. M., 50, 53
Shampine, Arlene, 133
Shawboose, Westbrook, 98
Shawboose Mays, Esther, 98, 117
Shawnee people, 13, 31
Sherrill, William, 195n11
Sherwood, Lincoln, 133
shoals: use of term, 3
Silas, Eliza, 67–68, 98
Simpson, Leanne Betasamosake, 178, 182n33
sites of dispossession: use of term, 2
Sitting Bull, 21, 22–26, 184n36, 185n41
Slater, Timothy, 148
slavery. *See* enslavement
Sloan, Thomas, 70, 73, 75–76
Smith, David, 165–66
Smith, Frederick M., 77
Smith, Paul Chaat, 174
Smitherman, Geneva, 147
Snyder, Rick, 167
Society of American Indians (SAI): Detroit convention, 72–77; dismantling of, 77–78; Minnesota meeting, 81–83; racial uplift discourse and, 68–69, 191n5; sovereignty and, 69–70; support for citizenship, 76–77
Society of Native Alaskans, 73
SouFy (student), 157
sovereignty: Cherokee and Creek leaders and, 41; cultural sovereignty, 96; educational sovereignty, 136–44, 151–58; freedom narratives and, 171; SAI and, 69–70; urban Indigenous feminism and, 115–22
Standing Bear, Henry, 70
Stanley, George, 39
Struder, Adolph G., 86–87, 88–89
Surkin, Marvin, 128

Tanner, Helen Hornbeck, 12, 56
Tax, Sol, 114–15
Taylor, Keeanga-Yamahtta, 112
TCF Center (Cobo Center), 174–75
Tecumseh, 13, 31
Testa, Jeff, 148
The Last of the Mohicans (Cooper), 16–17
Then and Now (Bange), 103
Third World Women's Alliance, 127, 201n53
Thomas, Clarence, 43
Thomas, Richard, 42–43, 51
Thrush, Coll, 18, 29, 34
Tionontati tribal group, 12
Tipi Order of America, 73
Tomahawk (1951), 105
Townsend, Charlotte E., 101
Trask, Kerry, 20
Treaty of Detroit (1807), 13, 41
Treaty of Greenville (1795), 183n9
tricentennial celebration, 191n64
Tuskegee Airmen Museum, 152

Underground Railroad, 16, 52, 86
Union League, 52–54

Universal Negro Improvement Society (UNIA), 96, 195n11
urban Indigenous communities: cultural formation and, 98–106; educational sovereignty and, 136–44, 151–58; as incompatible with cities, 104, 197n37; migration and, 98–106; narrative of dispossession and, 6–8, 182n27; Native people's agency and relocation, 104, 197n37; poverty and, 77, 131, 138–41, 149, 196n21; recognition of, 176; termination of land rights and, 104–6; urban education and, 144, 155–56. *See also* removal
urban Indigenous feminism, 115–22, 141
urban renewal: Black people and, 106–12; creative class and, 166–69, 206n5; housing and, 106–12, 196n21; Indigenous people and, 98–106, 185n56, 197n37; "internal colonies" and, 197n50; masculinity and, 29–30; racial capitalism and, 2–3, 107, 111–12, 179n4; settler colonialism and, 107–8, 110–12, 182n29; slum clearance and, 4, 106–12, 127; spatial segregation and, 4, 50–53, 72, 94–95, 106–12, 116–22; suburbanization and, 110–12
Utley, Robert, 21

violence: Detroit as, 12–13, 17, 50, 146; masculinity narratives and, 29–30

Walker, Yvonne, 137–38
Walpole Island First Nations people, 9, 36–41, 42–43
Ward, Charles, 34–35
Ward, Stephen M., 124, 201n53
Washington, Forrester, 52–53
Watson, Clifford, 147
wawaiiatanong (Waawayeyaattaanong), 11, 84–85, 166
Wayne, Mad Anthony, 152–53, 159
Webb, William, 50, 51–52, 53
Wekeshig, Peter, 39
West, Ralph, 100–101
West Centre Organization (WCO), 126–27, 128–30
Whalen, Kevin, 191n4
White, Richard, 12
Whitmer, Gretchen, 175
Wilson, Shawn, 159–60
Winnetou (May), 168
Wolcott, Victoria, 66
Wolfe, Patrick, 2–3, 120, 180n5
women: Afro-Indigenous women, 42–46; anti-blackness and, 42–46; Black radicalism and, 126–27, 128–30, 201n49; boarding schools and, 67–68; cultural maintenance and, 136–37, 139, 140; migration and, 65; political organizing and, 66–67, 127, 128, 201n53; Red Power movement and, 136–37, 139, 199n5; stereotypes of Indigenous women, 102. *See also* Black women
Woodland Indian Museum, 152
Woodson, Carter G., 144, 176
Wright, Russ, 138
Wyandot nation, 12, 13

Young, Coleman A., 6, 134, 191n5
Young, Edith, 153
Young Men's Christian Association of Detroit (YMCA), 85–91
youth: Camp Fire Girls, 90; Camp Ohiyesa and, 85, 88–91; Chi-Nations Youth Council, 177; dispossession of Indigenous youth, 148–52; murder rates and, 146; National Indian Youth Council, 116, 177; racial binaries and, 140; YMCA and, 85–91

ACKNOWLEDGMENTS

Trying to remember everyone who helped you write a book in small, medium, and ginormous ways is difficult. Conventional acknowledgments spend the most time thanking all of the scholars who helped the writer write the book. I'm going to flip that. Family first.

I want to thank my mother first and foremost. She did a helluva job raising five children. Who would've thought that I would still remain your favorite child after all these years? I'm sure the others will agree.

Thank you to my siblings for always acting out of order and ready to go 0 to 100 real quick on anybody who messes with their brother. Though I am not the youngest, I was always the most spoiled. Y'all remember when mom would take us to the movies on Saturdays after working well over forty hours a week at Pizza Hut? We would go to the movies and share that big ass bucket of popcorn, one large pop (pop! Not soda!), split it into water cups, and then sneak in candy from the gas station 'cause the snacks were too damn expensive (they're still expensive!). Well, mom also made y'all watch the movie *I* wanted to watch. I'm forever grateful for that. LOL. I love you, Shaun, Yaya, Twin, and J. Keep fighting, keep struggling.

I want to recognize my nieces and nephews—R. J., Hayden, Brandon, Cherish, JJ, Makiah, and D. J. You are incredible young people who are going to change the world. I know you all think I've done well for myself, but it won't be true unless you all continue in the fight for radical change in this society, in your own, collective way.

Thank you to my aunts Judy and Tracy, who were instrumental in helping me think about this book. I hope I make you both proud. Thank you for all the times I could crash on your couch and just spend time together talking about Detroit back in the day.

Now, I gotta give a big shout to my other fam. Dr. Geneva Smitherman, the Queen of Black Language, who continues to fight for the linguistic rights of Black people throughout the diaspora. Thank you to David E. Kirkland, Austin Jackson, AJ Rice, H. Samy Alim, Reverend/Dr. Jeffrey Robinson, and Ashley Newby. I've known these individuals since I was an undergraduate, and they have fundamentally shaped my views on the world. Thank you. We still argue into the midnight hour over race, politics, popular culture, how to get our freedom, and all of the Blackest of Black things that happen in our community. In my adult years, you all have shown me what academic excellence and social responsibility really means.

I must give a shout-out to Fred Hoxie and Holly. While Fred served as my advisor, he became a friend and a true mentor—a father figure. Holly has always accepted me into her home as one of her own, and I am forever grateful. Thank you, also, to my dissertation committee, including Robert Warrior, David Roediger, Coll Thrush, and Dianne Harris. And thank you to Tiya Miles, whose work has influenced my own thinking about Afro-Indigenous history since I was an undergraduate.

I have to thank my champagne and campaign fam. Bryce Henson, Kevin Whalen, and "E" Eddie Coronel, we been down like four flat tires since the University of Illinois. I wish we could have a few rounds at Murphy's and enjoy some swine-free Irish nachos. Thank you for being my brothas and helping me get through this project, the ups and the downs. I will forever have your backs. I also have to thank colleague and friend Veronica Mendez who always reminds me to have fun after writing all day!

A host of people have helped me think through this project over the years—meeting at conferences, reading material, having conversations, or writing dope books. I appreciate them all: Ned Blackhawk, Emily MacGillivary, Karen Marrero, and Matt Gilbert.

Dr. Adam Banks invited me to participate in the Smitherman/Villanueva Writing Retreat. I was able to learn from not only him but several writing elders and writing and rhetoric peer scholars who I admire and respect a great deal: April Baker-Bell (whose dope book, *Linguistic Justice* is next level good!), Aja Y. Martinez, David Green, Meredith Clark, Keith Gilyard, Jaime Meija, and the other fellows who were there. Thank you, Adam, for your vision and dedication to making sure that young faculty of color are prepared to carry on the burden of struggle for the next generation.

I need to give a shout-out to my peeps in the Department of African American Studies at UCLA. First, I want to give a huge thank you to the workers who make the place run: Eboni Shaw, Tricia Park, and Elliott Delgado. They don't get paid nearly as much as they should for all of their labor. I appreciate you. Second, I must thank Robin D. G. Kelley, a gem of a soul, who has guided and helped me in ways he knows and doesn't know. I want to thank Shana Redmond, Sarah Haley, Uri McMillan, Aisha Finch, Gaye Theresa Johnson, Peter Hudson, Jemima Pierre, and Marcus Hunter. Thank you, Cheryl Keyes, Brenda Stevenson, Scot Brown, and Bryonn Bain. Thank you to Safiya Umoja Noble, Kelly Lytle Hernandez, and Lorrie Frasure. Thank you to Eboni Shaw and Tricia Park for all of the amazing staff support you provided. I could make this list hella long, but I've learned a lot about UCLA and the importance of community. Thank you all.

I must thank my colleagues in American Indian Studies, including Randy Akee, Shannon Speed, Mishuana Goeman, Keith Camacho, Ben Madley, Erin Debenport, Teresa McCarty, Ananda Marin, Tria Blu Wakpa, Keith Camacho, Jessica Cattelino, Paul Kroskrity, Nancy Mithlo, Wendy Teeter, Peter Nabokov, and Angela Riley. Thank you for your support; I hope we can continue being one of the top places for Indigenous studies in the world.

Thank you again to Kelly Lytle Hernandez and Danielle Dupuy for helping me organize a book-manuscript workshop. Early readers included Dan Cobb, Angela Pulley Hudson, and Zandria Robinson. Thank you again for the feedback. It was so very helpful. Thank you to the two anonymous readers. The criticisms made the book better and helped me flesh out what I needed to say. Any errors in writing are my own.

During my postdoctoral fellowship at the University of North Carolina at Chapel Hill, I gained many friends and had plenty of time to write. Thank you to Sibby Anderson-Thompkins and Jennifer Pruitt, who helped me navigate the Carolina Postdoctoral Program for Faculty Diversity. Thank you to my mentor, Malinda Maynor Lowery. She was very supportive and helped me think through this book. I want to thank Keith Richotte and Jenny Tone-Pah-Hote (R.I.P.) and Steven, for letting me stay at the crib for a few nights before I left for Los Angeles! Thank you to Dan Cobb for his friendship and support. And thank you to the Department of History for hosting me: Cemil Aydin, Bill Ferris, Fitz Brundage, Kathleen DuVal, Miguel La Serna, Gena Rae McNeil, and William Sturkey.

When you move to a new place, it can often be lonely. Even though LA has mad shit to offer, it didn't become home until I met all the homies. More than that, I've developed family since I've been in LA. Muchos gracias to Liseth Amaya, the best artist in the game and always supportive. I gotta show love to my brothas, Rafael Leonor and Marvin Amaya. While you both get me into way too much trouble, and after a night with you two I question why I went out in the first place, I always come back for more. Thank you to Jessica Amaya and Sammy. Thank you, Kat and Emma. Big shout to my other brotha, Dr. Martin Jauregui. Though he works at that other school (USC) across the way, he's still my boy. Smart as a whip, and always down for bourbon and (James) Baldwin, as well as old-school hip-hop.

Shout-out to Liz's LA Crew on WhatsApp. Liz, the wine connoisseur. There's a rumor circulating that the price of wine goes up when you come back into town. Big shout to BellaMafia, an intelligent, young British woman who is going to be able to do whatever she wants well. Keep writing and I can't wait to read that novel. Lesly, keep staying positive. Mama Milli, thank you for the food and in-home haircuts. Big shout to Susie and Joel. I love the parties and bbqs. Big shout to Yolanda and Cami, thanks for keeping your home open and stocked with food! Edwin and Victer: Y'all are always down to kick it. Much love.

Thank you to Jennifer and Mayte Carrillo, the homies, and Mama Carrillo. Thank you for inviting me into your home during my first holiday in LA. That Salvie food was bomb. Jen, thank you for introducing me to one of the best people in the world.

Big shout to my Chicago fam. Thank you, Mike Staudenmaier and Anne Carlson. Thank you to some of my favorite Generation Zers, Sofia, Nico, and Brotha Malcolm. I know I will always have a home and family in one of my favorite cities!

With all of the cat and dog memes going around social media, I have to bring mine into the book. Big shout to my cat Ginger, aka "El Dón," aka G$. When I was writing, he was curled up either on my side or on my lap, discouraging me from writing. Big shout to his sister, Salchicha, "ChiChi." Both from Oaxaca, and though they be actin real extra sometimes, I couldn't do the work I do without them. Actually, I might get more work done, but, hey, it be that ways sometimes.

I appreciate those. Thank you, dear reader, for picking this book up. I hope you enjoy it. Finally, I want to thank my ancestors, both those forced to come to the Americas and my Saginaw Anishinaabe family. I hope I make you all proud.

Thank you to Keisha N. Blain and Bob Lockhart at the University of Pennsylvania Press for believing in this project and helping me get to the finish line. Keisha read drafts and helped me to become a better writer. Bob was a dope editor. He read every chapter and gave line edits and offered important criticisms that made the book better. If I missed anyone, I probably did it on purpose (smile). On the real, thank you to everyone I may have missed and to all of those who give me the motivation I desperately need to write every day. You da real MVPs!